Open Source Enterprise Solutions:

Developing an E-Business Strategy

Gunnison Carbone

Duane Stoddard

Wiley Computer Publishing

John Wiley & Sons, Inc.

NEW YORK · CHICHESTER · WEINHEIM · BRISBANE · SINGAPORE · TORONTO

658.05
C26o

Publisher: Robert Ipsen
Editor: Cary Sullivan
Assistant Editor: Christina Berry
Managing Editor: Marnie Wielage
Associate New Media Editor: Brian Snapp
Text Design & Composition: Benchmark Productions, Inc.

Designations used by companies to distinguish their products are often claimed as trademarks. In all instances where John Wiley & Sons, Inc., is aware of a claim, the product names appear in initial capital or all capital letters. Readers, however, should contact the appropriate companies for more complete information regarding trademarks and registration.

This book is printed on acid-free paper. ∞

This publication is designed to provide accurate and authoritative information in regard to the subject matter covered. It is sold with the understanding that the publisher is not engaged in professional services. If professional advice or other expert assistance is required, the services of a competent professional person should be sought.

Library of Congress Cataloging-in-Publication Data:

Carbone, Gunnison.
    Open source enterprise solutions : developing an e-business strategy / Gunnison
  Carbone, Duane Stoddard.
      p. cm.
    Includes index.
    ISBN 0-471-41744-0 (paper : alk. paper)
    1. Electronic commerce--Management. 2. Electronic commerce--Technological
  innovations. 3. Electronic commerce--Computer network resources. I. Stoddard, Duane.
  II. Title.

HF5548.32.C359 2001
658'.05--dc21   2001026451

Printed in the United States of America.

10 9 8 7 6 5 4 3 2 1

To my family who thought it was inordinately strange to whittle away my youth with countless hours in front of a computer screen but nevertheless encouraged me to pursue my enthusiasms.

GUNNISON CARBONE

To the memory of my grandfather, Ivan Stoddard, who I'm sure would have read the book from cover to cover, and to my family for their support.

DUANE STODDARD

Contents

Acknowledgments

The authors would like to thank Aleksander Lesniak for his contributions to the EAI and BerkleyDB sections and Ken McCorkell for his contributions to the CRM, Relata, OpenSourceCRM, and Sendmail portions of this book.

About the Authors

Gunnison Carbone

Mr. Carbone is currently CEO and President of Open3 Technologies. He co-founded the open source community, Open3.org, and is a faculty member of the Enterprise Linux Institute. Previously, Mr. Carbone was an e-business consultant to Lucent Technologies Bell Labs and to more than a dozen technology companies. Mr. Carbone has a Bachelor of Science degree in Computer Science and Mathematics from Metropolitan State College of Denver. Email: gun@open3.org

Duane Stoddard

Mr. Stoddard is an international integration specialist with projects recently featured in the Smithsonian. He co-founded the open source e-business integration community, Open3.org, and is currently CTO of Open3 Technologies. Mr. Stoddard has previously held lead e-business integration and development positions at SAGA Software and Lucent Technologies Bell Labs. Mr. Stoddard has a Bachelor of Science degree in Mathematical and Computer Sciences and a Bachelor of Science degree in Engineering from the Colorado School of Mines. Email: duane@open3.org

Introduction

Innovation defines human achievement.

From the stone axes chiseled by modern man 100,000 years ago, to the building of the great pyramids of Cheops in 2600 B.C., to robots that explore distant planets 90 million miles from the Earth, human innovation makes the evolution of technology possible. Innovation occurs for various reasons, including necessity for survival, curiosity, dumb luck, avarice, and ambition. Whatever the reason, the more people that communicate and participate in an inventive process, the more competition and collaboration that occurs to spur the rate of innovation. An increase in participation stems from the invention of language, printed books, the telephone, and the Internet. This communication affluence has caused innovation to grow at an incredible velocity.

Nowhere else in history is the momentum greater than with the creation of the Internet. The statistics are impressive considering its short existence. At the end of 2000, there were an estimated 350 million people online. Every country throughout the world has access to the Internet. It is predicted that by 2010, one half of the world's population will have admittance to the Web. This incredible communication and collaboration is creating a new age in innovation, one that will dwarf all prior periods of human achievement. It is incredibly exciting to be participants in this novel era!

As we move forward in the evolution of the Internet, we're seeing proof that great technology gives rise to new innovations. E-business and open source software are two of its most gifted progeny. E-business is revolutionizing the status quo for traditional business, bringing tremendous improvements in efficiency, speed of commerce, and ability to tap new revenue sources. Open source software is a tidal wave that has mega-corporations like Microsoft running for their bunkers. In fact, open source has enabled the Internet to be what it is today. Both of these inventions, producing prominent examples like Yahoo! and Linux, are made possible by the participation of a globally-connected community of individuals and businesses.

As children of the Internet epoch, e-business and open source are two inventions that assist each other in their continual evolution. E-business provides the demand for software and open source fulfills the requirement by the enterprise to build a secure, reliable, adaptable, and cost-effective IT infrastructure. E-business and open source are young and have many years of maturation remaining, however both will grow hand in hand; they've already begun to take their first steps together. According to the research firm, IDC, Linux represented 25 percent of the enterprise server market in 1999 and Apache Web Server powers approximately 59 percent of Web sites on the Internet. Both of these open source software systems have been adopted by and have aided in the creation of e-business.

Likely the best example illustrating the concurrent growth of e-business and open source is International Business Machines. IBM, the international powerhouse of computing for the past century and attaining $90 billion in sales in 2000, has embraced the potential of open source software. Many of its open source maneuvers appear to be aimed at enlarging the chinks in the previously impenetrable armor of Microsoft. In late 2000, IBM announced that it would invest $1 billion into Linux in an effort to surpass Windows NT market share by 2004. IBM is also significantly involved in Apache, contributing heavily to open source projects like Xalan and Xerces. At the core of IBM's strategy is enabling e-business through hardware, software, and consulting services. Strong evidence indicates that open source software will play a leading role in IBM's e-business initiatives.

Overview of the Book and Technology

This book explores the innovations wrought by e-business and open source and how they will shape the new economy. We'll discover what it means to really be an e-business. Many people have a limited view of the definition of e-business, something akin to selling books, toys, or puppies through a Web site. E-business is not simply e-commerce on the Internet, it is an enterprise-wide transformation through digital technology. We'll uncover the foundations of the IT infrastructure based on open source software including programming languages, protocols, operating systems, and application servers. Then we'll explore the five major components of e-business in detail including enterprise applications, enterprise application integration, business-to-business integration, business-to-business e-commerce, and business-to-consumer e-commerce.

We'll discuss the underlying business decisions for each of the five components of e-business that must be made before embarking on a particular initiative. Factors such as cost determination, implementation time, return on investment, risk analysis, and providing value to the customer are essential activities that create the foundation for the e-business strategy. Once we've attacked from the business side, we're prepared to tackle the arduous task of architecting the technology solution. We'll present dozens of quality open source software projects that will assist in building the e-business implementation. Once you've read this book, you'll have an understanding of what real e-business is and what open source software you can utilize to build a reliable, secure, and highly cost-effective technology solution.

Our motivation for creating this book stems from our personal experience in using open source software to embark upon the complex task of implementing e-business. It's frustrating to be faced with paying hundreds of thousands or even millions of dollars in software licenses before the task at hand has even been started. Take one piece of the e-business technology solution, the database, and the proprietary leader in the space, Oracle. An Oracle database license for one production machine can easily exceed $100,000. Now compare this to MySQL or PostgreSQL, two popular, reliable, high performing, and open source relational database systems. Their cost, $0! Any manager's eyes grow wide when they realize that they can build the same, if not better, technology solution at a fraction of the cost of proprietary software.

It is also our goal, as creators of open source software, to enlighten business and IT leaders about the merits of open source. It no longer resides solely within the domain of techies and hobbyists. Despite FUD (Fear, Uncertainty, and Doubt) tactics made by the hugely budgeted marketing arms of proprietary vendors which state to the contrary, quality open source is real software for real e-business. Open source doesn't need glamorous presentations or television commercials during the Superbowl, it is software that stands on its own merits. It is this simple fact, in a world filled with so much marketing drivel, that is refreshing to people who just want to get things done and done right.

The task of e-business is difficult enough without fighting against talented labor shortages, complex and expensive proprietary licensing schemes, and software that your enterprise is locked into without a key to get out. Open source solves these problems. IT talent has much easier access to open source software. For example, computer science students in college learn and utilize a database system like MySQL instead of Oracle, simply because of the cost factor. The cost-free admittance to the open source world produces a broader set of IT engineers skilled in this software. Open source licensing also permits the enterprise to distribute the software at their discretion. Since the source code is open and developed by a worldwide community, e-business initiatives are never locked into the whims of a vendor. Ever been held back by a critical bug that took your software vendor 6 months to fix? This doesn't happen with open source. As your enterprise stands at the gates of its e-business future, open source software is there to make the journey as painless as possible.

How This Book Is Organized

Implementing the right e-business strategy is a long-term effort for the enterprise. We've organized this book in a similar way to organizing an e-business project. Chapter 1 provides an introduction to e-business. We've structured e-business as a series of steps or tiers for the enterprise. Each tier, starting at Tier 0 and ending at Tier 5, is a metric that gauges the evolution of the e-business framework in the enterprise. We'll also introduce you to fundamental e-business concepts like enterprise applications, integration, and e-commerce.

Chapter 2 provides background on the open source software movement. In this chapter you'll learn about where, how, and why open source software is developed. We'll uncover concepts like cathedral, bazaar, and evolutionary software development and what they mean for information technology. We'll also investigate the potential pitfalls and benefits of utilizing open source software in the enterprise.

Chapter 3 details the low-level foundation of open source software. This chapter is designed to provide some background on the fundamental technology upon which your e-business initiative is constructed. We'll examine the core open source technology components including operating systems, protocols, and languages. For operating systems, we've provided insight for the enterprise on various Linux bundles including Red Hat, Slackware, Debian, SuSe, and more, and how they compare to the open source BSD systems including NetBSD, FreeBSD, and OpenBSD. For protocols, we investigate low-level protocols like TCP/IP and SNA, high-level protocols like HTTP, FTP, and SMTP, and also distributed environment and middleware protocols. We'll also explore various data, presentation, and programming languages like XML, XSLT, Perl, Python, and Java.

Chapter 4 builds upon the foundation created by Chapter 3 to present the next key technology layer in the e-business implementation. This layer is composed of Web, database, application, integration, and communication servers and often represents one of the most costly investments for the enterprise. Fortunately, the open source world has strong offerings in these technology areas. For each server type we'll uncover quality open source software like Apache, ArsDigita, Enhydra, JBoss, Open3, Sendmail, and Zope to build your e-business infrastructure.

Beginning with Chapter 5, we'll start to take an in-depth look at the five major components of e-business. In Chapter 5 we reveal enterprise applications and their importance to building an e-business strategy from the inside out. Enterprise applications provide automation of business processes such as human resources, accounting, and inventory management. We'll investigate open source software like OpenSourceCRM, Relata, Apache Jetspeed, and Red Hat Interchange for the enterprise application component of the e-business strategy.

Chapter 6 addresses the important issue of enterprise application integration. Typically, all but the largest of businesses choose to install enterprise applications in a gradual process. As the enterprise acquires more of these applications, it becomes increasingly crucial for those applications to share data. Application integration is essential for delivering effective business-to-business and business-to-consumer services through the Internet. We'll explore the business strategies and technology approaches for enterprise application integration. We'll also detail open source software like Open3, Enhydra, and JBoss for the technology implementation.

Growing from enterprise application integration, Chapter 7 presents the third major component of e-business, business-to-business integration. B2B integration provides a framework for communication external to the enterprise with suppliers, manufacturers, distributors, wholesalers, and retailers. The rise of the Internet has made it possible for a globally connected network of businesses to communicate seamlessly and in real-time. Automation of the supply chain through B2B integration represents one of the most fundamental and important strategies facing businesses today.

Leveraging the technology initiatives presented in prior chapters, Chapter 8 details business-to-business and business-to-consumer e-commerce.

E-commerce is the sale and purchase of goods and services through a digital medium. We'll explore the various categories of e-commerce distribution including fixed pricing, catalog aggregation, auctions, exchanges, and the rise of digital products. We'll highlight the coming age of mobile e-commerce, or m-commerce, and its impact on the enterprise's e-commerce strategy. We'll also describe several open source software products to build quality e-commerce applications.

Chapter 9 presents a hypothetical case study for the construction of an e-business solution. This chapter ties together the five major components of e-business with each stage built completely upon open source software. The case study is designed to show the progression of the enterprise through the e-business tiers and the associated challenges to both the business and technology implementation.

Finally, Chapter 10 provides a detailed listing of the major software vendors who sponsor and support open source software. These companies are at the forefront of delivering e-business solutions. Look to these companies for enterprise-level technical support, consulting, and product additions.

Who Should Read This Book

Technology innovates rapidly. As technology is evolving for use in business, it is also changing business. The two are becoming interwoven into the fabric known as e-business. Corporate management now faces the difficult challenge of comprehending the application of technology for the enhancement of business.

One area of technology that mandates attention is open source software. Major corporations like Home Depot are turning to open source for reliable and highly cost-effective software. Successful technology leaders are utilizing open source. As the business world moves forward in reaping the benefits of open source, will your enterprise?

E-business is forming the supporting pillars of every significant company on the planet. Business management must become e-business management. This book was created for those who must bridge the disciplines of business and technology and those who are attracted to the benefits of open source. This book is especially suited to CTOs, CIOs, Directors of technology, IT management, and others who are interested in applying open source technology for e-business initiatives. We've tailored this book for technical managers who face the formidable task of delivering solid, low cost, and adaptable e-business solutions for the enterprise.

One might believe that a book about open source is a book about computer code. This book deals with technical issues, but it is not about programming. However, software developers will find the book useful to improve the understanding of e-business and its implementation based on open source software. We provide an introduction and evaluation of dozens of open source products, which will furnish the programmer with an invaluable first step in utilizing the software.

What's on the Web Site

Innovation in e-business and open source moves faster than print. To keep pace with any changes, this book's companion Web site at www.wiley.com/ compbooks/carbone contains updated information and references to resources. Links to the software and Internet sites of all of the open source projects profiled in this book are on the Web site, as well as updated information about e-business, new open source projects, and open source companies.

Moving Forward

Moving forward is the mantra of innovation. In the ten chapters that make up this book, you will uncover real e-business and how open source software is charging to the forefront in providing e-business solutions. Major companies like IBM, Sun Microsystems, Dell, and HP are all engaged in open source initiatives. Open source is an undeniable tool that every smart e-business leader will, at a minimum, investigate.

Moving forward must also be the mantra of your enterprise. To survive and thrive in this emerging New Economy requires visionary understanding, strong business execution, and a rock solid technology infrastructure.

Innovation defines e-business success.

Introduction to E-Business

In 1439, Johannes Gutenberg made a horrible mistake. As a hand mirror businessman, he was ready to sell his wares to pilgrims leaving the city of Mainz, Germany. Unfortunately, poor market research led him to miss the date of the pilgrimage by a full year. He was then financially forced to begin working on an idea. That idea became movable type printing—the ability to reproduce documents, books, and paper for the masses.

Gutenberg's invention has become one of the most monumental events in the history of humankind. Printing has provided a whole new framework for the dissemination of information. It has enabled the spread of religion, the advancement of science, the development of formal business processes, and has even helped to promote democracy.

Today, more than 500 years after Gutenberg's invention, the electronic world is creating another information revolution. Computers and the Internet are shaping a global network of information, accessible in real time from virtually anywhere. E-business, short for electronic business, and open source software have emerged as two of the most important realizations of this connected world.

E-business has leading enterprises across the globe aggressively pursuing strategies to bring them successfully into the new millennium. Visionary companies are creating new rules in their industries by implementing e-business strategies.

To become a leader in this modern economy, business management must answer questions such as:

- Are you able to recognize the threats created by new and untraditional competitors?

- Do you understand how electronic commerce and the Internet are shaping your industry?

- Will your company become a rule maker instead of a rule taker in the New Economy?

E-business is quickly making its way into mainstream companies. Established companies must realize that their competitors are adopting e-business initiatives. Combining today's business with tomorrow's technology, however, is a significant challenge. Haphazard technology initiatives run rampant throughout the business world. So called quick fixes often fail disastrously in solving problems. A long-term e-business strategy must be organized, designed, and deployed for the long-term success of the enterprise.

It's a fact of the modern economy—e-business plays a significant role in corporate success. E-business latecomers will face difficult times.

Defining E-Business

E-business is redefining traditional business. Simply stated, e-business is the transition from manual business processes to digital, automated, and connected ones. E-business enables improved efficiency, an integrated enterprise for the seamless flow of information, better customer service, and new opportunities for revenue growth. Gutenberg's early business failure might have been a success if he had access to e-business technology, such as more reliable customer information and a customer relationship management system.

The first step in understanding e-business is to know exactly what it means. E-business is frequently used as a buzzword, and typically out of context. E-commerce, short for electronic commerce, and e-business are often mistakenly interchanged. E-commerce (electronic transactions of money for goods and services) is one component of e-business. E-business also includes the automation, integration, and organization of business processes internal and external to the enterprise.

E-Business is composed of four important components:

Automation. Technology applied to business processes in the form of hardware and software help to lower costs and increase efficiency.

Integration. Bridging automated processes and information throughout the enterprise. Integration is crucial for intelligent decision making and rapid communication between multiple departments, business partners, and customers.

Organization. To leverage an enterprise's most important asset—people—to take advantage of the benefits of an e-business revolution. The organization of the workforce within automated business processes enables new efficiencies for workflow.

E-commerce. Monetary and trade transactions executed in digital space providing for the most efficient and expedient methods possible for commerce. No modern business can ignore e-commerce.

The foundation of e-business is built on technology. Hardware, such as computers, networking equipment, and data storage provide the technological infrastructure. Software, enterprise applications, application servers, and information are the life force of e-business. Deploying reliable, scaleable, and manageable e-business software is the most critical, difficult, and potentially costly component of e-business.

Open Source Software for E-Business

Solid software is key for successful e-business. A majority of failed e-business initiatives stem from poor software design and deployment. Software failures fall into two general categories: software projects that exceed time, labor, and monetary constraints, and projects that are implemented with the wrong technology. Minimizing these risks is essential. Fortunately, software technology exists to do just that.

Open source (software that is publicly developed and available in native source code form) is revolutionizing the world of software development. Paying for expensive and proprietary software licenses does not guarantee e-business success—it only guarantees that your company will spend money. The cost and effort put into software projects should be focused on providing solutions that work.

Open source is rooted in the philosophy of enabling solutions. Open source provides what no proprietary software can offer—open code that is scrutinized by the world. It is a significant technological leap forward in the software development process. Generally, we think of technological improvements as advances in actual products. Open source is a technological improvement not just in the final product, but also in the process used to create that product.

The success of the open source development process is revolutionizing the creation of software. Open source software is built by a distributed community of experts from across the globe. Open source communities consist of a diverse and multi-talented group of individuals and companies, which pools its skills and resources to build solid, reliable, and high-performing computer software. The goal of the community is simple: build great software that solves problems now and can grow over time.

Open source is the spawning ground for cutting-edge technology. It is extremely difficult for a proprietary company to match the worldwide expertise available to open source projects. Open source projects like HTTP, HTML, and XML exist today as software standards because of their developmental and utilization freedom. Open source, due to its democratic process, allows for the most creative and useful advancements in software technology. Building an e-business solution in open source reduces the risk of being stuck with proprietary and potentially outdated technology products.

Utilizing open source also mitigates the risk of overextended software budgets. There is no cost to buy bits. The cost of using open source, as in proprietary software, is in developing the custom e-business solution. For the one dollar you spend to deploy an open source project, the whole one dollar goes to creating the solution. For the one dollar you spend for a proprietary-based project, an estimated 25 cents go to paying for software licenses.

Additionally, because the source code is openly available to software developers, the time and effort spent in developing an open source solution can be significantly reduced. Many software projects have been held back because of bugs in proprietary systems that can't be fixed. By its inherent open code nature, open source allows developers to fix problems and enhance the system easily.

It is commonly misunderstood that open source software resides in the domain of hackers. Open source has rapidly become mainstream. Today, commercial companies back all of the major open source projects and provide first-class service and support expected by software vendors. For example, Red Hat, a billion-dollar public company, provides service and support for Linux, Apache, Samba, and other open source software. Linux, the highly successful open source operating system, currently has over 10,000 developers working on the software. It is regarded as one of the most stable and quality software products available today. Linux is gaining wide acceptance in the enterprise and has the backing of vendors like IBM, Dell Computer, and Hewlett-Packard.

The benefits of using open source software are obvious. There is open source software that exists today to provide great e-business solutions. In the coming chapters, we'll explore open source software technologies and how to apply them to the various e-business components. We'll show you how to lower costs, reduce risks, and build e-business solutions that work now and over time.

Technology Foundation for E-Business

The four components of e-business (automation, integration, organization, and e-commerce) are needed to employ an effective solution. Technology is the foundation and the enabler of these four components. E-business technology solutions must provide the following:

Reliability. The underlying technological foundation must work consistently.

Performance. The technology must function to specifications.

Security. Critical business information must flow through e-business networks and must be secure.

Scalability. The system must be flexible and upgradeable to grow and change with business demands.

Accessibility. People who come in contact with the system—employees, business partners, and customers—must be able to utilize its features simply and easily.

Hardware is an important piece in the e-business implementation. Because hardware exists in a world of exacting specifications and ever-improving reliability, it is often the strong component of an e-business system. Our focus is on the potentially and historically weak link of the system—software—and specifically how open source software can forge strong e-business solutions.

There are six basic software components for e-business:

Development systems and programming languages. These systems are *software for software*, languages that permit the extension of existing software and development of new applications.

Proprietary examples: Microsoft Visual Basic and Allaire Cold Fusion

Open source examples: Perl, Python, HTML, and XSL

Communication languages and protocols. Software that enables communication between computers and applications.

Proprietary examples: COM and DCOM

Open source examples: HTTP, XSTP, BXXP, SOAP, and XML

Operating systems. The underlying software layer of a computer system that manages hardware resources and applications.

Proprietary examples: Microsoft Windows NT/98/2000, Sun Solaris, and HP UX

Open source examples: Linux, OpenBSD, and FreeBSD

Communication servers. Middleware systems that permit messaging for human communication, such as email and instant messaging.

Proprietary examples: Microsoft Exchange/Outlook, and AOL Instant Messenger

Open source examples: Sendmail, Qmail, and Jabber

Enterprise applications. Software applications for automating business processes and enabling e-commerce, such as customer relationship management or sales force automation applications.

Proprietary examples: Siebel, Vantive, SAP, Oracle, and Broadvision

Open source examples: Akopia Interchange, eGrail, Relata, and Zelerate

Enterprise middleware servers. Middleware systems that host applications and enable application integration.

Proprietary examples: BEA Systems WebLogic, ATG Dynamo, SAGA SagaVista, IBM Websphere, Netscape iPlanet, and Microsoft Internet Information Server

Open source examples: Open3, Zend, Enhydra, Zope, and Apache Web Server

The first two categories, languages and protocols, are dominated by open source software. Other software, such as Linux, Apache Web Server, and Sendmail, have strong penetration into the enterprise. Many other systems, such as Zend, Open3, eGrail, and Akopia, are beginning to make inroads into e-business. We are seeing the first wave of open source enterprise software and many more are in the works.

A broad range of open source applications can assist in building e-business solutions. Before jumping in and choosing an e-business application architecture, an e-business design must be formulated. This design provides the enterprise with an analysis of e-business needs, potential risks and benefits, and a long-term roadmap for success.

E-Business Design

The e-business design lays out the strategy for the enterprise. An e-business design must consider the end goal, the risks and rewards of pursuing that goal, and the costs and long-term effects of the design. E-business initiatives must be thoroughly considered because they will significantly influence the enterprise's future success.

The first question to ask when building the e-business design is "What are we attempting to accomplish to satisfy our needs?" Your needs may be immediate, such as, "We need this e-commerce Web site because we have three competitors that are stealing our business." Or your needs may be longer term, "Our customer service department is good, but we want it to be great. Let's investigate using technology to improve this in the future." Generally, your needs are dependent on how quickly your company needs to react to the e-business revolution. Visionary companies see needs evolving in the enterprise and build their business to meet this opportunity. Laggard companies see their more nimble competitors succeeding and must react swiftly to avoid losing market share and emerging opportunities.

Once you've identified the needs or vulnerabilities of your enterprise, you then must look at the potential risks and rewards of employing an e-business design. Evaluate the potential scope of your needs and to what extent e-business can assist. All businesses will benefit from e-business initiatives, but the type and implementation of these initiatives will vary from business to business. Fundamental and important risks inherent in employing an e-business initiative are time, labor, and monetary expenses. A business must assess the potential long-term rewards versus the cost of implementation.

In evaluating risk, you may need to answer questions such as the following:

- Do we have the time and money to implement this project?
- Is the scope of the project too ambitious or not ambitious enough?
- Does the technology exist to implement this project?
- Is our focus long-term or is this short-term fire fighting?
- Is this e-business initiative realistic or are we just blindly jumping on the e-business bandwagon?
- Are we trying to emulate our competitors or are we trying to do something new and significant?
- Can our corporate organization adapt to the demands of e-business?
- Do we fully understand our e-business initiative?
- In five or ten years, will we have built our e-business strategy to change and grow?

Translating the identification of needs and risks into real world e-business design is a significant challenge. There are several tiers of design to consider for your e-business initiative (see Figure 1.1):

Tier 0: What's E-Business? Businesses at this stage barely comprehend computers, technology, and the Internet, let alone the scope and complexities of e-business. Tier 0 companies either don't have the man-

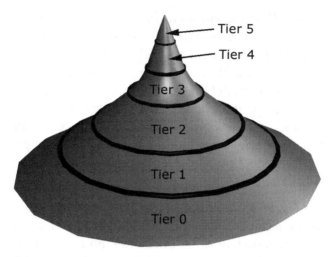

Figure 1.1 The tiers of e-business.

agement to recognize the need for e-business, have failed horribly with technology initiatives in the past, or are too tiny to consider e-business helpful. Few Tier 0 companies will survive in the evolving landscape of the modern economy.

Tier 1: Scattered Process Automation. Businesses at this tier begin to deploy enterprise applications into various internal business departments to replace manual processes. For example, a company may use an inventory management system to replace written recordkeeping. At this tier, a business is often reacting to immediate needs. They may also have a brochure-ware or other simple functioning Web site. Little consideration is given to the big picture or developing an e-business strategy that will grow over time.

Tier 2: Point-to-Point Integrated Process Automation. Tier 2 companies recognize the need for enterprise applications to share functionality and information. At this level, point-to-point integration scenarios are implemented to connect one application to another. Often these integrated systems are home grown and are tightly coupled to the systems they connect. This is fine if the systems never change and no new systems are added. Unfortunately, technology evolves and change is inevitable. Point-to-point integration is a Band-Aid solution to a short-term problem.

Tier 3: Enterprise Integrated Process Automation. Tier 3 companies are deploying solutions worthy of modern day e-business. Their applications are installed in disparate departments and are fully integrated through an enterprise-class integration solution. Enterprise integration provides a hub-and-spoke model that allows many-to-many integration solutions. The hub is the integration server and the spokes are the enterprise applications. As new applications are added to the enterprise, new spokes are simply added to the system. Tier 3 companies have deployed an internal "knowledge enterprise" and can react swiftly to market conditions.

Tier 4: Inter-Enterprise Integration. Companies at Tier 4 have developed strong internal e-business systems and begin to extend their e-business initiatives to external entities such as other businesses and customers. E-commerce transactions and information exchanges are conducted behind the scenes in real time across value-added networks (VANs) or the Internet. For example, companies at this stage may connect along their supply chain, tying in the purchase of materials with internal inventory and procurement systems.

Tier 5: Total E-Business Enterprise. Tier 5 is e-business nirvana. Reaching this level enables the enterprise to reap all the benefits of e-business. Tier 5 companies connect their fully integrated and internally automated e-business systems with those of business suppliers, partners, resellers, and customers. All facets of the enterprise are digital and automated, allowing the enterprise to react at the speed of light to resolve problems and tap into emerging opportunities.

Every business of moderate size or larger can become a Tier 5 company. Your e-business design must consider where your company is today and what you must do to reach Tier 5 in the future. Companies need not start at Tier 1 and work their way up. A strong e-business design enables companies to begin at Tier 3, the preferred starting point for a modern business engaged in e-business. A strong foundation at Tier 3 enables a business utilizing consistent effort to move to Tier 5, where business leaders of the new economy will reside. Will your company plant its flag on the Mt. Everest of e-business?

Internal and External E-Business Design

There are two major steps in the e-business design: forming a corporate strategy for e-business and developing a game plan and architecture to implement that strategy. The process of strategy formulation is carried out on two fronts, those internal and those external to the enterprise. Internal or intra-e-business projects are generally the starting point for established companies.

Internal E-Business

Internal e-business involves the deployment of applications like customer relationship management (CRM), human resources management (HRM), and inventory management (IM). Enterprise application integration (EAI) ties these applications together into a unified network. Effective internal e-business initiatives will (see Figure 1.2):

Improve speed. Business processes occur in real time without the wait for manual labor to accomplish tasks.

Lower cost. Automating tasks reduces day-to-day costs of doing business and expenses for the production of goods and services.

Figure 1.2   An integrated internal e-business.

Increase efficiency. Minimize waste and effort through a highly organized and automated enterprise.

Enhance customer service. An automated and integrated customer service department enables quick and accurate resolutions to problems.

Improve revenues. Information connection enables companies to better understand markets and customers to generate increased sales.

Internal e-business provides only a portion of the possible benefits. External e-business, through interaction with business partners and customers, extends internal initiatives to enable a total e-business solution. External e-business involves business-to-business (B2B) and business-to-consumer (B2C) initiatives.

External E-Business

B2B connects an enterprise's suppliers, partners, and resellers (see Figure 1.3). There are two basic categories for B2B interactions: one-to-one links between trading partners, commonly known as *extranets*, and connections to an e-marketplace or hub that provides links with potentially hundreds and thousands of business participants. B2B enables a company to streamline its sourcing, manufacturing, and delivery processes to lower costs and tap into new markets.

B2C connects an enterprise digitally with its consumers. The most common B2C initiative is the online storefront, where businesses extend their brick-and-mortar companies into brick-and-click companies that provide integrated sales through the combination of online shopping and traditional stores. Additional B2C initiatives look at utilizing the Internet and wireless technology for innovative ways to promote and distribute products and to enhance customer service.

Enterprise applications, EAI, B2B, and B2C form the basis of the e-business architecture. Understanding these concepts in more detail is crucial in formulating a Tier 5 e-business strategy.

Enterprise Applications for E-Business

Enterprise applications form the core functionality of the e-business design. These applications are often the first consideration made by a busi-

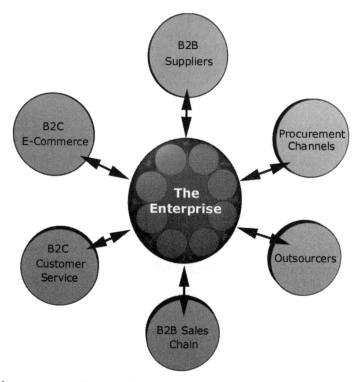

Figure 1.3   An integrated external e-business.

ness toward e-business. Enterprise applications are tailored to service a specific need in the business, such as managing employees or customers. There are several types of enterprise applications:

Customer relationship management. Customer relationship management (CRM) applications help manage interactions with customers. This may include using promotion, following sales leads, completing purchases and contracts, and following up with support and new offers.

Inventory management. Inventory management (IM) applications assist with tracking inventory and providing analysis on inventory supply, purchasing, and maintaining correct levels for optimal stock and profitability.

Human resources management. Human resources management (HRM) applications manage the day-to-day affairs of employees. This includes the management of paychecks, bonuses, commissions, raises, promotions, personal information, and internal activities that affect employees.

Supply chain automation. Supply chain automation (SCA) software assists with automating the process of acquiring raw materials, manufacturing goods, developing services, and the deployment of products.

Procurement management. Procurement software assists with the analysis and purchasing of goods and materials used by the enterprise.

Sales force automation. Sales force automation (SFA) software assists the workflow and processes involved to train, deploy, and manage the sales force in the enterprise.

Enterprise resource planning. Enterprise resource planning (ERP) assists with integrating various aspects of the enterprise architecture into unified system.

Knowledge management and business decision support. This software aids in various aspects of the business to assist with critical decision making and business analysis on data and information in the enterprise.

Accounting and financial. This software provides recordkeeping of business expenses and revenues and generates analysis, such as profit to loss ratios and income forecasting.

Workflow management. Workflow software defines the transactions that must occur to accomplish processes within the enterprise.

The utilization of enterprise applications is essential for effective e-business. Choosing and deploying those applications that will assist your business most effectively is a time-consuming task that cannot be ignored. Open source software is beginning to grab a strong handhold on the enterprise application market, with software products available in many of the application categories.

Enterprise Application Integration for E-Business

Software applications have traditionally been built to perform a certain set of functions, with limited ability to utilize or share features with other applications. This has resulted in many software packages speaking their own unique dialect. Software applications often appear as islands in the ocean of the enterprise, disconnected and limited.

Enterprise Application Integration (EAI) provides software known as middleware that is situated between disparate systems. Middleware is the bridge between software islands. It allows communication and interoperability between software applications and systems.

EAI connects diverse applications like CRM, HRM, SFA, Web servers, database servers, document management systems, desktop applications, legacy systems, and more into a unified and seamless environment.

EAI is essential to e-business. Tier 3 companies and higher build the foundation of their e-business initiatives on EAI. It is something that may be ignored temporarily, but not forever. If you're starting a new e-business initiative, integration must be at the top of your to do list. If your company is Tier 2 or lower, you must implement a game plan to begin building this crucial foundation. Businesses without a comprehensive EAI solution will be left with islands of information and processes that can only be linked by one solution—slow and error-prone manual labor. Manual business processes are yesterday's business processes. EAI creates automation for the modern generation of business. Middleware technology enables EAI and builds a continent out of a group of business islands.

There are various types of middleware technologies, each with functionality tailored to different integration scenarios. These technologies include message-oriented middleware (MOM), message brokering, object brokering, remote procedure calls, workflow servers, and others.

Diverse middleware technologies exist to service diverse environments. Ideal middleware systems support the following functions:

- To expose data in applications
- To expose methods and functions in applications
- To translate different data formats between applications
- To enforce business rules for data and function sharing
- To manage communication between applications

There are two ways to exchange data and functions, and middleware systems may provide one or both of these mechanisms:

Synchronous transfer. Synchronous communication requires a sending and receiving system to be tightly coupled. Therefore, the sender of data must wait for the receiver to receive those data before it can move on to other processes. Until the data are received, the sender is blocked. Typically, synchronous transfer occurs between two systems in real time. It is useful in business processes such as bank transaction that require, for example, the clearing of a check before money can be collected from it.

Asynchronous transfer. This form of communication allows loose coupling between systems. A sending application does not need to know where its receivers are and is not concerned if its receivers are even listening. This allows great flexibility in the design of the system. A sender does not have to wait for a recipient before it can continue to send messages. Asynchronous transfer is the communication of choice for diverse and multiple environments, and most modern EAI initiatives are built on this communication architecture.

Built on synchronous and/or asynchronous communication, there are two basic types of middleware integration systems (see Figure 1.4):

Point-to-point. This middleware connects two systems. An example of this software is a piece of code that can translate function calls of one application's API to another. Often this software is custom coded and is implemented as a short-term solution. Problems arise when data and functionality must be shared with a third application so two new software pieces must be written to talk to the first two integrated applications. If a fourth application is added, three new middleware pieces must be added to the system. This system quickly becomes unwieldy if more than a few applications must be integrated.

Many-to-many. This middleware system is a sophisticated piece of software machinery that provides a way for multiple applications to connect to each other. It often employs message-based communication, known as MOM. Applications have adapters that allow them to connect to the middleware server. Adding a new application to the system is simply done by using an adapter to connect it to the server, regardless of the number of other applications connected to the system.

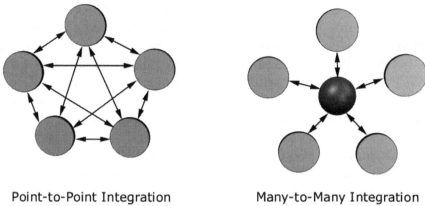

Point-to-Point Integration   Many-to-Many Integration

Figure 1.4   Point-to-point integration versus many-to-many integration.

MOM is often extended with message brokering capability, allowing features such as translation between different data formats and complex routing of messages through multiple applications. This provides for highly sophisticated function and data sharing throughout the e-business software environment. Many-to-many is enterprise-level integration software. Tier 3 and higher e-business initiatives extensively utilize many-to-many systems.

Therefore, in all but the most simple and limited initiatives, many-to-many integration is the obvious choice. Why, then, do many businesses continue to implement point-to-point integration? There are a few reasons. One is the cost to license the middleware software and another is the overhead in support personnel that are needed to develop and maintain the system.

The cost to license enterprise-level integration systems starts in the high five figures and is often $100,000 or more. Application adapters also generally require licensing fees, pushing the cost for software licenses for large projects into the seven figures. Many companies balk at paying $1,000,000 or more just to license software. In this case, management turns to a few programmers in the IT department to write some custom code to tie together the critical systems they want to integrate. This works temporarily with varying success, but many companies soon realize that they are reinventing the wheel and often devoting enormous resources to developing a system that has little long-term viability.

Additionally, expertise with expensive proprietary systems is rare. Standards, such as Sun's Java Message Service (JMS), are being utilized by more than 75 percent of middleware vendors. Standards make a greater force of IT talent available because a person can move from one standards-based system to another. Unfortunately, many of these systems build their own additional proprietary features on top of standards-based specifications, requiring software implementers to learn a whole new set of functionality for each system. The cost barrier to entry makes it difficult for software developers to use these proprietary systems, and consequently, this leads to limited expertise in the industry to provide the integration implementation.

Fortunately, there are strong open source projects that are solving the problems of cost and labor. Projects such as Open3, OpenJMS, and Enhydra are built to the same exacting standards specifications as proprietary products. For example, Open3 provides an implementation of JMS, additional message brokering functionality for complex integration scenarios, and a host of application and database adapters—all of which are open source and available at no cost. Eliminating the cost barrier tears down the knowledge barrier because software developers can easily get their hands (or minds) on the systems and begin using them.

Strong integration architecture is essential to succeeding at e-business. The availability of solid and reliable open source many-to-many integration systems makes the implementation of a custom point-to-point solution a poor choice. Open source enables first-class enterprise integration capabilities for all businesses.

Business-to-Business E-Business

B2B leverages the ideas behind enterprise applications and EAI to connect and integrate an enterprise with its business partners. B2B links a business with trading partners such as manufacturers, suppliers, and resellers to create an automated trading community. Once a business has completed essential portions of its enterprise application and integration initiatives, it can then begin to build B2B programs.

B2B transactions are enabled through message or document interchanges over value-added networks (VANs), virtual private networks (VPNs), and the public Internet. Typical message formats are Electronic Data Interchange (EDI) for VANs and eXtensible Markup Language (XML) for VPNs and public Internet exchanges. EDI has been in existence for decades and is gradually being replaced by XML. XML has emerged as the new standard for B2B transactions (see Figure 1.5).

B2B is conducted in two broad ways: by direct link to one partner or through trading hubs or e-marketplaces consisting of multiple participants. A direct link to one partner provides a highly personalized and customizable trading interaction. B2B through hubs is more generic but provides cost efficiencies and a standard framework for conducting business. Generally, a complete B2B e-business strategy involves both methods, and thus the system architecture must be designed to support the two.

In addition to these two general ways of conducting B2B, more specific initiatives exist such as the following:

Industry consortium marketplaces. These hubs concentrate buyers or sellers to negotiate the best price. In buyer-oriented marketplaces,

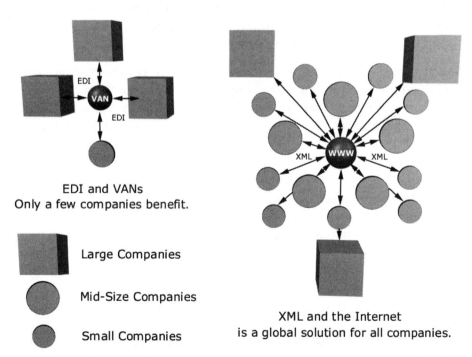

EDI and VANs
Only a few companies benefit.

Large Companies

Mid-Size Companies

Small Companies

XML and the Internet
is a global solution for all companies.

Figure 1.5   XML tears down the cost and technological barriers of EDI and enables a globally-connected marketplace.

smaller groups of business purchasers band together to increase their purchasing power and demand lower prices from suppliers. In seller-oriented marketplaces, groups of business suppliers pool their resources to provide great depth and selection of products. Monopoly, antitrust, and price-fixing issues are of concern in these industry hubs, but they are emerging rapidly in the modern economy.

Aggregate distributor. In this model a single entity unifies a fragmented buyer and seller marketplace. The aggregator takes product descriptions, price lists, and catalogs from a variety of sources and consolidates these into buyer-customized super catalogs. Buyers then purchase from the aggregator using a single purchase order. The aggregator's system is then responsible for parsing the order into smaller purchase orders and delivering these to the sellers. The sellers then deliver the products back to the aggregator or directly to the aggregator's buyers.

Procurement portals. Portals provide an integrated environment, generally through the Internet, to facilitate automated, efficient, and streamlined buying processes. Portals create a friendly environment for employees to negotiate and procure goods quickly and easily for the business. Procurement portals also provide catalog consolidation from multiple suppliers and integration with software for the analysis of the purchasing and spending processes.

Supply chain consolidation. This initiative often combines direct partner and trading hub links. The supply chain is the complex network of business partners that source, manufacture, promote, and deliver goods and services. Consolidation along the supply chain provides for the automated coordination of raw goods, manufactured materials, product information, and financial transactions.

B2B projects are more difficult to implement than intra-enterprise initiatives. The reason is simple—each business has its own particular way of conducting business. Adjusting to a common framework is difficult. Adding to the complexity is the variety of technology that may be implemented to facilitate B2B. The developments of recent standards, many which have been born in open source communities, are charging to call of a common system for B2B. These standards, like XML, are creating a new generation of frameworks for inter-business communication.

B2B Frameworks

There are many B2B frameworks that have been developed in recent years. B2B frameworks come in two flavors, horizontal and vertical. Horizontal frameworks apply broadly and shallowly to several markets. Vertical frameworks apply to a single market with great depth. Examples of horizontal frameworks include the Open Trading Protocol (OTP), BizTalk, Commerce XML (cXML), Commerce Business Library (CBL), and the Organization for the Advancement of Structured Information Standards (OASIS) electronic business XML (ebXML) community. Vertical frameworks include RosettaNet, and Information and Content Exchange (ICE). The Open Applications Group Integration Specification (OAGIS) provides a horizontal framework that complements several vertical markets. Many of these frameworks utilize XML to define documents, workflows, and transactions. Also common to these frameworks is management by business partners and industry allies so that the community develops the framework's specifications.

Choosing the right framework for your e-business design depends upon your business model, your industry, your business partners, and the required functional flexibility for long-term B2B success. RosettaNet has focused its efforts on the IT industry and suitably addresses the broad functional requirements of B2B. Open standards like ebXML, OAGIS, and RosettaNet are emerging dominant over commercially directed frameworks like BizTalk, Ariba, and Commerce One. Fortunately, there are many overlapping features of the frameworks, and some portions of the frameworks are interoperable.

The B2B project initiatives and the architectural framework depend upon the particular nature of the business strategy formulation. Top-tier companies demand successful B2B programs. Implementing a sound business strategy in the e-business design will provide the basis for developing the right technological architecture and corporate organization to make B2B in your enterprise a thriving reality.

Business-to-Consumer E-Business

E-business strategy focuses toward the customer-centric company. In a customer-centric company, the corporate organization, product development and deployment process, marketing, advertising, sales, and service are centered on the customer's demands. For the business that derives the bulk of its revenues from purchases by the end customer, a strong B2C e-business strategy is critical (see Figure 1.6). B2C strategies include online storefronts, online distribution and promotion, and automated customer service.

Online Storefronts

The online storefront is the most common B2C strategy. It is an Internet Web site that enables customers to browse and buy products. Online storefronts allow buyers to avoid crowds and long lines in department stores by shopping online from the comfort of their home.

There are several reasons to choose an online storefront strategy:

- To tap into the worldwide customer base of the Internet
- To increase profits or lower prices by reducing costs to sell

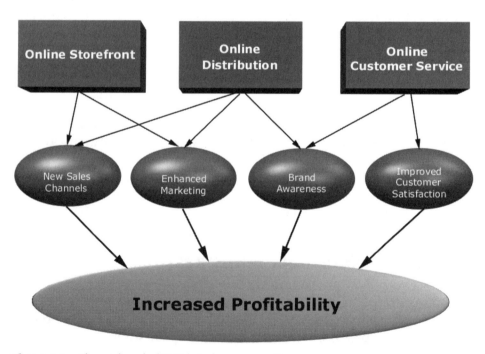

Figure 1.6 The end goal of B2C is to increase profits.

- To operate virtually and appear larger and more sophisticated than its brick-and-mortar counterpart

- To form the basis of a new business that operates solely through digital channels

- To provide an easy and convenient way for its customers to make informed purchases

In evaluating the e-business strategy, a business must answer the following questions:

- Will your customers buy your products online? Will customers buy books, groceries, golf clubs or women's dresses over the Internet? Is it reasonable that your products can be purchased without ever being physically seen or touched?

- How will you differentiate yourself from the entrenched competition? Maybe you're considering selling books online? How are you going to compete against giants like Amazon.com, Barnesandnoble.com, and Borders.com?

- Do you understand how the technology changes the way of operating a business online? Customers demand a greater amount of service and attention in the digital world. How will you figure shipping costs for sales around the world? How will you handle customer returns? Operating online creates many new challenges.

- Do you have the resources to devote to an online storefront? Can you afford the costs to build it? Maintain it? Upgrade it? Do you have employees to provide the additional customer service and the inventory, shipping, and receiving requirements?

- Are we doing this just to "join the crowd"? Will your business make money from this either directly or indirectly? Investing in an online storefront must be a business strategy and fundamental to the future success of your company.

Next, the enterprise must evaluate the technology architecture to implement. There are popular proprietary products such as Intershop, ATG Dynamo, and Microsoft Commerce Server. Growing in popularity are strong open source projects like Akopia and Zelerate for rapid e-commerce storefront creation, and development environments like Zope and PHP/Zend that provide a framework for building online storefronts.

The online storefront architecture is composed of two pieces, each critical to the success of the Web site. The first piece is the *back-end system*. This is engine under the hood that drives the Web site. The back-end software systems include the databases, content repositories, application middleware, e-commerce packages, fulfillment systems, and Web servers. These pieces must work together to deliver the second piece of the online storefront architecture, the front-end. The *front-end* is the Web site that the customer interacts with. The front-end requires software development for page layout, graphics design artists, writers for text content, and testers to measure the usability and functionality of the site.

Using only open source software, an enterprise can build a first-rate scaleable and reliable B2C storefront. If you were to buy all of the software from proprietary vendors, your enterprise is likely to spend up to six to seven figures. Open source, with powerful software at low cost barriers, has emerged as a very strong alternative in the B2C space.

Online Distribution and Promotion

The Internet is creating new ways to distribute and promote products. Software like Napster and Gnutella have turned the music industry on its head. The Internet enables distribution models that have never before existed. You must prepare your enterprise to tap into the realities of how the Internet is changing the business landscape of digital information distribution. Promotion to customers can be extended to the Web by utilizing open source software like Relata and OpenSourceCRM. These packages can be seamlessly integrated into your enterprise with a platform like Open3. Connecting web-based marketing to your Internet application is essential to the success of B2C initiatives. Online customer promotion has several benefits including cost reduction, personalized marketing, and rapid customer attention.

Automated Customer Service

B2C e-business initiatives leverage new frontiers in customer service. The Internet is redefining self-service. It permits customers to find information quickly and easily on their own. For example, Amazon.com provides an enormous resource of information for users browsing books online. They can read information from the book publisher and reviews from writers and general readers. Amazon.com also sponsors chats and interviews with the book authors. This level of information is not possible in a traditional bookstore. It enables book purveyors to make highly informed buying decisions without the need to ask a service representative. Customers are happier because they can help themselves in less time and feel confident in their purchase.

Customers that become self-reliant are more dedicated and require fewer business resources, improving short-term and long-term profitability. Enabling self-service requires creating a user friendly system with access to timely, correct, and complete content. Open source content management systems like eGrail and Apache Jetspeed can provide the information backbone for self-service Web sites. These systems can be extended with open source development environments like Zope and Enhydra. The creation of highly functional systems for customer self-service is a necessary and important task for B2C e-business.

Summary

E-business will become a significant component of future business activity. Many companies are faced with the daunting challenge of evolving toward e-business or be left behind by more agile competitors. The enterprise faces significant complexities in this transformation including adoption by management, acceptance by employees, changes in business activity, and increasing dependence on technology. Compounding these complexities is the fact that e-business is not simply the installation of a magic device that works perfectly forever. E-business is a long-term initiative and requires continual development internal and external to the enterprise. This ongoing development makes a reliable, cost-effective, and customizable technology infrastructure crucial to e-business success. Open source software can form an important mainstay for your e-business design.

In the following chapters, we'll show you the steps you need to take to begin building great e-business solutions using open source software. We'll look at underlying technology such as protocols, programming languages, and operating systems to build your IT architecture upon. Next, we'll investigate choosing open source enterprise applications and integration software for creating a unified system. Then we'll investigate open source B2B and B2C solutions. Open source is ready for e-business. Is your business ready to become a part of the modern economy? Great solutions are just a few pages away.

CHAPTER

2

Open Source in the Enterprise

The open source movement has changed and grown in the last 50 years and today is challenging the very foundation of the proprietary software hegemony. Open source software is being developed in several major software categories like operating systems, application servers, and enterprise applications to usurp proprietary competitors. Open source fear inside software giants like Microsoft has been publicly exposed. Major technology companies like IBM and Sun Microsystems are devoting significant time and effort to open source because they see smaller competitors like Red Hat and VA Linux speeding ahead in the software revolution. The activity surrounding open source is a boon to users worldwide. Open source delivers quality software at substantially lower cost and restriction than proprietary applications. More applications are being built through the dedicated involvement of software vendors and individuals worldwide. The enterprise can now significantly benefit from lowered costs, higher reliability and security, and easier maintainability by utilizing open source software.

Open source is software released in source code form that allows everyone free and unhindered access to it. There are several definitions and licenses for open source software, however, all recognized licenses support distribution and advancement through open code. Propelled by the success of Linux and Apache, open source projects are beginning to deliver world class software for e-business. In fact, without the acceleration of the Internet that has been primarily propelled by open source software, e-business would not be creating the new economy. Open source is a forefather of e-business. It makes sense that the two should work together.

The rise of open source has long been in the making. Understanding the value behind open source can be garnered from learning a bit about its history.

In the Beginning There Was Only Open Source

Open source was universal in the early days of software. In the 1960s, hardware was the primary source of revenues. Vendors like Digital Equipment Corporation (DEC) provided the software code free of charge to aid the sale of their hardware platforms. Hobbyists and students wrote programs (mostly utilities and games) and freely distributed the code on paper tape to any and all who wanted it. The idea of selling software, rather than creating it as a value-add to hardware or as a hobby, was rare.

A majority of software during this time was public information and publicly innovated; there were no limits to who could use or modify the software. As computer hardware became more sophisticated, so did the need for more complex and useful software. A few enterprising companies, such as Informatics, which in 1962 sold the first million-dollar software product, were the pioneers of the commercial software industry. Cullinane Corporation was the first software company to go public in 1978. It was during this era that the commercial software revolution was born, contrary to popular opinion that Microsoft was the first real software company. It was also during this era that proprietary and closed source software became a reality, replacing the early days of universal open source software.

The value in hardware, such as in a computer chip, is in its patent, design, and manufacturing process. Since hardware is tangible, it is much easier to protect than software. Software is easily replicated, especially when the software is distributed in source code form. This gave rise to distributing software in compiled or binary form that is unreadable by humans and difficult to decipher. Although the software can still be replicated in compiled form, the underlying functionality, the trade secrets of the program, are protected. Thus, closed source software was born. Good for commercial software producers, but bad for software users.

The Modern Era of Open Source

One person in particular, Richard Stallman, rose with fervent energy to denounce the closed source movement. Mr. Stallman was part of an early software sharing community at the Massachusetts Institute of Technology (MIT) Artificial Intelligence (AI) Laboratory in the 1970s. In this community of students, professors, and other participants, all software was made available in source code form. The goal was simply innovation, as good and as fast as possible. Open source, by providing peer-reviewed and peer-developed software to anyone interested, enabled rapid innovation. Coding in this community was without barriers, non-disclosure agreements (NDAs), or strict license agreements—a haven for developers to solve problems and invent useful programs.

In the early 1980s, as commercial companies began to grow in mass, many of the AI Lab's developers were hired away. Additionally, lab vendors now provided only closed source software. These factors ended the open source community Stallman had enjoyed.

Refusing to give in to the proprietary closed source world, Stallman founded the Free Software Foundation (www.fsf.org). His goal was to create a free and open source operating system like Unix. He chose the techie tongue-in-cheek recursive acronym GNU, for *GNU's Not Unix.*

Stallman defined *free* as not referring to price but as the freedom to use the software. He offered four tenets for free software. These four tenets have formed the basis for the modern open source software movement:

- You have the freedom to run the program for any purpose.

- You have the freedom to modify the program to suit your needs. (To make this freedom effective in practice, you must have access to the source code since making changes in a program without having the source code is exceedingly difficult.)

- You have the freedom to redistribute copies, either gratis or for a fee.

- You have the freedom to distribute modified versions of the program, so the community can benefit from your improvements.

In addition to promoting the open source philosophy, the GNU project involved the development of all parts of a robust operating system, such as the kernel, compilers, interpreters, and tools. Stallman left the kernel, the core component of the operating system, for last. He focused the community's initial efforts on the other components and developed successful software like Emacs and the GNU C compiler.

In 1991, the kernel component of the GNU project was still missing. At the time, Linus Torvalds, a Finnish computer science student, needed a more sophisticated operating system than the one he was using, MINIX. This led him, using GNU tools, to develop the first version of Linux. His early success and a foundation on the GNU community philosophy quickly brought other developers into the Linux project. Linux has become one of the most successful software systems ever built, many believe because it was rooted in the ideals of the FSF.

The GNU philosophy has almost a religious zeal for software freedom. Stallman is a very vocal opponent of any proprietary software. His stance has been viewed by some as too strict and incompatible for businesses to accept the use of open source software in their enterprise. To provide an alternative voice in the open source world, the Open Source Initiative (OSI) was formed.

Rebranding Open Source

OSI was spurred to creation by an industry-shattering event. On January 22, 1998, Jim Barksdale, the CEO of Netscape, announced that the source code of the browser clients would be released to the public. Barksdale cited Eric Raymond as being influential in Netscape's decision to go open source. A few days later, Mr. Raymond, a programmer and cultural anthropologist of the open source revolution, banded together with a group of open source veterans to form OSI.

OSI's goal was to rebrand open source from the negative stereotypes that were associated with the FSF. It determined the word *free* was damaging to open source software because the business world thought this was synonymous with *cheap*. The misconception arose because most open source software is free. Stallman never intended *free* to mean free in price but instead to refer to the free in *free*dom. Nonetheless, the open source community needed a voice to which the corporate world would be receptive.

OSI was to be the leader in a movement promoting the benefits of open source to big business, especially the Fortune 500. They sold positive aspects like reliability, strong security, lowered cost, and a better feature set found in great open source software like Linux and Apache.

OSI developed the Open Source Definition (OSD) and coined the term *open source* to define what was and was not an open source project. The strategy was to build a brand for the open source movement, something that business leaders and the press could use as a buzzword in promoting the effort. It was also a tactic that would prevent proprietary companies like Microsoft, battling against revenue loss from open source, from corrupting the movement. OSI could announce or denounce any project as open source and the world would stand up and listen. The OSI vigorously defends what open source means. It has sent many letters steering big proprietary companies in the right direction when they've incorrectly used the term.

The OSD provides a Bill of Rights for open source software. Based upon the GNU license, the OSD provides for unhindered access to the source code, unlimited distribution, and the right to make improvements to the software. Open source software can be given away free or sold for a fee. Anyone has the right to support it and provide services based on it. These liberal freedoms enable one important result—the software is more likely to become popular and a standard if the barrier of entry is low and the quality is high.

No cost and open code removes the barrier for a developer to learn and utilize the software. Many developers, wanting to gain experience with proprietary platforms such as the Oracle database, are blocked by the six figure price tags. These developers are turning to quality open source alternatives like the MySQL database. For example, the popular Google search engine incorporated into Yahoo! runs the MySQL database because of its low cost and strong performance. Since it is easier to get a hold of the software, and the performance of good projects meet or exceed their commercial counterparts, open source has the best opportunity to be adopted by the greatest number of users.

The efforts of the OSI have revolutionized the open source movement, bringing it from software developers to business leaders. The FSF espoused open source to the programmers. Once adopted at the grassroots level, the acceptance of open source software by the enterprise would gradually trickle up to management. Instead of the traditional bottom-up approach of promoting open source, OSI has been able to bring the software into the enterprise from the top down. Convincing the CEOs and CTOs of Fortune 500 companies of the merits of open source has rapidly spread its adoption. Major companies like Dell Computer and IBM have embraced open source software. Numerous private open source companies have started in the past two years, many well funded from the venture capital community, to form the next generation of open source software. The growing diversity of solid open source projects is enabling enterprise-wide e-business solutions.

The composition of the open source community enables its success. The OSI initiative has brought big business and strong media attention to the movement, creating a diverse mix of freedom coders and those who are capitalizing on the software. Understanding the character of the community is helpful to comprehend its dynamics and how it will grow in the future.

Character of the Community

Open source software began in the hacker and hippie community. The word *hacker*, misconstrued by the media as illicit deviants breaking into computer systems and spreading viruses, traditionally and correctly means a programmer, techie, or computer nerd who spends hours on end fiddling with software for benevolent reasons. These hackers and hippies, with their devotion to coding for creating software for the good of the public, have provided the seed and stalk for the open source movement. Today, open source has branched and blossomed with a varied group of participants. There are five discernible categories of people who contribute to and use open source software:

> **Hippie idealists.** Peace, love, and open code. Open source is free code and free information that provides the key to quality and innovation. Open source fights the greedy nature of proprietary software with a weapon that closed-source vendors are hopeless to counteract. Hippie idealists believe they create a better world through open source software.

> **Hacker all-stars.** Open source is the arena for geniuses of the tech world to show off their talents. The Internet has become the Coliseum and algorithms the weaponry for the open source software gladiators. A good example of these all-stars is the elite group of developers for the Linux kernel headed by Linus Torvalds.

Employee techies. Open source code gives developers freedom to do their job. They can tap into and utilize both the software and intelligence of the community to solve problems. These developers are happy to make contributions to open source in their daily course of work.

Cost- and quality-oriented management. As the open source movement has matured, management is increasingly looking to open source for two main reasons. The first is the cost reduction, not just in licensing revenues but for the increasingly available skill set of open source techies in the workforce. The second is quality software. Since open source is developed and scrutinized by a worldwide community, active and successful projects are typically more reliable and secure than their commercial counterparts.

Business strategists. Increasingly, open source is being adopted as a business strategy. Consulting, service, and support companies are looking to open source as a model for developing and profiting through software expertise.

This diverse mix of attitude toward the usefulness of open source paints a motley canvas of varied benefits. There is something for everyone in the movement. Because open source has moved solely from the hippie/hacker realm to include a business-friendly component, it is becoming more broadly adopted. Increasing acceptance is driving resources to build more and better software. Many of the all-star developers are now paid for their work, such as Linus Torvalds at chipmaker Transmeta, or Brian Behlendorf of Apache at Collab.net. Salaries for hackers let them pursue open source initiatives full-time. Red Hat employs many of the kernel developers on the Linux project and releases all of their work back to the open source community.

The success of open source is largely owed to the community that supports it. Open source community development has defied traditional thinking about what constitutes a proper environment for the creation of successful software. It is this community, composed of the five categories of people above, that is enabling strong open source alternatives to proprietary software.

Open Source Community Development

Imagine a software project with 10,000 developers. The size and complexities of such a project are enormous. How do you coordinate 10,000 developers into a coherent system? 1,000 managers? Maybe, but then you'd need managers to manage the managers. And managers to manage the managers that manage the managers. You get the idea. Fred Brooks created Brooks' Law in *The Mythical Man-Month* (Addison-Wesley, 1995), which states that as the number of developers, n, increases, the complexities of the project increases n^2. The reasoning behind this is that the number of pathways of communication between developers must grow by the total number of developers each time a new developer is added. This means that a project with any more than a few developers is too complex to complete efficiently and effectively. Many experienced project managers have found Brooks' Law to be undeniable, and have learned from trial and error that adding more developers to a project often delays its completion date rather than the intended effect of finishing it more quickly.

Remarkably, the Linux project has defied Brooks' Law. As many as 10,000 developers have actively contributed to the software. The Linux community accomplished what no other proprietary company has been able to do—mount an effective offensive against the Microsoft Windows operating system. They've been able to do this because the project accomplished the seemingly insurmountable feat of pooling the resources of thousands of talented developers from around the globe.

Linux and other open source projects defy traditional programming practices by employing fundamental tools, including the Internet, evolutionary development, and a bazaar, or open source, community. The Internet enables n^2 communication with only n effort. A programmer posts code, documents, and bugs to a central repository that everyone can access from anywhere. All communication is publicly open, so before a person asks a question he or she can refer to a repository to see if it has already been answered. The broad dissemination of information helps to eliminate duplicated efforts. Open source evolutionary development mimics the design process of evolutionary biology. Stephen Jay Gould, acclaimed professor of zoology at Harvard, defines biological evolution as "adaptation to changing local environments." In software, the *local environment* is the area of industry in which a particular software lives. For example, Linux lives in the operating system space. Adaptation is Darwin's "survival of the fittest." Fit software adapts to survive in changing environments. Open source development mimics biological evolution through constant pressure for selection. Open source is publicly open and new code becomes available worldwide overnight. This extreme openness, as opposed to proprietary software that remains in its caves for months, provides constant pressure and continuous viewing and refinement by the community to select the best code.

The computer age moves at the speed of light. One year in the computer age is like a million years in biological evolution. Imagine a short-haired bear, surviving in a comfortable temperate environment, that decides one day it will hibernate for the next 500,000 years. When it awakes from its slumber, the landscape has changed to a frigid snow-covered landscape. Evolved bears have grown great wooly coats to protect them from the cold. The short-haired bear is no longer fit to survive.

Proprietary software is just like the short-haired bear. It hunkers down in a secretive development phase for months, if not years, before it emerges in the world and can be tested against the current environment. Whether or not the software survives depends on two factors: the ability for the developers to predict the emerging environment and the quality of software in that emerging environment. Before the era of open source, poor software survived because its competition was even less fit. Now that open source software is out in the world, constantly being refined, fixed, and updated, it is adapting at levels that cannot be replicated by proprietary software. Closed systems are dinosaurs and open source evolutionary development is the great meteorite that has struck the landscape. Extinction of proprietary hegemony is imminent. Building e-business solutions on open source are solutions for long-term survival.

Eric Raymond, in his seminal work *The Cathedral and the Bazaar* (O'Reilly and Associates, Inc., 1999), describes closed source development as a *cathedral faction* and open source development as a *bazaar community*. Proprietary firms subscribe to cathedral development, so named because of the similarities to the secluded and secretive nature of monks. Cathedral development is characterized by teams of developers that hunker down in their cubicles, withdrawn from the eyes of outsiders, to produce software. Open source is quite the opposite—its bazaar style encourages everyone to participate in an open process.

The definition of a bazaar, a marketplace of various shops and diverse customers, is characteristic of the open source development process. In the bazaar, sellers compete for buyers. Sellers succeed when they peddle their wares at high profits. Buyers succeed when they've purchased their goods at low cost. Bazaars work because they encourage competition between both buyers and sellers. High-priced and low-quality vendors don't earn profits. Very thrifty customers waste their time without making a purchase. There are many shops and many customers and only some are successful.

Like these buyers and sellers in the bazaar, code in open source exists in a highly competitive environment. The sellers are the developers and the buyers are the users (some of which are also the developers) of the software. Good code succeeds, and bad code is pruned or fixed. Bugs are like dishonest vendors that are quickly recognized and removed. The software is released frequently and is constantly tested in a haphazard, yet highly effective manner. Bugs become shallow, and their removal occurs early in the project development process. This is highly desirable for e-business solutions because open source produces highly reliable and secure code. Completed versions of open source software are significantly more finished than proprietary Cathedral software that has been seen by few eyes and quickly rushed to market. Highly reliable and secure software is the most important reason to adopt open source solutions.

As open source is reaching new heights for use in business, it is breaking ground as a fundamental business strategy. The business strategy is based in the ideals of open source, publicly developed software, and a shift from locking customers into an endless cycle of upgrades to providing solutions that work. This shift is proving, through successes like Linux and Apache, a phenomenal disruption to the status quo in the software industry. Recognizing this shift is essential to the types of e-business solutions that your enterprise adopts.

Disruption to the Entrenched

The history of business and technological success is based on disruption. Disruption creates new rules in the industry. Open source software and e-business are two strong modern disrupters. Open source is redefining the software business and is emerging as one of the most revolutionary advances ever in software development. E-business is a disruptive force that is changing traditional paradigms for conducting business.

Disruption occurs through two main factors: significant new invention and unique ways to satisfy and create new demand. New inventions are at the cornerstone of many businesses capitalizing on technology. Invent something, patent it, and your business has a monopoly for nearly two decades. New invention has traditionally been leveraged as fortification for the enterprise. Open source turns the tables on this conventional strategy. Open source is about creating products that everyone invents. The significant difficulty and complexity in developing solid software is solved when experts from around the world can contribute to a particular application. Likewise, e-business leverages invention in a similar manner. There is no single protocol, programming language, or piece of software that magically produces e-business. E-business is a conglomeration of the best technology the world has to offer.

Open source and e-business also utilize unique ways to satisfy and create new demand. Open source satisfies demand by solving difficult technology issues with robust and low-cost software. It also creates new demand by lowering the barriers of entry, especially through the lowered cost and open licensing, to new technology. Smaller companies and developing countries can afford the solutions that open source enables. E-business satisfies demand for greater efficiency, lowered cost, and new revenue sources. It creates new demand by creating new business models, such as Yahoo! or eBay. Disruptive forces cannot be denied. When the landscape changes, your enterprise must leverage the new models to succeed.

Shift to Service

Open source is a business strategy being adopted by both big and small enterprises. Large companies like Sun Microsystems, IBM, and SAP have invested a portion of their resources in open source. These companies are pursuing hybrid strategies with their proprietary models. Open source dedicated companies like Red Hat, Caldera, and VA Linux have had strong initial success and have garnered significant public stock valuations. Several smaller private companies have based their entire strategy on open source. Companies like Lutris Technologies, Open3 Technologies, ActiveState, and Zelerate have grown in the past few years to provide open source enterprise systems and applications.

As open source becomes more prevalent in the software world, it is disrupting the industry marketplace. For example, Linux has been the only effective competitor to emerge against Microsoft Windows NT. Before Linux landed strong blows in 1998, Windows NT enjoyed great success in taking market share from Unix platforms. The disruption in the industry by Linux has caused Microsoft to shift strategies to new licensing models.

The new open source landscape is causing a paradigm shift in the way companies generate revenues. Instead of selling software licenses, open source companies sell turnkey, support, and custom solutions for software. The industry is changing from selling bits to selling services that make those bits work.

A new breed of consulting companies use open source as a strategic advantage over large competitors like Accenture, MarchFirst, and Sapient. These companies are founders of open source projects and lead their sponsorship in the community. Their strategy is simple—use the low barrier of entry created by open source to gain market share. These companies leverage the initial expertise and brand created to pursue lucrative contracts. It's a strategy that has worked extremely well for Digital Creations. Their open source Zope project for rapidly building Web sites has become very popular. Digital Creations is so busy that it can't handle all the requests for Zope contracts and must offload its business to other companies.

In addition to causing a shift to service, open source is enabling the commodity era in software. Commodity software is based on enabling highly customizable but rapidly completed technology solutions.

Enabling the Commodity Era in Software

In the later part of the 1980s, the personal computer platform evolved from proprietary systems to commodity systems, whereby a computer could be built entirely from third-party components and easily customized. IBM and Apple failed to recognize this and quickly lost share to commodity players like Dell and Gateway. The commodity era in software is now approaching, replacing bulky one-size-fits-all applications with custom software built from libraries of smaller components.

There is no universal application or set of applications that will accomplish an e-business initiative. Every business operates differently and has varied e-business objectives. A retailer may find value in an e-commerce consumer Web site, while a construction company may find more value in a B2B supply portal. Even companies that compete in the same industry operate differently, with diverse business partners and unique business processes. It is this uniqueness that enables companies to succeed. Extending uniqueness to the e-business implementation is a prerequisite for continued success in the modern economy. Custom solutions are absolutely necessary for e-business to work effectively and efficiently. Commodity software is the enabler of custom solutions for e-business.

Open standards and open source are enabling the commodity era in software. A solution built on open standards may use pluggable software from a variety of vendors. One of the most successful open standards to emerge in recent years is the Java 2 Enterprise Edition (J2EE) platform from Sun Microsystems. J2EE is a platform for building distributed and integrated applications that function on both the back-end and front-end of e-business. The platform includes popular features like Enterprise Java Beans (EJB), Java Message Service (JMS), and Java Server Pages (JSP).

Large companies like IBM, Oracle, BEA Systems, and Art Technology Group have adopted the J2EE platform by building implementations of it. Applications built on J2EE can run on any J2EE-compliant implementation. This allows the developers of e-business solutions to pick J2EE components from a variety of vendors to build their technology base. Open standards provide flexibility in choosing technology for custom e-business solutions.

Open source projects built on open standards, like Open3 built on the J2EE Java Message Service API or the J2EE Enhydra implementation, go one step further by allowing significant benefits to proprietary solutions. Access to the source code guarantees the highest level of customization. Development by a public community means that good open source software has been rigorously peer-reviewed and peer-tested. Custom e-business requirements that go beyond the features of the open standards can be accomplished much more quickly and effectively with open source. Additionally, the price of open source software can't be beat since many proprietary vendors of open standards like J2EE carry a five and six figure price tag.

Open Source is the epitome of commodity software that enables the greatest flexibility for e-business solutions. The rise of open source in commodity software is redefining the software industry and is a significant change from expensive and proprietary systems.

Risks and Benefits of Using Open Source in the Enterprise

In the modern world people have a tendency to look for magic cures that will solve medical ailments. We have medicine for depression, anxiety, weight loss, weight gain, hair removal, hair growth, and most everything else diagnosed as a medical problem. Some of these drugs do work for the quick fix that people labor for. Unfortunately, the mindset of a quick fix is translated to many problems that don't have an easily definable solution. E-business won't magically fix the poorly functioning enterprise. Open source won't instantly solve all technology problems. E-business and open source will solve many problems, but they won't do so overnight. The following are several risks in utilizing open source for the enterprise:

The enterprise fails to understand what problems a particular software technology can and cannot solve. This risk is inherent to both open source and proprietary software. However, let's make one thing clear: Open source succeeds only on its own merits and not the marketing hype accompanied with many proprietary products. Therefore, no matter how many slick sales and marketing people hype a proprietary product, it won't solve every issue that a business faces. Such is the case for open source software. It has limitations. Mitigating the risk of using the wrong technology or expecting too much means having a full understanding of the capabilities and limitations of the software.

The enterprise adopts a careless attitude of "It's free and it's open source, so let's use it." Maybe your enterprise has succeeded with open source in the past and had developed a "let's go for it" attitude. It's important to understand that because something is open source doesn't mean that it's automatically good. It's the same with proprietary software. Some proprietary systems function well and others don't. Your enterprise must only accept open source solutions that deliver the reliability, security, and robustness that mission-critical e-business demands. Unless your enterprise plans to finish and customize a particular project, utilize open source software that is production ready.

The enterprise utilizes open source software that has poor or non-existent documentation. There are thousands of open source projects. A majority of these are simple tools and applications that have been developed by a single person. Software developers are notorious for not documenting their work. Open source developers are no different. Even though the software is open source, documentation provides a substantial reduction in the learning curve for the application. It is difficult to assess the features and limitations of software without documentation. Trusting your enterprise to a poorly documented application can have deleterious effects. Most quality open source projects are well documented. Make it a requirement in your enterprise to only use software that you can fully comprehend.

The enterprise deploys open source software without adequate third-party support. Software development and e-business implementation come with difficulties. It's a part of the trade. Expert support is extremely helpful when the IT team becomes stuck on a problem. In critical e-business projects, speed and efficient use of resources are necessary. Deploying open source software with adequate support helps to ensure that these needs are met. There are two potential ways to solve support issues with open source. First is to utilize the message boards of the project community. Generally, helpful participants are available to assist with your problem. These individuals will vary in their expertise and how much investigation they're willing to do, so it's hit or miss whether the community will solve your problem. The second way to solve support issues is through commercial companies. Generally the best companies are those that sponsor particular projects, like Digital Creations for Zope, or companies that actively work with the projects, like Kaivo for Zope. Solid commercial companies will endeavor to solve the most difficult of your support issues—for a price. Often the cost is significantly less than the time and effort your IT team will spend in attempting to solve the problem on their own.

The enterprise engages open source software that has not been adequately tested. Quality assurance is one of the most highly ignored components in the software engineering process. Products have frequently been shipped with little testing to meet corporate timelines. Proprietary products are released prematurely for commercial objectives, and some open source software may never have a formal testing process in the first place. Smaller open source projects, those of a handful of developers or less, are focused on writing the code. Inadequate attention may be given to testing the product on various platforms and configurations. This can result in software that functions well on one particular configuration but has bugs when used in other setups. However, this problem is generally evidenced in small open source projects or projects early in their software lifecycle. The very nature inherent in the wide distribution of open source can make the software extremely reliable. Linux is an excellent example.

The risks of using open source primarily extend from the historical roots of the software growing from a discontinuous group of individual developers. Times are changing. Open source developers have begun to focus on additional aspects of the software engineering process, like formal quality assurance, rather than just the development effort. Companies contributing to and sponsoring open source projects are basing their commercial success on the quality of the software. Therefore, necessary attributes like testing, documentation, and support are inherent to quality open source projects. The open source community is aggressively addressing risks and working to alleviate them.

Throughout the chapter, we've discussed the many benefits of using open source. These benefits include the following:

The enterprise unleashes itself from an endless cycle of upgrade churn. One of the most profitable strategies of proprietary companies has been to develop products with multiple generations or versions. This practice makes sense; after creation of a product, feedback from the user community, and the advancement of technology, the addition of new features makes the product a better one. However, problems arise when advancements are intentionally stifled to prolong the lifetime and profitability of the product. Additionally, users must wait months or years to enjoy the new features of the product. Software vendors make strategic decisions based on their business goals. These may not be the same goals that are best for their users.

Open source eliminates several potential deleterious effects of upgrade churn. First and foremost is that the software is never held back, features are added constantly based upon user demand. Therefore, open source projects may have dozens of smaller lifecycles in the space of one large lifecycle by a proprietary vendor. Features are made available to users more quickly, helping them do their jobs better and more efficiently. The second advantage (one that delights upper management) is that most open source software doesn't require a constant and expensive outlay from the corporate coffers. Proprietary vendors generally offer lower cost upgrade prices to its existing customers. However, this doesn't mean that the cost is cheap. A $100 upgrade for 5,000 users costs the company $500,000. Everyone agrees that this is a substantial expenditure. The decision to use an open source product of comparable quality to a proprietary one becomes a no-brainer when looking at the cost factor.

The enterprise has unbounded ability to customize the software. This is a great benefit if your company has the desire or expertise to customize the software. Often, remarkable gains in efficiency can be achieved by custom tailoring a product to the enterprise's workflow. By having access to the source code, this possibility becomes a reality.

The enterprise engages software that has been designed and tested by a worldwide community. This is a significant and extremely important benefit. Broad and active open source software projects have the critical mass to be developed and tested by a global peer-reviewed community. When a community reaches this critical mass, the software engineering process attains its peak in quality. Bugs are found and fixed quickly. Features are added, reviewed, and tested in time spans of hours and not weeks or months. Security flaws are rapidly exposed and expunged. Quality software is essential for e-business and strong open source projects are known for producing some of the best software available.

The enterprise realizes a lower cost of utilization. This benefit stems not only from the lowered cost of the open source software but also from the savings reaped by a reliable product with a knowledgeable IT user base. Reliability has been a significant issue for several major Internet companies like eBay. These companies can lose millions of dollars of revenues in just a few hours of downtime. No business can afford for its software to fail. E-business creates a dependency on the technology and reliability ensures that the cost of technology won't increase through lost business.

Another cost factor for open source is its low barriers of entry for every IT person to utilize the software. This creates a much wider workforce that is knowledgeable and trained on the product. In a tight labor market for skilled technology talent, this is a significant advantage. Savings are realized through training and from the efficiencies gained by an expert workforce.

The enterprise is unshackled from restrictive licensing. Proprietary licenses can be a nightmare. You may make one copy but only for backup purposes. This license is for developer use only; you must purchase an enterprise (and expensive) license to use this software in production. This language is common in the proprietary licensing scheme. The licenses have been designed to maximize the profitability for software vendors. This means maximizing the cost for its customers. Licensing issues have also caused delays in many software projects. Failure to obtain the correct or enough licenses slow the development and release dates of the projects.

Time wasted is money, especially in e-business. Open source eliminates all of these licensing issues. For example, you may buy one copy of Red Hat Linux for its printed documentation and additional ease of use; then you can install that copy throughout your enterprise, give it to your friends, install it anywhere and everywhere. You'll be amazed at how well your enterprise can run when the ball and chain of proprietary licensing has been eliminated.

Summary

Open source is changing the landscape for software development and distribution. The ideology is a radical paradigm shift from the one espoused by proprietary vendors. Instead of keeping the intellectual portion of the software secret and locking customers into software that they can't change, open source is a democratic process that creates the best features from a public community. Businesses around the world, after struggling with proprietary software and high-cost upgrade churn, are rapidly moving toward open source solutions that best enable their ability to succeed.

E-business does not rest solely within the walls of the enterprise. It demands collaboration with other companies. Therefore, e-business requires that business partners agree on standard systems of technology. Open source, because of its public development and low barriers of entry, provides a strong offering for modern companies. Since businesses will come to accept and utilize open source software more easily, these applications have the best opportunity to emerge as standards. In coming years, open source software will be a major, if not the most significant, enabler of e-business.

The following chapters present a blueprint for building the technology of e-business on open source software. The next chapter will present the foundation of this technology such as protocols, programming languages, and operating environments. These lower-level pieces such as XML, Perl, and Linux form a basis to build out the e-business with enterprise applications, integration, and e-commerce between businesses and customers.

The Foundation of Open Source Technology

Computer systems are built and arranged just like many other traditional products. Most products do not exist as a stand-alone one-piece product. To manufacture a car, for example, a frame, a good engine, an exterior body, and many other components are required. Many of these components may not even come from the same vendor. Computer systems are not much different. They, too, must rely on several components before the whole system is useful. This chapter examines the many pieces and components that provide the groundwork for current e-business computing systems.

The frame or core component of any computer system is the hardware. Often the hardware will dictate what type of software can reside or operate within the computing environment. Additional hardware can be the answer to certain computing problems, if the systems have been architecturally designed correctly. Because the computing industry has essentially "solved" this portion of the problem, an in-depth discussion of the various hardware components required in any enterprise system will be left to another book. New systems require a careful examination of available hardware options. Software will function poorly if it does not have the proper hardware environment within which to operate.

To begin this exploration of the various components that exist in the common computer systems, one must start at the bottom and work toward the outermost layer. It helps to have an understanding of the underlying components of a computer system when selecting or designing an integration scenario. This chapter will look at those core components.

The Operating System

Using the previous automobile example, a computer operating system (OS) provides the engine that allows all the programs of that system to operate. Just as the hardware provides the frame of a system, the OS defines how a program will execute and interact with that underlying hardware. Several operating systems exist in the current marketplace for different hardware configurations and specific application requirements. Microsoft emerged from a small startup company by providing an OS and OS solutions to companies and individuals. IBM commonly provides both the hardware and the OS environment for their enterprise-class mainframe solutions.

For an enterprise-class system, your OS choice is important for the IT operations of the business. The system should be usable, expandable, stable, secure, and provide all the services and features required within a standard corporate environment. Clearly, some operating systems excel in these areas. Since Ken Thompson and Dennis Ritchie's inception of Unix, circa 1970, the Unix platform has reliably provided most of these capabilities. The only real weak point with most Unix-style operating systems was the usability factor. Typical users required a great amount of knowledge to feel comfortable within a standard Unix environment. Most Unix vendors and environments now provide a GUI-style interface that rivals the Microsoft and Apple interfaces. Unix is still more complicated to use but not enough to preclude its use given added benefits like scalability and stability that it provides.

Mainframe operating systems also have their place within business enterprise systems. Operating systems such as OS/390, OS/400 (for the AS/400), and VAX/VMS have a great deal of backing from vendors and user communities. In the past, the mainframe was the only true enterprise-class solution for a business. This idea is rapidly changing. As knowledge increases and the systems evolve, Unix platforms can offer a very competitive option for the enterprise solution. Mainframes are still reliable workhorses and handle multiple batch style jobs well, but the Unix platforms offer an expanding assortment of enterprise class features. Unix systems are also typically cheaper and easier to maintain.

Given the price tag and availability, more of the development community has transitioned to and are familiar with Unix environments. IBM realized this and even provides a Unix environment for their OS/390 platform known as Open Edition or Unix System Services (USS). This low barrier to entry has also created an open source community that primarily uses and prefers Unix environments. This community has given rise to several Unix-style operating systems. The most common of these, Linux, OpenBSD, FreeBSD, and NetBSD, will be covered in the sections that follow. These open source OS solutions provide functionality that matches or even exceeds the proprietary operating systems. If the open source development community sees a feature that it doesn't like or that does not exist, it will quickly be corrected.

The biggest drawback for mainstream corporations has been the lack of knowledge and support surrounding the open source solution. In the past, companies utilizing an open source OS needed to obtain the hardware from various vendors and install the OS in house. Many complex features, including multiple machines, fail-over, and other enterprise-class features needed to be manually designed, configured, and tested by company personnel. Although the OS supported such features, it was a major project for a company to take on. When the same type of solution is purchased from a mainstream vendor, this complex setup process is usually handled by the vendor. For example, when you purchase an enterprise-class system from IBM, IBM provides many setup and training options beyond just shipping the hardware and software.

The environment has changed and this lack of support or knowledge no longer exists. Therefore, it is not a limiting factor for corporations. IT managers can choose to have a system designed and setup by a third party. Many companies exist to provide the total solution or pre-installed server quality packaged solutions such as VA Linux and Cobalt (recently purchased by Sun Microsystems). Mainstream hardware providers including IBM, Compaq, Dell, and others all provide support or solutions for open source OS installations. If the work is still to be done in house, the company employees no longer have to wade through several disparate sources to find the information needed. Companies have been created primarily for support issues and general architecture consulting services such as Linux-Care. The distribution companies providing the open source software have also created a support environment to assist with any problems that arise.

Once a choice is made to utilize an open source Unix-style system, the proper system must be selected. Although Linux is the most abundant and enjoys the largest development community, the OS choice should be made carefully. Each system has its pros and cons, and each system is furthering development to eliminate some of the cons. The one thing that all of the systems have in common is that they are all Unix-like operating systems. Just as Unix comes in many different flavors, so do the open source versions.

Another important factor in the open source OS decision process is the distribution package that is used for the installation, setup, and maintenance of the OS. Several distributions exist for the different open source varieties. Most distributions are created and maintained by a commercial entity. These distributions usually consist of the software on a CD, setup programs, and documentation to make the process easier. Certain packages will also come with support from the vendor. These distributions and the various open source operating systems will be looked at in the following sections.

Linux

Linux is arguably the most successful open source project and as such has been the example by which most open source projects follow. The Linux source code is available under the GNU Public License (GPL), which is the most common open source license, as detailed in Chapter 2, "Open Source in the Enterprise." The Linux community currently consists of thousands of active developers and users numbering into the millions. It is useful to understand Linux and the Linux community to understand some of the other open source projects that exist.

The Linux effort was started in August 1991 by Linus Torvalds on a Usenet newsgroup. The effort was initially approached as a hobby for bored developers "without a nice project" to work on in their spare time. The goal was to create a MINIX-like, and hence Unix-like, OS. The project has grown to thousands of developers, but Linus Torvalds still maintains an active role with Linux and the Linux community.

The term *Linux* is used to describe a multitude of components, systems, and applications that are actually not Linux. The Linux project is focused primarily on the kernel and system components that make up the *core* Linux environment. Beyond the kernel, this includes the thousands of drivers that have been written to interact with the different hardware components and devices. The current goal of the project is to create and maintain a Portable Operating System Interface for Unix (POSIX) and Single Unix Specification-compliant OS implementation. This implementation has been ported to many hardware platforms including x86-based PCs, Compaq Alpha AXP, Sun SPARC and UltraSPARC, Motorola 68000, PowerPC, ARM, Hitachi SuperH, IBM S/390, MIPS, HP PA-RISC, Intel IA-64, DEC VAX, and others.

Given the large development community, Linux has a relatively high number of available drivers when compared to traditional operating systems. This has lead to the ability to support many different hardware configurations. Linux has been compiled and successfully run on everything from a wristwatch to a CRAY computer system. The only devices that usually aren't supported include certain proprietary devices for which drivers are only available from the vendor. One example of this is the Win Modems that are available for the Windows platform exclusively. These modems require that the OS handle much of the data processing reducing the cost of the hardware components. The drivers for these modems require extensive work and knowledge of the device itself. The vendors typically keep this information closed to the outside world. The power of the Linux movement has caused many of these devices to disappear. To *increase* sales, many vendors now provide Linux drivers with new products.

Beyond the core components, Linux is commonly bundled with many other open source programs and software applications. The bulk of these components come from the GNU software bundle created and maintained by the Free Software Foundation (FSF). This software bundle, some of which was created prior to Linux, includes most of the core OS tools that make the underlying OS usable. The GNU tools have been closely coupled with Linux since its creation, although the majority of these tools are designed to run within all modern strains of Unix-like environments. These tools include the important command level interpreters, or shells that make Unix what it is. The GNU environment provides many programming tools including the make utilities and compilers that are actually used to compile and build the Linux kernel. Beyond these required tools, GNU has several useful utilities and even games that make the OS complete.

Recently, great effort has been extended to create a user-friendlier Linux environment. Much of this effort is focused on the creation of an easy to use Graphical User Interface (GUI). The GUI endeavor is being lead by two different open source projects, GNOME and KDE. Both of these environments utilize the XFree86 organization's X Window System capable of running on most Unix and Unix-like operating systems. Since both projects are stable and provide a full-featured environment, it is left to the reader to select a platform of choice.

Much work has also gone into the development of an easily installable and configurable system. Distribution vendors are developing various configuration tools and distribution methods in an effort to create a user-friendly end product. A typical Linux distribution will consist of the Linux kernel and core drivers, the GNU tools, some X11 GUI environment, and usually vendor specific value-added products. These value-added products distinguish the various releases. A majority of the distributions offer both a GPL (or freely available) version and a commercial version. The commercial version will usually have more custom tools and will come with manuals and support. Close to one hundred distributions currently exist, but some of the more popular distributions include Red Hat, OpenLinux, SuSE, Slackware, and Debian. This section will outline the differences between these distributions, but again it is left to the reader to decide what flavor to use. Other distributions that deserve a mention due to their growing popularity include Turbo Linux, Corel Linux and Linux-Mandrake.

Red Hat

The Red Hat distribution is the most popular and widely available distribution. It was one of the first distributions available to the Linux consumer and has, therefore, had the most time to mature. Red Hat's goal, from the start, has been to make the product more user friendly and to simplify the installation process. This fact, along with strong commercial backing, can help to explain its wide use. The distribution is aimed toward both desktop users and server administrators utilizing Pentium-compatible, Alpha, or SPARC hardware. The current package includes a graphical installation utility that allows the user to select one of the installation types: Workstation, Server, or Custom.

Red Hat has made several advancements in the packaging and distribution of the Linux bundle that other distributions either use directly or have modeled their distributions after. Red Hat created the Red Hat Package Manager (RPM) and encourages other distributions to utilize the technology by making the RPM software packaging tool open source. RPM allows Red Hat to bundle the distribution into several distinct packages. For example, the XFree86 standard SVGA video drivers are available in a single package. This method allows the user (or the installation tool) to install only certain options. The user can easily see what packages have been installed and install updated or new packages downloaded from the Internet.

Advancements in the configuration of the OS have also created an easier to use environment. Red Hat provides a graphical configuration tool called the *control-panel*. This tool allows the user to control many of the system settings such as printer setup, networking, and system time. *LinuxConf* is another commonly used tool that eases the configuration process. This tool provides four basic interfaces including text, Web, X Windows GUI, and command line. Both of these tools hide some of the Linux environment complication from the user. Nearly all of the configuration parameters used by Unix applications and modules are stored in plain text files. The configuration tools simply create and edit the files for the user. This approach tries to appease both factions; one requesting ease of use and the other, limitless system control.

Support is also high on the list of customer expectations, and Red Hat does not fall short in this category. The level of support varies depending on the package purchased. Even if no package is purchased, you still have access to the fairly vast resources available on their FTP site and Web site. The most basic packages can include preferential Web-based support and telephone support for installation. Support is available through email and mailing lists. The bigger packages can include enterprise-class support, such as training and 24/7 server-down support.

Even with everything Red Hat has going for it, the Red Hat distribution is not the best solution for every situation. Red Hat is somewhat limited in the number of packages that are included with its bundled distributions (when compared to some of the other distributions). The most common ones are included and any other packages needed may be downloaded from the Internet. Other complaints include its post-installation configuration tool *control-panel*. It is useful to a point; however, other tools or methods are required to fine-tune the system.

OpenLinux

Caldera Systems provides the OpenLinux distribution product line, which is targeted toward corporate users and administrators. Their packages support Pentium-class and compatible hardware. Caldera is considered the most "commercial" of the distributions. This is due to its extensive enterprise-class support services and bundled commercial value-added products. Support services range from the basic email support to unlimited

24/7 telephone support. Caldera also offers unique packages for Novell NetWare solutions that other distributions do not. Depending on the specific package, OpenLinux comes with several useful commercial and open source applications.

Given the commercial emphasis of OpenLinux, many claim it is the easiest to install. It has a simple graphical setup process that automatically detects most hardware components for the user. The installation GUI utilizes the same underlying technology as the K Desktop Environment (KDE) window environment, so the look-and-feel is familiar to most users. Once installed, the eDesktop package even has an Internet Connection "Lizard" (instead of Wizard) to easily connect with any Internet Service Provider (ISP).

Somewhat more complicated installations are also made easier by Caldera. The option to create a dual boot machine, or one supporting multiple OS environments, is available to the user during the installation process. This is done by bundling PartitionMagic with the Caldera products, so the user can easily resize any Windows partitions. System administrators also have the option of creating an installation server connected to the company LAN. This server can then be used to easily create several identical installations by inserting a floppy disk and booting any connected computer. The software will automatically handle the installation.

While the post-installation configuration utility is one of the weak points with the Red Hat distribution, it is one of the stronger points of OpenLinux. OpenLinux uses the RPM technology for packages, but adds its own package manager to manage and update installed packages. The Caldera Open Administration System (COAS) allows the user to configure most of the system without resorting to a text editor. For central administration, the OpenLinux distribution can also be managed by using the Webmin Web-based management tool.

The biggest strength of the Caldera design can also be its greatest weakness. Because the GUI configuration tools provide simplicity by hiding details, the user may not know what is going on behind the scenes. This isn't an issue until the system has problems. The lack of knowledge provided about what is done behind the scenes makes troubleshooting the installation relatively difficult. This issue could be resolved by expanding the configuration tools to handle nearly all circumstances and providing a meaningful reporting system.

OpenLinux also does not handle many of the older hardware configurations. If the installation program doesn't like a particular configuration, it will not proceed with the installation. This should not be a problem if the system requirements are matched carefully, but it is an added distraction.

SuSE

One company has made a name for itself by providing an international flavor of the Linux operating system. SuSE (pronounced "soo'-sah"), a German-based company started in 1992, originally provided only a German language distribution of the Linux OS. The distribution has grown to become the most popular distributions in the overseas market and is beginning to break into the U.S. market.

SuSE Linux has been touted as the Red Hat of Europe. Like Red Hat, it is focused on the desktop and server administrator market supporting primarily Pentium-compatible, Alpha, and PowerPC hardware components. This is, however, where the comparison ends. SuSE provides one of the most complete distributions available, bundled with an abundance of tools and utilities.

One of SuSE's stronger points is its available documentation and international support. Most documentation and technical Web site help is available in English and at least two other languages, mainly French and German. Installation can proceed in any one of over a dozen languages. Some of the information is even available in Spanish and Czech. Two different technical support packages are included with the two available products including 60 days of telephone installation support for the personal edition and 90 days for the professional edition.

The installation and maintenance process is somewhat harder than either Red Hat or Caldera's but is still manageable with the help of the installation manual. YaST (Yet another Setup Tool) is used for both the installation and package maintenance activities. This tool utilizes RPM technology to manage and maintain the system configuration. The user is presented with several predefined installation scenarios to choose from, or a custom installation may be created. SuSE also uses its own graphical post-installation configuration tool called SaX for SuSE advanced X Configuration Tool.

The only glaring shortcoming of the SuSE distribution is its installation process for novice users. Although not overly cumbersome, the installation process requires that you know about your hardware prior to installation. Also, because of the large number of available packages, the custom configuration can be somewhat difficult to complete.

Slackware

Although the Slackware distribution offers several benefits, it is primarily for the skilled Linux user. Slackware is the most popular commercial distribution whose target market is aimed directly at those who love Linux. It doesn't offer an easy graphical installation interface for novice users, but is instead focused on providing a fast and stable end product. But because it is Linux, the average user should be fine once the system is up and running. And for those who do require installation assistance, Slackware provides both telephone and email support to customers.

Slackware's main goal is to provide a solid product that is the most Unix-like distribution available for Pentium-class systems. Given this goal, the installation process is relatively unpolished, but it does give the user full control over system setup and maintenance. You aren't left wondering what is going on behind the scenes when problems arise. Slackware also does not bundle unstable or untested components with their releases. This means that the "latest and greatest" may not be included, but what is included has been tried and tested reducing any security or stability problems. This makes the distribution ideal for stand-alone solutions, for example, in the ISP industry where the machine isn't necessarily used by general users.

Because the Slackware distribution does not contain any of the bells and whistles packaged in most of the other distributions, it requires much less installation space. Companies requiring a robust minimal system that provides complete control over the OS should consider Slackware.

Debian

The Debian distribution is available from the same people who maintain the GNU projects, the Free Software Foundation (FSF). The FSF is a not-for-profit organization allowing for Debian to be the only purely non-commercial distribution available to consumers. The full distribution is available for download from their Web site or from several resellers who provide it on CD at a nominal cost. Some distribution vendors, including Corel Linux, even use Debian as the underlying technology in their product offerings.

Debian provides one of the largest collections of tools and packages of any of the distributions, but like Slackware, it is not the easiest to install. Debian is also one of the few distributions that does not utilize the RPM packaging method. They have created a separate packaging utility called *dpkg*. This command line utility, or *dselect* (the menu-driven version), provides the ability to update software via automatic Internet upgrades.

Given its non-user friendly installation and maintenance procedures, Debian is best left to developers, power users, and knowledgeable server administrators. The only support available is through the Debian mailing list. But because the product is backed by the GNU creators, it supports many more platforms than most of the other distributions including Alpha, ARM, Intel x86, Motorola 680x0, PowerPC, and SPARC.

BSD

The open source Berkeley Software Distribution (BSD) community is separated into three distinct BSD releases including NetBSD, FreeBSD, and OpenBSD. For those counting, that makes four distinct open source Unix-like platforms. At this point you may be asking yourself: Why so many? Wouldn't it be better if all the effort could be combined into one project? These valid questions will be answered in this section.

To understand why the various flavors of BSD software exist and how they differ from Linux, it is helpful to understand some of the history behind their creation. In the late 1970s, UC Berkeley began to adopt the AT&T Bell Labs version of Unix partially due to the emphasis of Ken Thompson. Developers at Berkeley soon began adding features to make the operating system much more useful. Throughout the 1980s programmers at Berkeley and other institutions rewrote so much of the code that little of the Bell Labs source remained.

A group of developers tried to capitalize on this circumstance by forming a company called Berkeley Software Design, Inc. The company wanted to replace the remaining Bell Labs code to remove the licensing restrictions. Legal action from AT&T prevented this attempt from being completely successful, but the ideas proliferated and in 1993 a second BSD-based system was released called 386BSD. Two development groups used this new license-free version to create the first two BSD projects. The NetBSD faction wanted to make the software usable on all hardware platforms while the FreeBSD project wanted to create a highly reliable and stable product for the Intel platform.

OpenBSD was started later in 1996 from the NetBSD code base. Its goal was to become the most secure OS available. Because of the different goals and directions of the three teams, the projects have never been combined.

Each of these BSD projects has succeeded, for the most part, in attaining their individual goals. NetBSD supports as many, if not more, platforms than the Linux OS. It is especially useful for older hardware configurations, for which few operating systems are available. The FreeBSD software has evolved into one of the fastest and most stable operating systems available for the Intel platform, outperforming Linux using similar hardware configurations. Several companies and organizations have selected FreeBSD for use in high-reliability servers. Companies like Yahoo!, USWest (which is now Qwest), NASA, and even Microsoft's Hotmail servers all use FreeBSD. OpenBSD is well-known as being one of the most secure operating systems available. The project developers continuously perform security audits of the entire software base in an effort to eliminate any security problems that might exist. Many companies use OpenBSD when security is of great concern.

Even given these different goals and development directions, all of the OS projects utilize many of the same components. They all use the XFree86 windowing platform for providing a GUI. Because of this, any machine utilizing the various operating systems looks and feels much the same. Emulators also exist for the BSD platforms to run any of the Linux software. Most of the GNU tools are available for any of the platforms, and all the operating systems utilize them to some extent.

The largest problem surrounding the use of any of the BSD systems is in the distributions' availability and support. Because Linux has received a great deal of attention lately, it has had more commercial companies huddled around the technology. This has led to many different distribution companies and support organizations available to customers and the corporate environment for Linux products. Typical BSD vendors will bundle the software "as is" directly from the individual project sources. The support structure for the BSD releases is not as prevalent and consists mostly of mailing lists and Web site assistance.

The BSD releases offer a valid solution for companies for which commercial support and "simplified" installation processes are not issues. Given the rapid development and changes occurring in the Linux community, more problems may actually be included in Linux distributions than in the BSD releases. Although these problems will most likely be noticed quickly and fixed, it is an issue to consider. Table 3.1 summarizes the differences between the various BSD platforms and Linux.

Table 3.1 Operating Systems Comparison

	LINUX	NETBSD	FREEBSD	OPENBSD
Development Community Size	Excellent	Fair	Fair	Fair
Hardware Compatibility	Good	Excellent	Fair	Good
Speed	Good	Good	Excellent	Good
Security	Good	Good	Good	Excellent
Reliability/Stability	Good	Good	Good	Excellent
Support Options	Excellent	Poor	Poor	Poor

Protocols

Computer protocols provide the common methodology that allows each OS and program environment to communicate with one another. To refer again to the automobile industry, they are similar to the use of common specifications on the gas tank inlet, for example. Without a common specification, every manufacturers' vehicle would have to get gasoline from different providers since the nozzles or delivery mechanisms would all be different. In the computer world, common protocols have also arisen to prevent similar problems. They provide the "rules" by which participating computers use to transmit information. Without the ability for computers to talk to each other using common procedures, the Internet could not exist.

Protocols are included in this book because they differ greatly in their functionality. These differences limit the usage and capabilities that may be allowed by the various technologies utilizing the different protocols. A rational software decision cannot be made without at least a rudimentary understanding of the underlying technologies. Many different protocols exist, but some have also been developed or used for the common proliferation of information in Internet or integration scenarios. For the purposes of this discussion, only these protocols will be analyzed.

None of the software communication protocols can reach beyond their own machine without a physical connection. This physical connection can be in the form of a direct connection, such as two computers connected via their serial ports, but more often the connection is much more indirect. Commonly, a computer is equipped with some hardware device (like an Ethernet card). This hardware component can then be connected to a network or hardware routing device to provide the physical connection. If the network that is being connected to also allows for Internet connectivity, the machine will be able to connect a vast number of machines. The Internet is simply a large network of loosely connected machines and cooperating networks.

At a high level, most networks, including the Internet, work much like the telephone system. When you make a telephone call, you do not know exactly how your call is being routed, but you are able to communicate with your desired destination. Your call may be directed through satellites or across several central office switching areas, as shown in Figure 3.1a. All that was required on your part was the specification of the recipient telephone number. Most computer networks including the Internet operate in a similar fashion, which is depicted in Figure 3.1b. Only the recipient of the information must be known to actually open a communication channel.

Communication channels are often represented and described by using a common networking model. The models are depicted using various layers to describe particular services within the communication channel. The most popular model, and the one that will be used here is the Open Systems Interconnect (OSI) model. This model contains seven distinct layers within the communication channel:

Physical. The physical layer consists of the physical connection between various machines or networks. It is the most tangible layer and, therefore, often the easiest to understand.

Data link. This layer is responsible for error-free transmission of information using frames. It is responsible for maintaining the reliability of the physical layer. This layer defines the procedures used to transmit data using the physical connection.

Network. The network layer is primarily used for routing information to different addresses or components using the data link layer. This layer essentially provides or coordinates the map or directions to get from one resource to another.

Transport. The transport layer reliably handles and delivers the data packets to the various components or applications within a given network resource.

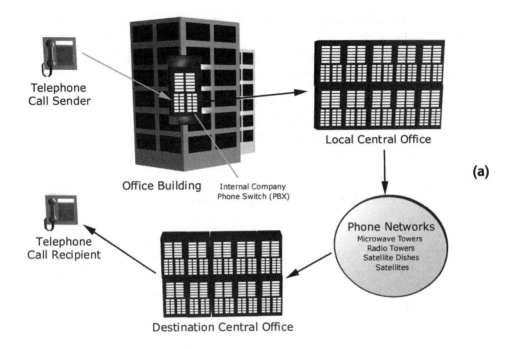

(a)

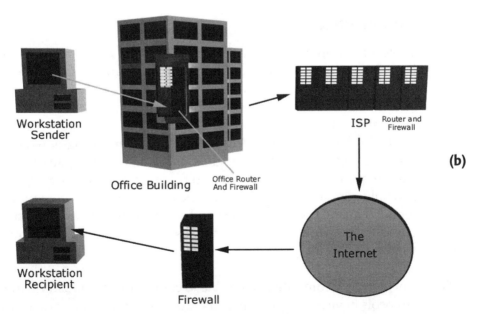

(b)

Figure 3.1   Telephone system (a) compared to computer network (b).

Session. This layer creates a single communication channel between two endpoints within the transport layer. The session layer defines weather the channel operates using a full-duplex, half-duplex, or simplex communication method.

Presentation. The presentation layer is used to "present" the data to the application layer. It handles the compression or encryption technologies used on the information before and after transmission. Gateways commonly exist in this presentation layer.

Application. This layer provides the interface that allows a user application to transmit data to another application.

Typically the first two layers, the physical layer and data link layer, are handled by hardware components like routers, hubs, and Ethernet cards. The point-to-point protocol (PPP) specification operates on the data link layer, but many hardware components have embedded software to handle these two layers. Because protocols will often cover multiple layers, for discussion purposes, the remaining layers can be simplified further into two primary categories. Low-level protocols are those that facilitate the network, transport, and occasionally the session layer. High-level protocols are protocols that operate in the application, presentation, and also occasionally the session layer.

Low-Level Protocols

Several protocols or architectures exist to provide the low-level services required for the transmission of data between applications. In the early computing years, vendors had their own protocol or communication architecture that each one used. This was done for two primary reasons. Each solution was more or less independently created since no common standard existed. Vendors could also lock in a company into using only their technology. As the computer industry grew, this was no longer an option. The Internet required the need to have common and open protocols so computers could communicate with each other. Customers also demanded that systems be able to work together and to share information. Standalone systems were no longer of any benefit as the enterprise and computing needs grew.

Given this need for computers to be able to communicate industry wide, several protocols have managed to become the standard. Protocols such as TCP/IP, SNA, IPX/SPX, Banyan VINES IP, NetBIOS, and AppleTalk may be familiar to anyone in the networking industry. TCP/IP is the technology used to create the Internet and is therefore the most prevalent. SNA may also be contained in the enterprise since it is IBM's proprietary communication architecture. Most of the other protocol types, each pushed by a specific vendor, have either given way to TCP/IP or methods exist to use them in conjunction with TCP/IP. Because of these reasons, TCP/IP and SNA are arguably the most relevant for the purposes of enterprise integration and Internet services.

TCP/IP

Of all the low-level protocols, Transmission Control Protocol/Internet Protocol (TCP/IP) is by far the most commonly used networking protocol. TCP/IP gained its popularity because it is the basis of the Internet and all of its associated applications. TCP/IP is available for nearly all operating systems included with the OS or available for a small fee from the OS vendor. Most operating systems now use TCP/IP by default including Apple Macintosh, IBM's AS/400, various Unix platforms, and Windows 2000. If an enterprise happens to have technology that does not utilize TCP/IP, many gateways or translation software exists to make the protocol work with TCP/IP.

TCP/IP grew out the necessity of the government to create robust communication links between various military installations. Throughout the 1960s, the Department of Defense funded research done in several major universities across the United States. These efforts lead to the creation of the Advanced Research Projects Agency Network (ARPANET), the forefather of the current Internet. TCP/IP was not the original protocol but was designed during the ARPANET project to accommodate the requirements of the network. It has become a highly flexible, open networking standard.

The ARPANET required that data transmission be available even in the event of a war that destroyed portions of the connecting infrastructure. This requirement has made TCP/IP reliable and scalable. The network utilizes a technology known as *packet switching* to transmit data packets. This is slightly different from the circuit switching technology used for telephony. Circuit switching establishes a physical connection between two points every time the connection is needed. Although the connection may be different with each consecutive use, a physical connection must exist. Packet switching is more of a "connectionless" environment, where a clear path or connection is not established between the connecting parties. The information is instead "bounced" around the network always attempting to get closer to its destination. Each individual data packet is then able to take a different path creating the capability to account for changes in the network that may occur during transmission.

TCP/IP itself, does not refer to a single protocol but instead is used to describe a suite of protocols. At the network layer, TCP contains several specifications including IP, ARP, RARP, ICMP, and IGMP. TCP and UDP (which will be discussed shortly) exist in the transport layer. The TCP/IP suite also contains several protocols that exist at the high-level layers, some of which will be discussed in the *High-Level Protocols* section that follows. Figure 3.2 demonstrates how these different protocols relate to the OSI Reference model.

The IP in TCP/IP refers to Internet Protocol. This protocol uses packet switching techniques to route and coordinate the transmission of information throughout the network. This portion of the protocol suite is entirely

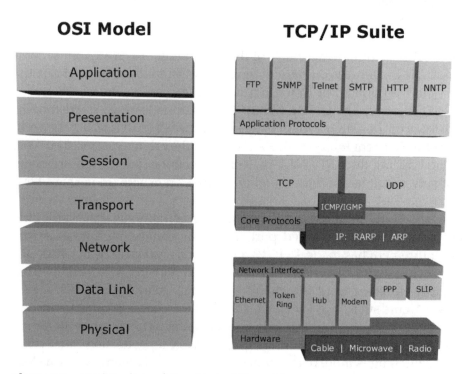

Figure 3.2   TCP/IP suite's relationship to OSI model.

connectionless, which means the communication channel is not left open. Each data packet contains address information and the associated data that is to be routed and each packet may be routed along a different path to the final destination.

The ARP and RARP are used throughout the network to create a telephone directory style of address resolution. ARP stands for Address Resolution Protocol while RARP adds the ability to do "Reverse" address resolution. IP addresses are mapped to physical hardware locations and vice versa thereby allowing the transmission of data to an actual physical end point.

The Internet Control Message Protocol (ICMP) is a background protocol used for network maintenance tasks. It allows computers on a network to communicate status and error information. The Packet Internet Groper (ping) utility common to most TCP/IP environments utilizes this protocol to test data connectivity between machines.

Internet Group Management Protocol (IGMP) provides the ability to use IP multicasting. IP multicasting allows for the transmission of a single message to several recipients. The router or network component participating in multicasting will handle sending the data to the end clients.

Built on top of all these network layer protocols are two distinct transport layer protocols. The TCP/IP suite has defined both a Transmission Control Protocol (TCP) and a User Datagram Protocol (UDP). The standard data packets are shown in Figure 3.3. The primary difference between these two protocols is the connectivity that is required. UDP provides a simple data transmission method that does not rely on message acknowledgements. TCP does use acknowledgements and it also maintains the transmission sequence. This allows large messages to be broken into several smaller messages. Because of these differences TCP is used when a high-reliability full-duplex connection session is required, while UDP is used when transmission speed is more important.

SNA

The Systems Network Architecture (SNA) is different from TCP/IP in its origins and what it accomplishes. In the mid-1970s, IBM created SNA in an effort to provide the framework necessary to connect previously incompatible IBM components. Given the proliferation of the IBM mainframe, SNA has been used as the groundwork for corporate-wide area networks. SNA was developed to provide a high-reliability, mission critical network environment.

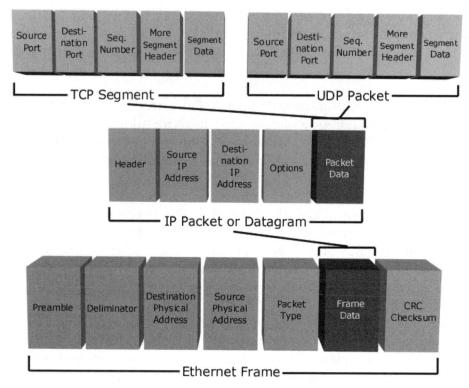

Figure 3.3   TCP/IP data packets.

Because of this, SNA may still be used in companies that first networked mainframe systems.

The original SNA model did not allow for peer-to-peer communication methods. This capability was added later as the need arose. A SNA network consists of a collection of nodes. Various node types exist and each node typically represents a specific machine. These nodes are assigned a Network Addressable Unit (NAU), which is similar to TCP/IP's use of an IP addresses to distinguish resources.

Three NAU types exist in the current SNA architecture. These types include logical units (LUs), physical units (PUs), and control points (CPs). LUs provide access to network resources and manage the data flow between end points. PUs monitor and control attached network links and other resources within a given node. CPs are similar to PUs in that they also manage nodes and their associated resources.

Originally, PUs were implemented using Virtual Telecommunication Access Method (VTAM) on a mainframe. As the requirements of networks grew beyond the capabilities of a centralized network utilizing a single mainframe host, communication controllers were developed which utilized a Network Control Program (NCP). The communication controllers would handle several of the tasks previously done by VTAM and allow for connections to remote resources.

CPs differ from PUs because they decide what action should be taken while PUs actually cause the action to be carried out. Each main host, or mainframe, will typically have a System Services Control Point (SSCP). The SSCP provides high-speed communication links to disks, tapes, and other communication controllers.

Connections between these NAUs provide the physical layer of the SNA network. Several protocols then utilize this physical layer to provide the data link layer including the standard Synchronous Data Link Control (SDLC) protocol and the Qualified Logical Link Control (QLLC) protocol used for communication over X.25 networks. These protocols are similar to those used in TCP/IP at the data link layer such as PPP.

Traditional SNA required the explicit definition of all resources thereby eliminating any discovery requirements (which the ARP and RARP protocols provide for TCP/IP). This design has evolved to support peer-to-peer communications via Advanced Peer-to-Peer Networking (APPN). APPN allows directory services to maintain the resources within given remote networks. APPN provides the network layer and portions of the transport layer as defined by the OSI model. These functionalities are described as path control and transmission control respectively in the SNA model.

The presentation layer, session layer, and the remainder of the transport layer are handled by a single protocol within the APPN SNA network model. This protocol is known called LU Session Type 6.2, or more commonly as LU 6.2. This protocol corresponds to the TCP or UDP portions of the TCP/IP model. The SNA model maps closely to the OSI model, as shown in Figure 3.4.

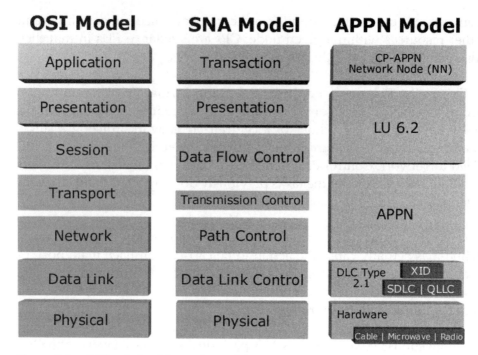

Figure 3.4 SNA's relationship to OSI model.

Unlike TCP/IP, all datagrams are guaranteed to be delivered. By using UDP over IP, the TCP/IP suite allows for communications without the burden of message acknowledgments, thus making it more efficient (at the cost of reliability). SNA also does not provide the capability to reroute data packets if a problem is found during delivery like TCP/IP does.

Even given the differences between TCP/IP and SNA, both networks can be used within the same enterprise environment. To achieve this coexistence, an SNA gateway can be used to provide TCP/IP access to certain SNA resources. SNA communications can also be bundled inside TCP/IP data packets. Given these possibilities, companies can utilize the technology that already exists within the enterprise and simply expand on it, without the need to necessarily replace it.

High-Level Protocols

A multitude of high-level protocols exist in the current computing environment. The reason for this protocol diversity can be attributed to the differing needs of applications. High-level protocols are those that provide the communication services necessary for a particular application or genre of applications. Most widely excepted protocols in use today all stem from some openly available standard. Many have even been the creation of open source organizations or groups, such as the World Wide Web Consortium (W3C).

Entire books have been written on the subject of protocols. To limit the discussion here, this section will focus on those protocols that are most relevant to the open source world, the Internet, and the integration arena. This information is not meant to be a comprehensive guide to protocols, but instead a primer into what differentiates particular protocols.

TCP/IP Suite

Beyond the low-level protocols in the TCP/IP suite, several presentation and application layer protocols are specified. These include most of the common functionality used on the Internet including file transfers, mail transfers, newsgroups, and Web pages. Even if you have never heard of any of these protocols, if you have used the Internet, you have used them.

The most basic file transfer mechanism includes the File Transfer Protocol (FTP). The protocol and services it provides are often built into web browsers. Operating systems will normally provide an FTP utility bundled with the TCP/IP package. FTP uses TCP typically on port 20 to facilitate the data transfer using either a binary or a straight ASCII transfer method. A UDP version known as Trivial FTP (TFTP) also exists. FTP abstracts variations in the file storage methods used on the different machines. An FTP application gives the user a set of standard commands that are used to transfer files between a client and host machine.

The email system is created behind the existence of three primary protocols. The Simple Mail Transfer Protocol (SMTP) provides the ability to exchange email messages as ASCII information. Because of the ASCII limitation, binary mail information must be encoded using one of the acceptable encoding methods. The Post Office Protocol (currently version 3, POP3) is used by client software to download email messages from a server. Another protocol that provides the ability to download email messages from a server is the Internet Message Access Protocol (IMAP). IMAP differs from POP in that it provides extended features, such as the ability to search email messages on the server. Neither POP nor IMAP provide a method for sending email to a server. All three of these protocols utilize TCP to create the current email system that exists on the Internet.

Telnet is another TCP-based service that allows users to access the resources on a remote machine. Telnet sessions are typically started on the remote Unix-like host and the user is presented the information using one of a number of terminal emulations, like VT100. Unlike FTP, the Telnet protocol was not designed to transfer entire files between systems although programs do exist to accomplish this task. Several protocols, including FTP and SMTP, utilize the Telnet protocols to initiate a connection with the remote host.

The Internet news system is created through the use of the Network News Transfer Protocol (NNTP). NNTP utilizes TCP to transmit news messages throughout the Internet. These news messages can be downloaded and read by users connecting to a news server.

The Web system or Internet Web pages are transmitted via the Hypertext Transfer Protocol (HTTP). This application-level protocol is designed to distribute HTML and other Web-based documents. HTTP is more relevant to integration issues and therefore deserves a closer look.

The HTTP protocol utilizes TCP to create a request/response style of communication. Although TCP is used, HTTP is considered a connectionless communication method. The client machine creates a request, in the form of a message containing a URI, request information and client information, and occasionally client content. The server receives the request, processes it, and replies in the form of a response message. Often the response will be a Web page that is then displayed by a Web browser and presented to the user.

Client requests can take several forms under the HTTP specification. The most common requests, those for documents, typically take the form of either a GET or a POST. These methods are relatively similar in that both are used to transmit a request and associated client data to the server. The server interprets the request and formulates the response. The main difference in the two methods is that the GET method may contain various user request parameters in the URI while the POST method contains the additional data in a separate section of the message. A POST typically requires further server side processing, using a Common Gateway Interface (CGI) script or Servlet for example. Once a connection is established to the server, the following GET requests can all be used to obtain the index page from the www.open3.org Web server:

```
GET http://www.open3.org/index.jsp HTTP/1.0

GET /index.jsp HTTP/1.0

GET / HTTP/1.0
```

The client is also able to include various options or request modifiers depending on its needs. A Microsoft Internet Explorer (version 5.5) uses a request similar to the following:

```
GET / HTTP/1.1
Accept: image/gif, image/x-xbitmap, image/jpeg, */*
Accept-Language: en-us
Accept-Encoding: gzip, deflate
User-Agent: Mozilla/4.0 (compatible; MSIE 5.5; Windows NT 5.0)
Host: www.open3.org
Connection: Keep-Alive
```

After each of the previous three requests is serviced, the TCP connection is severed. Note that in the last example the client is requesting a connection type of "Keep-Alive". For most servers this will cause the connection to be left intact so the client may make additional requests without reestablishing the TCP/IP link.

Distributed Environment Protocols

Another important protocol genre for the purposes of integration is the collection of component services protocols. These protocols are used to create what are known as *distributed computing environments*. Utilizing a distributed environment, a client program on one machine can request the services of an object or component located on the same machine or a remote machine.

One of the first protocols to provide the ability to access the logic of remote components was the Remote Procedure Call (RPC) protocol. This protocol provides the ability to make a function call across a network to a remote object. Unix-style Network File Sharing (NFS) mounts utilize RPC. Most of the other distributed environment protocols either use RPC directly or are based on RPC techniques to accomplish similar tasks. The most prevalent RPC architecture is the Distributed Computing Environment (DCE) specification maintained by the Open Software Foundation (OSF).

From the programmer's perspective, most of the RPC call is handled automatically by the underlying RPC subsystem. Typically RPC packages include libraries or methods that must be incorporated into a program to participate in the RPC environment. The calling program may have to load the RPC libraries or otherwise set up the environment, but then the program essentially makes a function call, similar to any other function calls. This function call is actually transmitted through a client stub or proxy program. This stub is the client side representation of the called object. The data is encapsulated into data packets and transmitted to the called object. This called object also has a "demarshalling" stub that turns the data packets back into useful information for the object to process. The response is sent using the reverse method. Figure 3.5 depicts the various components in a typical RPC environment.

To allow for several different languages to access the same objects, regardless of the object language, a common access language is required. Most RPC-style implementation relies on some form of the Interface Definition Language (IDL) to solve this problem. Every remote object has its interface defined using IDL. Calling objects then build the request based on the IDL information and receive a response using data elements from the IDL language.

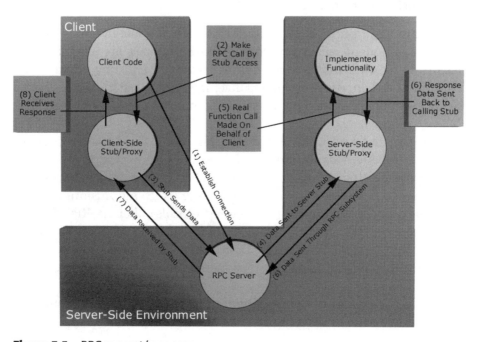

Figure 3.5   RPC request/response.

Callable RPC objects are typically managed or maintained in a centralized object repository. This requirement is what allows the object environment to call the remote object on behalf of a remote client. The environment differs depending on the RPC installation, but they all provide similar functionality. Most environments support some form of security and directory services. Other services or options may also be included and range from explicit thread usage to time services. Three major RPC programming paradigms exist and are heavily used in the current computing environment:

CORBA. Common Object Request Broker Architecture maintained by the Object Management Group (OMG).

DCOM. Distributed Component Object Model maintained by Microsoft.

RMI. Remote Method Invocation included with Java and maintained by JavaSoft.

The CORBA environment utilizes a protocol called the Internet Inter-ORB Protocol (IIOP). The environment is maintained and coordinated by an Object Request Broker (ORB) to connect all the given CORBA objects. All service requests are handled by the CORBA servers. The client does not need to know anything about where the object resides or how it works. Several vendors provide the CORBA server and associated environments for several platforms.

DCOM is the technology currently used in the Microsoft Windows line of products. It uses a protocol known as Object RPC (ORPC), which is essentially an extension to the DCE RPC model. Calling an object connects with the DCOM server to obtain a reference to an instance of the remote component. The object can then call the various functions that have been exposed through the DCOM interface. The capabilities exist to use a DCOM object in a transaction process.

Although the environment is used primarily on Windows platforms, certain vendors have created the ability to communicate with DCOM objects on several platforms including Unix and mainframe environments.

The Java version of RPC, RMI operates in a similar fashion to the other remote object environments. It uses the Java Remote Method Protocol (JRMP) to communicate. An RMI server manages the various object instances and makes calls on behalf of the client. Java has the built in ability to serialize most objects, and RMI relies on this fact heavily to transmit information. RMI also has the capability to transmit entire classes if they are not present on the client side. This feature does no exist within most of the other distributed environments. Since RMI is a key part of the Java language, it is available within any Java programming environment. Technologies such as Enterprise Java Beans (EJB) and Java Message Service (JMS) may also utilize it to communicate.

Two new distributed environment protocols are on the horizon, with developers ready to use them. Both utilize the power of XML for the transmission of data and information. The XML-RPC protocol is based on RPC techniques, but uses HTTP for communication (rather than directly using a TCP/IP socket). This ability allows the protocol to be used in Web server environments that currently exist on the Internet. Microsoft, along with IBM, DevelopMentor, and Userland Software, has noticed the benefits of this technology and has created its own XML and HTTP capable distributed technology called the Simple Object Access Protocol (SOAP). The SOAP protocol has been submitted to the W3C and is gaining acceptance. SOAP allows for distributed object usage over an HTTP channel utilizing XML to carry the data. As XML and the Internet evolve, additional protocols will likely be created.

Middleware Protocols

Beyond the protocols previously discussed for the Internet and distributed environments, other protocols exist and have been developed for messaging services. These protocols are not contained in the TCP/IP suite but are gaining in popularity and usage. They are relevant to integration scenarios as they provide *open* messaging protocols specifically designed for data transmission and client communication.

The repeated transmission of data amongst several connected components is different from the functionality covered thus far. For speed of transmission, clients often require a communication method that has the ability to remain connected. The HTTP protocol does not allow for this style of communication nor does the distributed component architectures previously discussed. The remaining protocols in the TCP/IP suite are focused on specific applications and don't lend themselves to create a middleware style of client communication easily. For these reasons, additional protocols are required.

One such open source protocol is the XML Streaming Transfer Protocol (XSTP). This protocol has been designed to accomplish two primary tasks.

Most importantly it needs to be able to handle communication and data transmission in a middleware-type setting. The second primary design goal was that it be highly portable among the various computing platforms.

To provide a communication channel capable of providing middleware-style communication methods, the XSTP protocol allows clients to connect using either a persistent connection or a connectionless environment. Persistent connections are a necessity due to the speed requirements of most messaging systems. With a persistent connection, the server may send data to the client when received. Using a connectionless environment, the client is required to poll the server to obtain messages. This is actually one of the problems found in the original HTTP specification, which did not allow for a maintained connection. Every request required the client to reestablish a connection to the server, creating unnecessary network overhead. For pages that included images, for example, each image on the page required a new connection to the server. This has been changed in the new HTTP specification, but the architecture is not designed to maintain server connections for any great length of time.

To make XSTP highly portable, the specification utilizes several different techniques. The most relevant is the use of a TCP/IP connection using only valid XML messages. TCP/IP is available on nearly all OS platforms. XML messages enhance the TCP/IP connection by defining the type of data and character encoding that will be used. XML has the ability to define the character set used to encode the XML document adding to the portability of the protocol. XSTP also supports the two most common messaging paradigms: point-to-point messaging (queue style) and publish-and-subscribe messaging. To further enhance portability, the protocol is designed to transport JMS messages easily. Although not a requirement, this makes the protocol easily adaptable to a Java platform, which arguably has the highest level of portability of any programming language.

Other messaging platforms also exist and are in use for message transport and delivery purposes. Several instant messaging (IM) platforms exist to facilitate the delivery of instant messages throughout the Internet or in internal network environments. These platforms include commercially supported systems such as AOL Instant Messenger (AIM), ICQ (pronounced "I-seek-you"), Microsoft Messenger, and Yahoo! Messenger. Open source projects also exist including Internet Relay Chat (IRC) and a growing Jabber IM community.

IM is similar to email services, in that a user is typically sending a message to another user. The main difference is that instead of sending the message to a mailbox typically located on a server, IM sends the message directly to the user. This also requires a persistent connection to the server. If no persistent connection existed, then all the systems would be just different email platforms. The commercial protocols are not valid choices for a middleware-style messaging environment since they are closed technologies. The open source protocols could be used, but features required in a standard middleware environment, such as security, message acknowledgment, and persistence, are not available.

One final open source protocol to examine is the Blocks eXtensible eXchange Protocol, or BXXP (pronounced "beep"). This protocol is used as a protocol's protocol. The BXXP movement was founded on the belief that many applications will need to create their own protocol. The BXXP creators realized that although this may be true, nearly every protocol contains features required by all protocols. These features include the need to transmit data and provide authentication, transportation security, and error reporting. BXXP provides these abilities and allows programmers to extend the protocol to change how these tasks are accomplished. BXXP also uses XML for its low-level communication but does not require protocols built on top of it to use XML. BXXP is an interesting idea and should be watched closely to see how it will be used.

Common Open Source Languages

Programming languages are as diverse as the programmers that use them. The first computers utilized the most basic programming techniques, which consisted of hardwiring a set of processing instructions directly into the machine. As computer technology grew, these instructions were encoded into punch cards or other formats that could easily be translated directly into processor instructions. Thus, the programming industry was born.

From these simple processor instructions grew an assembly language that allowed programmers to abstract certain machine instructions into basic statements. People soon realized further abstraction could make programming easier, giving rise to high level languages. Each language provides its own set of features and benefits, but as with most things, programming languages contain tradeoffs. No one programming language is the best, at least not yet.

When selecting an implementation language for use in an enterprise or on a particular project, the properties of the language should be analyzed. For enterprise environments, some of the most important aspects of a language are its maintainability, an object-oriented (OO) design, and developer support.

Maintainability is highly relevant for most enterprise projects. The cost of creating an internal application is high, and to maintain a high rate of return on that investment, company programs should be easily maintainable. The costs to maintain programs created using poorly maintainable languages can soon grow higher than the original development costs.

An OO program paradigm might not seem that important at first. However, for enterprise projects that are expected to exist for any length of time it becomes extremely important. These programs should be designed using OO techniques and utilize a language that also supports this paradigm. This OO nature of the programs makes them easier to change in the future. As the company grows, the functionality of the programs may be needed throughout the company. If the program was developed using an OO language, certain modules or program sections may be easily extracted from the original programs and reused. This functionality can be added into packages, libraries, or placed inside of a distributed environment. This demonstrates the mantra of the OO supporters.

Developer support is also a key deciding factor when selecting an implementation language for enterprise use. It is unwise to select a language without the ability to find accomplished developers that can implement the program. Even if a particular language seems like the best fit, managers should consider the ability to find people to carry on the project and maintain it in the future.

This section focuses on languages that are relevant to the current computing environment. The languages discussed comprise the suite of languages most commonly used by open source projects and within the enterprise. As shown in Figure 3.6, these languages have been separated into three categories: presentation languages, system languages, and scripting languages. *Presentation languages* include programming languages and formatting languages that are used to present information directly to a user. *System programming languages* include those languages that are used to create applications or system components. *Scripting languages* can be thought of as utility languages, used for tying elements together. It should be noted

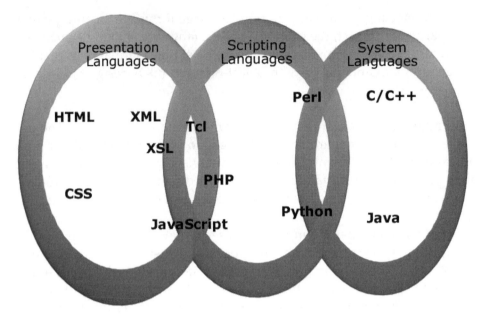

Figure 3.6   Language separations.

that certain scripting languages could fall under either the scripting or the presentation category. For discussion purposes, the *primary* purpose of each language defines the assigned classification.

Presentation Languages

Presentation languages are used for just that purpose—to present information or data to users in an easy to interpret manner. This separation of languages into presentation layer and application layer has been brought about due to the rapid growth of the Internet. Given this growth and the need to share company programs and program functionalities, companies soon realized that the data should be separated from the way it is presented. This realization corresponds to the growth of multi-tiered application designs that have lead the enterprise computer development environment.

HTML

Hypertext Markup Language (HTML) was invented by Tim Berners-Lee in 1989 at the CERN energy research laboratory near Geneva. It was designed to be a simple language for the display of documents across a variety of computer systems at CERN. The system was launched in 1991 and the Web was born. Interest grew quickly and popularity surged with the creation of the Mosaic browser by Marc Andreessen and Eric Bina.

Today, most Web pages display information formatted in HTML. HTML is a non-proprietary language derived from the parent language, Standard Generalized Markup Language (SGML). The visual foundation of a Web site is based on HTML. Its specification is maintained and advanced by the W3C (w3c.org).

HTML is a relatively simple language. It uses tags, formatting rules enclosed in brackets (<>), which describe the layout of a Web page. These tags are used in tandem with textual and graphical information to build a page. One of these tags provides for hypertext references, the ability to click on a link and be taken to a different part of the page or a different page altogether.

Hypertext is the essence of navigation on the Internet. It takes standard text and connects it with other documents to enhance the understanding for the reader. For example, a Web page may display:

```
Application and data integration is one component of e-business that has
enabled Dell Computer (DELL) to become one of the great modern hi-tech
companies.
```

When clicked, the hypertext link <u>Dell Computer</u> may take the user to www.dell.com and <u>(DELL)</u> may take the user to a stock quote. This ability to click on links enables the reader to gain greater depth about the current subject. A complication of hypertext is that it can cause a reader to jump from document to document, without ever fully reading or understanding any one of them.

HTML has driven the growth of the Internet and is a necessary component of an e-business strategy. HTML is implemented to help build corporate intranets, enterprise information portals, B2B exchanges, and e-commerce Web sites. Knowledge and implementation of HTML is essential for many e-business applications.

Currently, HTML is being updated with XHTML, a reworking of the HTML 4.01 specification in XML. XHTML enables HTML to be integrated with XML-aware applications, furthering its usefulness for e-business.

XML

The eXtensible Markup Language (XML) is a data language for structured documents and communication of information. XML is written in the SGML standard. SGML and XML are international standards and are owned by the public. SGML is a meta-language, a language that defines other languages, and XML is an abbreviated and simpler version of it. This enables the extensibility in XML, the ability to create custom markup for a document. An XML document is also human readable, enabling the ease of developing software and communication systems for the transmission and processing of the data. The flexible and legible features of XML have enabled it to become widely adopted in the last two years.

An XML document is composed of tags, attributes, and data. XML uses tags to differentiate document structures, such as <xml></xml>. Attributes inside of tags encode additional information, such as <xml document="123">. Data is contained between opening and closing tags, such as <xml>here is the data</xml>.

XML documents must be well-formed and valid. To be well-formed, a document must follow these guidelines:

- Every beginning tag must have a matching ending tag unless it's an empty tag.
  - For example, the beginning tag <xml> has the ending tag </xml> or the beginning tag is also the ending tag, known as the empty tag <xml/>.
- All beginning tags must line up with ending tags.
  - For example, this is valid: <xml><tag></tag></xml>
  - But this is not: <xml><tag></xml></tag>
- All attribute values are quoted.
  - For example, <xml document="123"> (the 123 must be quoted "123")
- All entities, reusable pieces of data, must be declared.

To be valid XML, the document must be described by a set of rules or grammar that defines the tags and attributes and their appropriate positioning in the document. A valid document must either have a document type definition (DTD) or XML schema that defines this grammar.

XML is primarily useful for providing structured metadata for data. This means that the data in an XML document is described by something informative. Determining what data means in HTML is difficult and XML is quickly replacing HTML for delivering content over the Internet. For example, text in HTML is placed in between nondescript body tags like <body>George Washington</body> but can be placed between informative tags in XML, such as the following:

```
<US_President>
    <first_name>George</first_name>
    <last_name>Washington</last_name>
</US_President>
```

You can quickly see that XML makes interpreting data much easier than with HTML.

XML provides a system with the ability to separate data from business logic and presentation. Data are independent from the operating algorithms and the displaying system. This makes the system loosely coupled and easily updated. Therefore, describing all data in XML format enables a highly desirable architecture for e-business systems.

Beyond describing legible content for the Internet, XML is used for data communication. Repositories, such as BizTalk or RosettaNet, are composed of thousands of DTDs and XML schemas that define documents used for business transactions. XML provides a common language for different business partners to communicate information. XML is becoming the de facto language for data and must be supported by the modern e-business.

CSS

Cascading Style Sheets (CSS) is a language for adding style to a Web page. It is managed by the W3C. CSS is typically used to style HTML but can also be used for XML. CSS is particularly useful in allowing a Web site to display a uniform look and feel across pages with a minimum of HTML coding effort. CSS rules include formatting instructions that detail fonts, margins, colors, spacing, and other features of a Web page. Simply applying one style sheet to a set of Web pages enables style to be applied across an entire site. CSS allows the look and feel of a Web site to be quickly changed through utilizing updated style sheets. This feature is useful in e-business to create a site that is visually dynamic and constantly appealing to users.

CSS also enables HTML pages to be written with device independence and have CSS pages applied for device dependent styles. For example, style sheets may be written for sites to support mobile computing devices, such as cell phones or PDAs. Style sheets have many advantages and are an important application of technology to be considered for e-business initiatives. CSS' counterpart, XSL, is a much more robust style language that is used to fulfill more complex formatting requirements.

XSL

eXtensible Stylesheet Language (XSL) is a language to express style sheets for XML. Scott Boag and the Xalan group at Lotus IBM were the early founders of the XSL standard, which is currently managed by the W3C. XSL is composed of XSL Transformations (XSLT) and XSL Formatting Objects. XSL is used to transform and format an XML document into virtually any other format.

A typical use for XSL is transforming an XML document into HTML for display on a Web page. This allows the data of the web page, encoded in XML, to be separated from the presentation of the page. Utilizing XSL allows the XML data to be easily represented in any format just by writing a new style sheet. For example, an XSL stylesheet may be written to display data for wireless devices utilizing Wireless Markup Language (WML) or to format data for a spreadsheet.

XSL is also frequently used in integration scenarios for application integration and B2B transactions, such as transforming from one XML document to another. For example, a B2B trading hub with diverse participants may be using different XML documents to convey information. XSL can be utilized to format a foreign document into one that is immediately recognizable by a company's software.

As XML becomes an increasing standard in e-business, so will XSL. XSL is an integral component to utilizing XML and its knowledge and use in the enterprise is critical.

JavaScript

JavaScript was originally invented by Brendan Eich at Netscape. JavaScript is a language for extending the capabilities of a Web page beyond HTML and offers a basic feature set found in most programming languages. It was originally used in the Netscape Web browser version 2.0. In turn, Microsoft created a similar language known as JScript for its Explorer browser. There were many incompatibilities between the two versions and programmers had to write and debug two separate programs to support both.

In June 1998, the European Computer Manufacturer's Association (ECMA) created a formal specification based on Netscape's JavaScript named ECMA-262, simply known as ECMAScript. Netscape, Microsoft, and other browser developers have adopted ECMAScript as a standard. The ECMA standard has helped to eliminate incompatibilities between different browsers. Despite the new name of ECMAScript, it continues to be known popularly by its original name, JavaScript.

JavaScript provides programming capabilities to Web pages, enabling business logic, Dynamic HTML (DHTML), and communication with other Web components such as Java applets. It can also be used to develop logic that runs on the server.

JavaScript is not Java; it is only syntactically similar so that a Java programmer can learn it quickly. Although JavaScript is also technically a scripting language, it is included in the presentation languages since that is its primary purpose. Its most common use is in DHTML to provide dynamic elements such as drop-down menus and animated buttons. It is also useful in validating forms, for example, to ensure that a person has entered 16 numbers in a credit card field. JavaScript enables Web pages to communicate across different browser windows such as in frames or between separate windows. It is a versatile language and an essential tool for more complicated Web sites.

In addition to JavaScript, Visual Basic Script (VBScript) is a programming language used in Web browsers and on Web servers. It is most commonly used in conjunction with Microsoft Active Server Pages. Explorer supports VBScript; however, Netscape Navigator does not. Unless all of your users are running Explorer, VBScript is not a viable option for extending Web pages. It is proprietary software and controlled by the Microsoft empire. JavaScript is a much better choice for adding logic and features to Internet applications.

PHP

PHP (officially "PHP: Hypertext Preprocessor") is an open source presentation scripting language embedded in HTML to create dynamic Web pages. It was invented by Rasmus Lerdorf in 1994. PHP is the open source alternative to commercial packages like Microsoft Active Server Pages and Allaire Cold Fusion. PHP works with Apache Web Server to deploy Web sites on the Internet. Netcraft estimates that there are over three million sites today running on PHP. PHP is currently in version 4.x and is consistently upgraded with new features and support.

The PHP language parser is called Zend. The Zend parser was first written by Zeev Suraski and Andi Gutmans in 1997. Zend is the engine that powers a PHP-based Web site. The Zend engine is open source and free for use but is owned by the commercial company Zend Technologies. Therefore, Zend exists in the middle ground between true open source software and proprietary software.

PHP is an example of *server-side execution*. This means that the server processes the PHP code before sending it to the browser. This is opposed to *client-side execution*, such as a Java applet or JavaScript, that executes its functionality on the client's computer inside their Web browser. This enables processing to be handled by powerful servers and quickly delivered to the less powerful client systems.

PHP code often interacts with databases to perform tasks like retrieving customer information and cataloging products. PHP supports over 20 database systems, including proprietary databases like Oracle, Sybase, and DB2 and open source databases like MySQL, PostgreSQL, and InterBase. This broad support enables the strong acceptance of PHP into the enterprise.

PHP can also communicate to other services using a variety of protocols such as POP3, IMAP, NNTP, and HTTP. This enables PHP, for example, to communicate directly with a mail server to deliver email messages to customers who have just placed orders from a Web site.

PHP's broad appeal and constant upgrade development along with its database, protocol, and system support make it a strong choice for developing Web-based applications in the enterprise.

System Programming Languages

System programming languages, although often used to present data, are also capable of much more. These languages provide strongly typed environments that create the ability to easily produce large stand-alone end products. Strong data typing allows many developers to work on the same project by preventing potential data type errors. Often the capabilities of these system languages are only limited by the programmer's imagination or abilities. The languages analyzed in this section are primarily those used in open source projects.

Why do open source developers select these languages? This is a good question that all enterprise decision makers should ask. It is important to look at what languages are selected when a development team is given absolute choice. Sometimes a language is selected simply because of its "cool" factor. This should never be a major deciding factor for any project. These languages should instead be selected for valid programming reasons, whether it be speed of the end product, portability, maintainability, or developer support. Currently the two most common system programming languages are C/C++ and Java. Each of these languages has its pros and cons, which must be carefully examined when selecting an appropriate development environment.

C/C++

The C language was developed by Dennis Ritchie in 1972 at Bell Laboratories. It was used originally for the development of the Unix OS. Its popularity quickly grew and it is now possible to write C language programs for nearly all operating systems. C is a procedural language that has become the language of choice for most programming projects.

C++ is everything that C is, plus the ability to program using OO techniques. Bjarne Stroustrup, also from Bell Laboratories, developed the C++ language as an extension to standard C in the early 1980s. Because of its design, the C++ language can be used either as a procedural language or as an OO programming language. This ability has made it a standard in the curriculum of most computer science courses, increasing the number of programmers who have at least some familiarity with the language.

One argument for the use of these languages, either C or C++, is that they provide access to low-level resources. This gives the programmer much more control over all elements of the programming environment including memory allocation. This ability, however, can also be a double-edged sword. Since programmers are required to handle their own resource allocation and deallocation, the language is more difficult. The improper handling of resources often leads to spurious bugs, or problems difficult to find because they only appear sometimes. A powerful capability can quickly become a necessary liability.

Another reason C and C++ have enjoyed such a long life and are still in use today is because of their ability to be compiled into highly optimized executable image. The ability to be optimized is even greater when using only the C portion of the language. Because of the languages' relative simplicity and the requirement to handle resources left up to the programmer, compilers don't have to add any behind the scenes code sections. The code often compiles directly to machine instructions for the processor.

The fact that C/C++ is not an interpreted language also increases the speed of the end product. The code executes directly using instructions understood by the processor. No interpreter is needed to change the compiled instructions into something understandable by the environment. This also means that any program written using C/C++ must be compiled specifically for the environment on which it will execute.

The fact that each program must be individually compiled for the environment has created many problems with portability, since all C/C++ environments are slightly different. A program that compiles and executes fine on a Windows machine may not work in a Unix environment, either because of compiler issues or missing libraries. Careful programming and lots of testing on various platforms can reduce these problems, but some issues may always exist.

C/C++ will continue to be a standard in many computing environments because it still provides features that are not yet available with other languages. When speed of the end product is the most important factor, C should definitely be considered. If your project requires great control over resource usage, it is also a valid choice. Most operating systems are now written using C, including Linux and Windows. If you are considering the language only for its OO environment, other choices should be looked at.

Java

The Java language was originally developed by James Gosling of Sun in the early 1990s. The language was intended to be used for the creation of platform independent embedded applications. These applications could run, for example in a phone, television, or VCR. These originally requirements lead to the creation of a highly portable language with the ability to process multimedia material in a networked environment all built into the language.

Java's high portability is due to the way the language works. Java utilizes a Virtual Machine (VM) environment to abstract the differences with the various hardware components that may be present in a computer system. The source code is compiled into a standard byte code that is then executed by the VM. This allows programs to be created without having to deal with changes in the underlying hardware. It also, however, means that there is an extra step in the execution process that slows the overall speed of the end product.

This has been one of the major issues with Java. Although the design can easily create code that is faster than an interpreted language (one that is not compiled at all), it is still slower than a language that is compiled directly to processing instructions that the OS can directly execute. Most of the advancements in this area have lead to better VM environments. Certain environments will read the byte code and produce code that is much closer to the processing instructions required. As work continues, this is becoming much less of a problem. IBM even claims that on their mainframe environment, they can create Java programs that run as fast as the equivalent C programs.

Java is similar to the C language in structure and format. One major difference in the Java language is that it requires the use of OO programming to write code. Even to create a simple "Hello World" application, the programmer must use a class. Java also handles all the garbage collection required by the program, thereby eliminating the programmer's responsibility to explicitly deallocate resources. Programmers must still take care though, because poor use of objects can lead to memory problems that are equally hard to track down.

To expand on the usability of the language, Sun has continued to add features to the language. Multimedia and networking have been included from the start, but Sun has continued to build the language. Java now includes specifications and functionality that make it relatively easy to use in an enterprise-computing environment. It has the built-in ability to create a distributed computing environment through the use of RMI. If programmers do not wish to create their own distributed environment, Java contains a specification for a standard environment known as EJB. To assist in standard middleware messaging, Java also provides the JMS specification. The expansion of the Internet has lead Sun to create Servlets, which provide an environment to create dynamic Web pages.

Scripting Languages

Scripting languages, in one form or another, have been included in most operating system environments, since their creation. Utility languages are often required to tie together system components or applications in a meaningful way. DOS has its batch files and Unix has its shell script. Given these beginnings, three scripting languages have evolved to become the standard for script-style programs across multiple platforms: Perl, Python, and Tcl.

Scripting languages are often loosely typed. This means that you can mix and match your data or variables easily. This feature makes creating small, usable programs easy. It also means that implementing a large project using them becomes increasingly difficult as the size of the project grows. Another benefit to scripting languages is they are relatively powerful. With only a few lines of code, you can accomplish tasks that may take several lines of code using a system language. This inherently makes the program execution somewhat slower since more functionality is being provided behind the scenes. Depending on the situation, not all of this extra functionality may be needed. Scripting languages are useful when used properly.

Perl

Perl was originally developed as another scripting language for the Unix environment. It could efficiently process text, execute system commands, and prepare reports. Perl was the Unix system administrators dream language. Through ever expanding use, the language has grown to be much more than just a text processing engine. It now provides an OO programming capability along with many open source libraries to make previously complex tasks relatively easy.

Perl is often associated with CGI programming, although this is simply a side effect of the features the language provides. Text processing and data access are the primary requirements of any Web page creation environment. Perl happens to be a relatively simple way to provide such capabilities. Since Perl is an interpreted language, it is considered slower at most programming tasks, but it rivals even C when it comes to text processing and file manipulation.

The portability of Perl rivals that of Java. Because Perl has a high number of open source developers behind it, it has been ported to a number of platforms. This fact has also lead to an increase of knowledgeable Perl developers.

One of the major drawbacks of Perl has been its relatively high learning curve. Although the language is powerful when understood, it is relatively cryptic to read. This readability problem is also hindered by the strange variable symbols, utilizing characters not commonly used in other languages. This, however, is part of what makes the language more powerful. The variables can be accessed and used in a variety of ways. The cryptic nature of some of the statements is also what allows fewer lines of code to be used.

Python

The Python presence is currently smaller than either Perl or Tcl, but it is growing. The Python development team, lead by Guido van Rossum, created an interpreted, interactive, OO programming language. Python is much like Perl and Tcl given its portability and quality of implementation. Because of its OO approach, Python is often considered more suitable for structured programming projects.

Python is often touted as the more aesthetically pleasing of the three scripting languages for larger scale projects. For the neophyte, Perl is much more difficult to read. Tcl, although easier to read on a small scale, becomes rather cumbersome on a large scale. Readability is a large factor determining the maintainability of programs created using a language. This would seem to suggest that programs written using Python are more maintainable than either Perl or Tcl.

Python has several high-level data types built into the language, similar to Java. Extensions can also be added by implementing new modules in C or C++. These extensions can add new data types and functionality to the base Python implementation.

Because Python is OO, expandable, and portable its usage will undoubtedly continue to increase as a scripting and development language. Several system administrator and CGI programmers are deciding to use the language for their purposes, but the Python community is still relatively small (when compared to Perl and Tcl). Given its smaller following, Python programmers may be harder to find, but the language use is growing.

Tcl

The Tool Command Language (Tcl) takes an approach similar to Perl. The Tcl mantra, "everything is a string" has made the language relatively easy to learn and use. Early version of Tcl did treat everything as string, including the code sections. Every statement is viewed as a command followed by some arguments. The statement would be parsed when it was reached.

Because it views everything as a string, it is somewhat difficult to process common control and arithmetic activities. Performance is also reduced by interpreting all data as string elements. Some of this view is being changed slightly. Code sections are now usually parsed ahead of time to create byte-code, similar to the Java compilation method. The Tcl interpreter is evolving into something closer to a virtual machine that processes the byte code.

Tcl is best used as an extension language for products and other languages. It can be embedded in products or used with other languages to provide scriptable functionality. Two important extensions to Tcl help demonstrate this. Expect automates character-based interactions, while the Tool Kit (Tk) provides the ability to easily build GUIs. If Tk is bundled with a commercial product, for example, the product can easily be customized for the given environment.

Summary

The hardware, operating systems, available protocols, and underlying programming languages all contribute to the core components of the e-business foundation. Careful selection of these components is particularly important during the construction or modification of your enterprise environment. Once technologies in these categories have been chosen, a company and its computing systems begin to become dependent on them. It becomes increasingly difficult to change the environment as the company grows. Just like an automobile, you can only modify the core components to a certain extent. After this limit, the entire system and potentially the existing applications that use those systems will need to be replaced.

This chapter examined the deciding factors that can be used when selecting new core technologies for the foundation of your computer environment. Many different solutions exist for similar problems, but the current environment and future needs of the enterprise determine the proper implementations.

Using these same principles, the next chapter will explore the mid-level solutions available to build on the foundation discussed here. Like foundation components, mid-level or infrastructure solutions quickly become imbedded in the day-to-day operations of the business. Users and applications become dependant on their functionality. Selecting the proper infrastructure software elements can also only be done through in-depth analysis and cautious consideration.

Open Source Infrastructure

Open source software is founded on the premise that if something has been created that someone else might need, why not make it open source? Projects generally begin because a developer or group of developers finds a problem for which no solution or only costly solutions exist. To correct the situation, the group takes it upon itself to implement the necessary solution. Once the project is finished, or has reached mid-stream point, the developers realize that others may suffer from the same problem and could assist in the development of the solution.

This chapter is devoted to projects that are capable of providing the infrastructure within the enterprise—from basic company communication software to complex multi-application systems. These applications can all be used to provide the necessary services that a company relies on for day-to-day computer operations. Several open source projects, like Apache and Sendmail, have grown to become invaluable enterprise capable applications.

The enterprise infrastructure components described in this chapter are separated into four basic categories: database systems, Web servers, communication servers, and application and messaging servers. These systems represent standard components within any current enterprise environment.

Comparable proprietary systems can cost a company thousands—or possibly hundreds of thousands—of dollars to purchase and install.

Database Systems

Although the principles behind database systems are relatively simple, the methods used to implement those systems can vary greatly. At its most basic level, a database is simply a means to store, sort, and retrieve data elements. However, there are numerous ways to accomplish this task. Many database systems exist, both proprietary and open source. The right solution for your enterprise will depend on your requirements.

Usually the most relevant features of any database system are stability, scalability, and of course speed. All of the following systems are capable implementations, but each excels in different categories. This can be attributed to the foundations of the different products and the development community behind them. With most proprietary systems, some level of support is usually assumed. Support does not generally come with open source products, since they are free, but it can be purchased. These issues, and others specific to your situation, should always be considered before selecting an implementation.

MySQL

The MySQL database implementation is one of the most widely used open source database solutions. It is a reliable and fast relational database system. The project did not start as an open source initiative, but has changed with the evolving computing industry. For certain applications, the MySQL product offering competes with such big names as Oracle and Microsoft's SQL Server. Certain teams at NASA have even selected MySQL to replace Oracle.

MySQL dates back to as early as 1979 when a Swedish company, TcX, started the project as a screen and report building tool. In the beginning, the project goals were to create fast and reliable low-level data access routines. During the 1990s, the project was expanded to include an SQL accessible application programming interface (API). The first attempt used the mSQL database management system (from Hughes Technologies) to access the underlying data access routines. Because of speed and flexibility issues, the MySQL team elected to create a new SQL engine, but used the mSQL API model as the basis for the new API.

The first version of MySQL was released to a limited number of people using a license similar to the Ghostscript product, a popular open source PostScript interpreter available from GNU. In October 1996, the product was freely available in binary form for the Solaris platform. Linux source and binary distributions were available soon thereafter. In June 2000, the license was switched to a true GPL license. A new company called MySQL AB was formed to coordinate the product development, support issues, training, and consulting. This is also a Swedish company, and as such they have formed partnerships with companies in the United States to provide similar support and consulting offerings.

Given its open source nature and vast international support, the MySQL project has created a relatively diverse product offering. MySQL supports access via several standard programming APIs including C, C++, Eiffel, Java, Perl, PHP, Python, and Tcl. ODBC and JDBC drivers have been written to access MySQL databases. The product has been ported to and is supported on a number of different computing platforms. The database supports several different character sets and multi-lingual error messages and documentation.

Even given these strong benefits, MySQL does have some shortcomings that may exclude its usage for certain situations. The most obvious of these limitations includes foreign keys and triggers. The MySQL team has decided that both of these items decrease overall database performance with little gained in functionality. It also lacks full ANSI SQL92 compliance. Certain common queries, such as subselects or nested selects are not recognized. But since this is an open source project, once the community notices a problem that it would like to change, it will soon likely disappear.

Until recently, MySQL only offered table locking. The table locking mechanism, as shown in Figure 4.1, was chosen to achieve high lock speeds but precludes the possibility of easily implementing transactional support. Table locking also creates a problem in high concurrency applications since the entire table is made inaccessible during certain operations. The open source community, however, realized this was a problem and has expanded MySQL to use BerkeleyDB tables. With BerkeleyDB tables, row locking is available, as well as true transactional support. MySQL tables may now be configured to use any one of five table types. Different table types can even be used in the same database, allowing the user to select the appropriate type depending on the application needs.

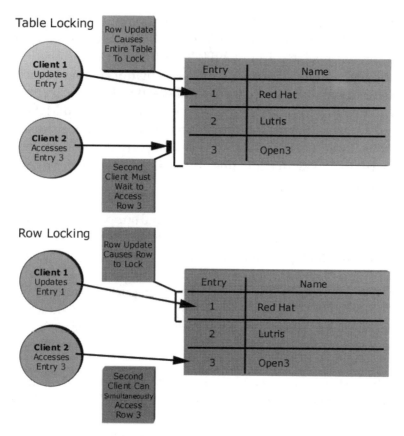

Figure 4.1 Table locking versus row locking.

Although features like multiple processor support and data replication have been designed into MySQL, it does not have the database management capabilities and advanced tools of other more expensive database systems. Oracle, for example, provides the ability to manage multiple database instances easily from a single configuration or management tool. Many of these proprietary database systems also have complicated failover and multiple redundant components to increase data reliability. MySQL can be setup to do some of this, but it is not automatic and does have limitations. The big name vendors usually provide these options as expensive add-ons to their database products. While MySQL does compare in quality and capability to the core database products, it does not currently have the value added tools that other vendors can provide.

However, given the open source nature of the project, this could be changed if enough people within the community request it.

As companies learn about the power of open source products, MySQL grows in usage and developer community size. As Linux and Apache have grown to capture much of the Internet server marketplace, companies have begun to take interest in other open source products for use within the enterprise. Database systems are usually closely tied to company Web sites, and as such MySQL is often examined as a valid option. Several companies now use the database system, either as a stand-alone product or bundled with other products. Companies like Yahoo! have selected it as one of their internal database systems. MySQL provides a very fast database solution that compliments the Linux and Apache products.

PostgreSQL

PostgreSQL is an open source Object Relational Database Management System (ORDBMS). The project has grown from collaborative efforts of students and professors at UC Berkeley. The current version is no longer associated with the university, but the name hints at its history. PostgreSQL is currently one of the leading open source database products comparable to the MySQL offering.

The first relational database project started at UC Berkeley was called the INteractive Graphics REtrieval System (INGRES). This code was developed throughout the late 1970s and early 1980s until it was adopted by Relational Technologies/Ingres Corporation. This company turned Ingres into the first commercially successful RDBMS product and was eventually acquired by Computer Associates.

From this project, the Postgres project was formed. The new project did not use the original code base but maintained some of the leading members, including Michael Stonebraker. Postgres was used as a testbed of various techniques and technologies for the university. Again, a commercial company took notice and used the database to create a commercial product. This company, called Illustra, was eventually purchased by Informix and the product integrated into their offerings.

Eventually SQL capabilities were added to the product by two students, Jolly Chen and Andrew Yu, and the name was changed to Postgres95. In 1996, the source was no longer being maintained by UC Berkeley but by an outside open source community. Shortly thereafter, the name was again changed to PostgreSQL to reflect the SQL capabilities of the product. Since then, it has enjoyed a strong development community that has tried to turn this university database test suite into an enterprise capable database system.

This diverse history has led to more than just name changes. It has allowed the product to grow and transform over several years into a feature rich database offering. The database can be used just as any standard relational system. It has several interfaces to access the database and offers true transactionality and concurrency support.

At first glance, the PostgreSQL project looks similar to the MySQL project. In some ways this is true, but upon closer inspection, the similarities lessen. Both offer a capable relational database accessible through various APIs and access methods, including SQL. They also both offer sophisticated feature sets including data replication, multi-user support, and various optimization options. PostgreSQL, however, offers stored procedures, triggers, and foreign key support, where MySQL does not. PostgreSQL is also highly extensible offering user-defined operators and types.

The differences between the products arise mainly from their differing histories. MySQL has been designed to be fast and stable, and it is for most applications. PostgreSQL, on the other hand, was originally a testbed of technology and has endeavored to create an enterprise ready system. This has created a feature rich product that has suffered in the past with stability. The stability and other problems in PostgreSQL have definitely been reduced making the product able to compete with proprietary solutions. Due to these design differences, MySQL is best used when speed and simplicity are of the utmost importance. PostgreSQL is usually best for projects where high concurrency or complicated features are requirements.

BerkeleyDB

BerkeleyDB is an embedded database system with roots going back to development work in the early 1990s done by Margo Seltzer and Ozan Yigit on a new hash access package to replace the Unix-based *dbm* and *hsearch* methods. Hashing involves the association of key-value pairs, where the key is used to retrieve an element of data from the hashtable. The new hash package was a superset of original Unix functionality because it combined the functionality of disk-based and memory-based hashing along with various optimizations.

By 1991, BerkeleyDB was released. This release included the original Hash and a new B+tree database type. Work on BerkeleyDB continued, and in 1996, Seltzer and Keith Bostic founded Sleepycat Software to support BerkeleyDB for a growing user base of commercial customers.

The current BerkeleyDB implementation owes much to its hash roots, and extends the original key-value pair paradigm. All data is stored using a unique key. This approach to data storage is different from a SQL-based RDBMS where data are stored in relational tables, or in an object database where data storage is tightly coupled with a language such as C++ or Java. BerkeleyDB actually support four distinct storage types, optimized for different applications:

Hash. The Hash type optimizes data retrieval times while maintaining reasonable data storage requirements. This type may be used where fast access to a large set of data is needed, the keys are known ahead of time and updates to the database are rare.

B+tree. The B+tree type tends to be slower for data retrieval in a large database than the Hash type, but this is balanced by relatively fast insertion and searching. This database type may be used when the database will be used for dynamic storage, retrieval and where key values may be searched. It is also good in situations where a range of keys must be retrieved.

Queue. The Queue is a specialized database type that optimizes retrieval and storage times for data are stored and retrieved in sequential order.

Recno. The Recno type is a specialized access method that is optimized for dealing data that can be stored and retrieved as a sequential list.

BerkeleyDB is an embedded database; the data are accessed through an API rather than through SQL statements. As a result, BerkeleyDB is typically linked into the target application either as a static or dynamic library. This means it is not normally used as a stand-alone system and does not support native query execution, or the type of data management one would expect from a relational database. It is a database engine that can act as a data store for a SQL engine, an OO database, or some other application. BerkeleyDB aims to be small, robust and scalable. It is aimed primarily at a software developer rather than a database administrator.

For development purposes, the BerkeleyDB implementation presents several features that make it worthy of selection. The entire database has a small footprint and supports several platforms and languages. The design is also scalable. BerkeleyDB can be thought of as a minimalist's database designed to be simple and optimized for speed, reliability, and scalability.

Comparable to stand-alone systems, it provides transactionality, concurrency, and recoverability in case of a failure. Because supporting these features can be relatively costly, Sleepycat provides three different versions depending on how the product will be used. The standard Data Store version supports multiple reads but only single data writes with no transactional support or recoverability. The Concurrent Data Store offering adds multiple write functionality. The third version, BerkeleyDB Transactional Data Store, is designed to be used where high concurrency, data integrity, and recoverability are critical. It provides transactionality and utilizes write-ahead logging to provide recoverability.

One other item to note about the BerkeleyDB implementation is the distribution method and licensing surrounding the product. Sleepycat distributes BerkeleyDB in source form freely, but to obtain a binary distribution you must purchase a support contract. This normally does not pose a serious problem since the product is typically used within other development efforts. The license, however, is slightly more troublesome depending on your needs. The license does make the software open source, but it limits the distribution of the source and the distribution of products developed using the database. Applications using the database are required to provide a freely available version of the application in source form. A commercial and distributable license can also be obtained from Sleepycat.

BerkeleyDB provides a small, fast and robust database engine that can be integrated into an application. Although it does not provide querying features that are the mainstay of RDBMS systems, it provides advanced functionality such as transactionality that make it a viable solution for applications where reliability and scalability are chief concerns.

Web Servers

Web server technology is the key component in the current Internet environment. These servers provide the functionality that allows users to obtain and download Web pages and other material from Web sites all across the World Wide Web. Every Web site requires a Web server to handle client connections and distribute the Web pages.

The first real Web server was a basic Unix daemon, or stand-alone background process, that listened for socket connections from clients requesting a document. The requested document, or Web page, was then sent back to the client using the opened connection. Soon clients were built into Web browsers, which eventually made Netscape and Internet Explorer common words known all across the world.

This technology was first created by the Software Development Group at the National Center for Supercomputing Applications (NCSA). They also created the first widely used Internet client, originally called NCSA Mosaic. As the Internet industry has advanced, several proprietary Web server platforms have been created. Such well-known companies as AOL, IBM, Microsoft, Netscape, Oracle, and many others all have a Web server platform of some form or another. Nearly from the start though, only one open source Web server product has excelled above all others—Apache. Apache is usually the Web server of choice for not only the open source community but also for the typical enterprise.

Apache

The Apache project was born out of necessity from a public domain HTTP daemon created by Rob McCool in the mid 1990s. By 1995, the NCSA httpd program had become the most popular server software on the Internet, but it was no longer being managed or developed. Webmasters and users began developing patches to correct problems or optimize portions of the code, but no common entity was managing or coordinating the development effort.

Soon, the Apache Group was formed to handle the management tasks. The name actually refers to the original server being "a patchy server" based on the NCSA httpd. This group created a plan to overhaul the original program to create a robust, commercial-grade, and full-featured implementation. Version 1.0 of the Apache server was released on December 1, 1995, and within a year surpassed the NCSA server as the most popular HTTP server on the Internet.

The Apache server project is now managed by the Apache Software Foundation (ASF), which was created in June of 1999 as a not-for-profit corporation. The server is one of several projects that are not headed up by this open source organization. The ASF also manages several Java server projects and XML projects including Cocoon, SOAP, Xalan, and Xerces.

Due to their excellent ability to manage projects, companies and developers have handed off certain projects to Apache to be managed as open source initiatives. The ASF is arguable the best managed open source organization to date.

Compared to the original NCSA httpd program, the Apache server is still very similar in functionality. A client requests a connection and the server responds to the requests, as depicted in Figure 4.2. The primary changes have been in optimization, security enhancements, reliability, and scalability. The server is now highly configurable. Web site administrators can configure access to various directories and set up fairly complicated security rules. The core Apache product is capable of serving static content and executing CG-style programs. By adding on the Tomcat extension, originally developed by Sun, the server can also handle JavaServer Pages (JSP) and Java Servlets.

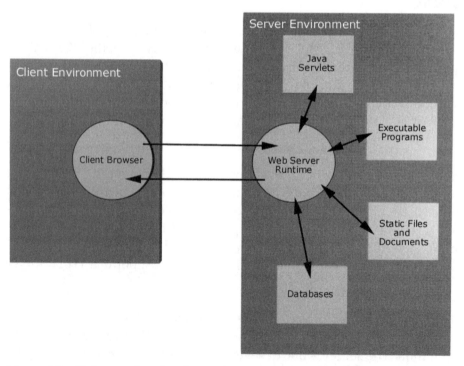

Figure 4.2 Web server functionality.

Apache is used on more than twice as many Web sites than its nearest competitor. Apache is used on over 15 million total sites and six million active sites worldwide. Companies have selected the Apache server because it is one of the fastest and most reliable Web servers available. It also has one of the widest feature sets and platform supportability of any HTTP server. Considering that most commercial servers can cost several thousands of dollars, a free Web server that performs comparably seems like an excellent option.

The HTTP server and many of the other Apache tools come bundled on most of the Linux distributions. It is a standard option and feature available to the Linux distributors. The Apache server has helped to make the Linux platform what it is today.

Communication Servers

Communication servers are an important component of the enterprise infrastructure. They comprise the technology that allows employees, customers, and other people associated with an enterprise to communicate electronically. Currently these servers come in two main forms: email and instant messages. Both of these services allow the employees within an enterprise to work and communicate with other employees, customers, and suppliers effectively.

The distinction between email and instant messages is sometimes slightly fuzzy. The main difference is that email is designed to be used in an asynchronous or delayed fashion. Instant Messaging (IM), although still asynchronous, is designed for near real time communication. Email is sent to an individual's mailbox or server-side message queue, which is checked periodically. With IM, messages are sent directly to an application typically running on the recipient's machine. The information is displayed immediately and is normally not saved in a mailbox.

The notion of sending text messages between users on a computer system has been around as long as multiple users of computer systems have existed. The first real email was adapted for use on the ARPANET in the 1970s. Instant messaging was also available during this time in the form of chat type applications. Both of these communication methods have grown since then into the form we know today.

In the past, people did not typically have access to a computer network constantly. Thus email allowed for participants to communicate when they could. Messages were saved until the recipient was able to read it. Given the number of people constantly connected to the Internet, the popularity of IM has risen recently.

Although similar in nature, the technology involved with the two communication mediums is quite different. Email servers play a double role, in that they must act as a message database for each mail recipient and as a relay station for delivering sent messages. They do not notify clients that new mail has been received. The client must connect with the server to check for new messages. Instant message servers simply act as an intermediary between clients. Clients typically maintain a connection with the server and are instantly notified of incoming messages. As the need for connectivity and communication continues to rise, it will be interesting to see how these paradigms grow and possibly combine.

Sendmail

The sendmail application is one of the oldest and most widely used mail transport agent (MTA), or email server, in use today. The original version was written before the Internet was standardized to handle the delivery of mail messages on stand-alone servers. It is now estimated to handle approximately 75 percent of Internet email traffic. Although typically hidden from the average user, most companies could not operate without an email server.

The earliest sendmail program was actually called delivermail. This application was developed by Eric Allman, while he was a student at UC Berkeley, before TCP/IP networks were commonplace. The first version, shipped with BSD 4.0 in the late 1970s, used FTP protocols to transfer messages between machines. As the ARPANET grew the standards changed and new protocols, including TCP/IP and SMTP, were developed. These new protocols caused Allman to re-examine his delivermail application, and thus sendmail was born.

As Internet standards have grown and the needs have changed, sendmail has continued to evolve. Several versions were created throughout the early 1990s to suit the needs of specific individuals or organizations. This led to an increase in the different versions of the product and created great confusion for system administrators. Most of the relevant features of these versions were combined into one version, and by 1996 entirely new features were being added once again by Eric Allman. This new version is the one that is typically used in most enterprise environments.

Email accounts and mailboxes are similar to postal mailboxes. Users typically have a single account. An account is identified by a name and an address using the @ (at) symbol as a separator. The address identifies the computer and the name identifies the account or the mailbox. Users can have several names or aliases that all point to the same account. They can also set up forwarding so all the mail delivered to a particular account can be automatically forwarded to a second account, possibly on another computer network. This functionality is depicted in Figure 4.3.

In this scenario, sendmail acts as the post office. When a user sends a message, sendmail examines the message to find the address. The address is looked up using a Domain Name System (DNS) to determine the IP address that identifies the recipient's server. Once this is found, the mail is sent to the receiving MTA normally using the SMTP protocol. The receiving email system will sort the mail and place it in the proper mailbox.

Beyond the basics required of any email server, sendmail offers many more features that make it the MTA of choice. Sendmail is highly scalable and manageable. It is also extremely robust and fairly secure. Much of this

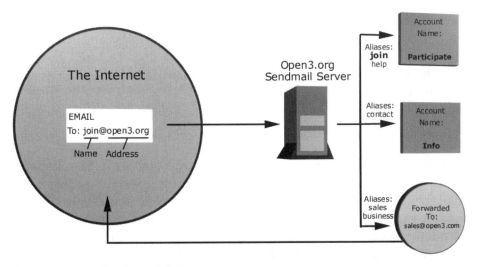

Figure 4.3 Sendmail email delivery.

can be attributed to the open source nature of the project and its many years of existence.

The sendmail project, currently managed by the Sendmail Consortium, is entirely open source. A strong community of developers, including Allman, works constantly to add features and fix bugs in the email server application. A commercial company, Sendmail, Inc., has also been created to offer bundled products and commercial grade support for the project. This company uses the open source version along with various add-on tools to create several customized versions pre-configured for different needs. Sendmail is also included in most of the Linux and BSD distributions that are available.

Jabber

Jabber is an open source system for IM, which allows users to send text and binary messages quickly to other users. The rise of the Internet has made IM popular, and it is becoming a useful addition to email. Several proprietary IM systems include Yahoo!, America Online, ICQ, and Microsoft Network. Unfortunately, these proprietary systems do not provide a bridge between each other. Therefore, a user on one system is unable to communicate with a user on another system. Jabber aims to solve this problem by not only providing a universal open source IM system but also by integrating with the various proprietary systems.

The Jabber system contains the central server, client applications, and various transports for other IM systems. These components of the system communicate with each other by using XML messages. The central server handles communication between other servers, clients, and transports. Client applications provide an interface to the user to send messages through the server to other users. Transports translate between foreign IM systems and the Jabber server. The transports allow a user, for instance, to send a message from a Jabber client to an ICQ client. There are currently several Jabber transport projects for all major IM systems.

IM is useful in e-business for enhancing communication between employees and business partners and providing a secondary avenue to email for customer support. IM between employees can facilitate communication for those working in disconnected environments. Jabber being extended to work with mobile appliances, like the Palm Pilot, would allow field consultants to converse with the home office. Jabber is also useful in business-to-consumer e-commerce. Real-time communication with customers can provide, for example, assistance with a purchase while online.

Jabber also has potential uses beyond simple text messaging, such as providing for the transmission of voice and video files and conducting e-commerce. Purchases can be made through an interactive IM client that adds personalization and interaction to the average e-commerce Web site. Jabber's ability to connect with e-commerce systems and to be linked with the enterprise applications is greatly enhanced through the Open3/Jabber adapter that integrates Jabber with the Open3 server. This enables Jabber, through Open3, to connect with a product like Akopia Interchange that can enable e-commerce transactions through the IM client.

Application and Messaging Servers

The final category of infrastructure components discussed in this chapter includes those products and applications that assist in the integration of existing applications and new development efforts. These products go by many names such as application server, integration server, messaging server, or middleware server. The combination of eager marketing departments and the evolution of a new market have caused the lines between these terms to become blurred.

No matter what they are called, these servers all have one thing in common. They use a multi-tiered design to create a common framework for access to applications within the enterprise. They tie together disparate systems in an effort to allow access to those applications more easily. The extent to which each individual product assists in the integration problem may vary, but each product does have its purpose.

Because the terms used to describe these products can differ, some clarification is required. Two primary classifications exist within the application integration arena. This book will use the terms *application server* and *messaging server*. A server that falls into either of these classifications may also be referred to as an *integration server*. The definitions of these two classifications are as follows:

Application server. The most basic definition of an application server is a program that manages and assists in the communication with applications. Most application servers are designed to assist in the rapid deployment of Web sites, but some are capable of much more. Usually application servers operate by managing various modules within the server environment. These modules will typically provide some new functionality or tap into existing legacy applications or data sources. A common access method can then be used to execute all of these modules from some thin-client application, such as a Web application.

Messaging server. A messaging server, using its most basic definition, is an application that manages the delivery of messages from one client to another. These messages can take several forms, but typically one access method will be presented to clients for communication within this messaging environment. Programming modules for these servers are typically written to run externally to many of the core server components. These modules can also be used to communicate with legacy applications or data sources.

These two paradigms together make up the bulk of integration products in the current computing industry. Although these definitions are simplistic, they point out the major differences in the two classifications. Beyond the general principles of the integration servers, various toolsets or features may be included with particular products possibly making them more or less suited to your particular needs.

Open3.org

The Open3.org team has created an open source integration platform that allows disparate enterprise applications, databases, legacy systems, and other applications to communicate with each other easily. The main efforts of Open3.org have been directed toward the implementation of the Open3 E-Business Integration Server. In the founding of the project, it was observed that the main problem with integration is the proprietary nature of most platforms. This situation is not helped by purchasing more proprietary tools to connect existing proprietary packages. The Open3 project for integration enables companies and individuals to contribute open source solutions that benefit all the users of the community, ever increasing the usability of the integration platform.

The server architecture has been designed to be highly portable and scalable. The core messaging server uses XML messages to communicate on standard TCP/IP socket connections. This allows nearly any platform or programming language to communicate with the server. The server is also written in Java to increase portability. Several APIs, and access methods are currently being created to access the Open3 server architecture. The project currently provides a J2EE JMS-compliant open source implementation for client access. The Open3 integration platform provides a standard point-to-point message queuing paradigm and a publish-subscribe style of messaging, shown in Figure 4.4. These messaging styles can be used individually or together to take advantage of each method's strengths. The server offers persistent message delivery with standard message acknowledgement methods. The persistence engine supports many database systems including MySQL, MS Access, MS SQL Server, and Oracle.

The Open3.org platform is more complicated than a basic messaging platform. It provides features commonly found in commercial message broker software packages that often sell for several thousands of dollars (some even ranging into the hundreds of thousands). A message broker differs from standard messaging platforms in that it allows certain business logic to be established within the server. This business logic commonly consists of message filters and conversion utilities. An adapter or

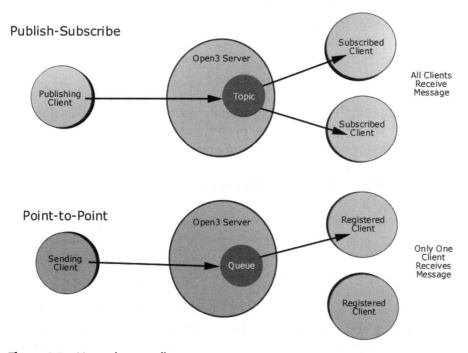

Figure 4.4   Messaging paradigms.

connector framework is also provided which allows easy integration with various software packages.

These features make it much easier to integrate disparate software platforms by placing much of the integration logic in the messaging platform. Fewer "custom" client programs must be written. The adapters or connectors can instead connect with the external software package and consume or provide messages in the appropriate format for that package. It is up to the message broker to filter and manipulate messages according to the integration scenario desired.

The Open3 project is only a couple years in development but is quickly gaining popularity. The feature set and available adapters are also growing as usage increases. Companies that are considering using a messaging platform for integration purposes should definitely consider examining the Open3 E-Business Integration Server for use within their enterprise.

Enhydra.org

Enhydra.org is a software community dedicated to building Java-based and XML-based application development platforms. Enhydra.org has commercial backing from Lutris Technologies, which sponsors the community and invests heavily into the development of its software. Enhydra and Lutris may seem like strange names. They refer to the scientific name, Enhydra Lutris, for the California Sea Otter, a mascot for the Enhydra project like the penguin is for Linux.

Enhydra's mission is to build completely open source Java-based application servers that meet and exceed proprietary systems. This is no simple task. It is competing against large proprietary platforms like ATG Dynamo, BEA Weblogic, IBM Websphere, and Allaire JRun. To compete against these large and entrenched players, Enhydra.org is bringing together individuals and companies from around the world to develop its application server platform. Its completely open source solution, and benefits like open code, no license cost, and a large support community, is helping it to gain a foothold in the Java application server marketplace. Enhyra.org contains two application servers, Enhydra and Enhydra Enterprise.

Enhydra is a Java Servlet implementation. Its architecture supports the development of high volume Web sites in an enterprise setting. Enhydra contains a leading generation data and presentation separation system known as the eXtensible Markup Language Compiler (XMLC). XMLC has been designed as a replacement for Java Server Pages with the goal to detach data from presentation logic.

Enhydra is most useful in building Web sites, particularly for B2B portal, B2C e-commerce, and content and information sites. Enhydra has broad platform and application support. The Java-based Enhydra server can run on any platform that supports modern versions of the Java Virtual Machine (JVM), including Linux, Unix Solaris, Windows, and several others. It supports several Web servers, including Apache and Microsoft IIS. It utilizes Secure Sockets Layer (SSL) for transactions involving e-commerce and other secure transmissions of data. Applications based on Enhydra can access database systems like PostgreSQL, MySQL, and Oracle through JDBC. The strong multi-platform compatibility of Enhydra makes it a strong choice for deploying in an enterprise setting. Enhydra contains several development tools like XMLC, Data Object Design Studio (DODS), and the Servlet Debugger. XMLC enables all business and database logic to be completely isolated from how information is displayed, making it easy to change the look and feel for the presentation of information, such as a Web site. DODS is a graphical environment used to build and map the application's database layer. The Servlet Debugger provides for live monitoring of requests and responses between the server and the application.

Enhydra's technological base on Java and XML, its multi-platform compatibility, and toolset enables leading generation development for Web sites. Web applications are built around a component model that encourages reuse across projects. The component model, extended with XMLC, provides for multi-tier application development, as depicted in Figure 4.5. Database operations, business logic, and presentation format are separated. It enables database experts to handle the database logic, developers for the business logic, and page designers for the presentation. In other platforms, like Allaire Cold Fusion and Microsoft Active Server Pages, all of this logic is jumbled together into a single Web page. This makes it difficult to change one set of logic without affecting another set. Enhydra applications are a leading example of architecture necessary for first-class e-business solutions.

The second platform of the Enhydra.org project is Enhydra Enterprise. This platform aims to become a fully compliant J2EE server that is extended with Enhydra specific technologies. The Enhydra Enterprise Application Server (EEAS) contains J2EE implementations of EJB, Java Naming Directory Interface (JNDI), JMS, RMI, and Servlets. The Enhydra community has many of the EEAS containers, but it has also partnered

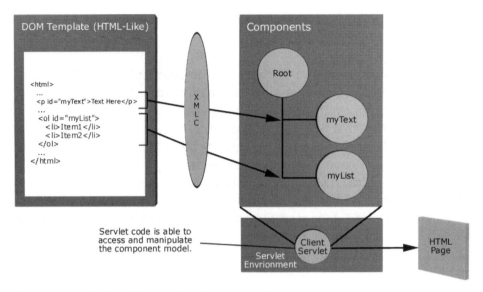

Figure 4.5 Enhydra XMLC and Servlet relationship.

with other projects like Evidian for their JOnAS EJB implementation. Enhydra specific additions include the Enhydra Scheduling Service (ESS), Enhydra Logging Service (ELS), XMLC, and support for wireless applications through WML. J2EE is emerging as a strong development platform for e-business solutions. J2EE dominates market share in the application server market. The J2EE platform allows for the development of highly distributed applications that scale easily as system demands grow. BEA Systems, IBM, and ATG are leaders in the J2EE space. Enhydra Enterprise represents the most robust open source J2EE implementation available.

Both Enhydra Enterprise and the applications built on it function as modular components or services. The kernel of the system, called the Enhydra MultiServer (EMS), is the core code that manages services. Services run within their own environment separate from other services. This enables enterprise-class security and prevents services from malicious external access. The modular service architecture also allows significant customization to the server, providing versatility in its deployment for custom solutions.

Design features like deployable and configurable services on a live server enable rapid development and constant production uptime. Programmers can develop Enhydra Enterprise applications quickly and live applications can be adjusted while in production. For load balancing and fail over, multiple Enhydra Enterprise instances can operate in a cluster that is spread over several machines. This allows for a highly scalable and reliable system for applications, a strict demand for e-business solutions.

JBoss

The JBoss community is a group of several hundred developers with a similar mission to Enhydra Enterprise—to build an open source implementation of J2EE. The currently completed system, JBoss/Server, is a J2EE-compliant EJB application server. The community also features other J2EE projects in the works like JBoss/JBossMQ (formerly spyderMQ) (JMS), JBoss/Apache for the Apache Tomcat project (Servlets, JSP), and JBoss/Jetty for the integration of Servlets, JSP, and EJB into one JVM. Another significant project in the community is the JBoss/TestSuite that is a testing framework built on top of JUnit to ensure compliance and functionality of the JBoss/Server. Strong quality assurance in this open source project aids in validating its operation in the enterprise environment.

The JBoss/Server represents a mature implementation of EJB, supporting Session and Entity Beans. It has been designed to be highly modular to support system customization through the Java Management eXtension (JMX) API. This modularity allows features of EJB to be removed from the system that aren't being used by applications. This benefit enables an increase in performance and a reduction in application footprint.

JBoss is progressing toward the J2EE goal but is not as mature as the Enhydra Enterprise project. However, JBoss has made giant strides in their work and is a significant open source community developing enterprise-class software.

ExoLab Group

The ExoLab Group is another open source community that is building many of the features in J2EE. This includes OpenEJB (EJB), OpenJMS (JMS), OpenORB (CORBA), and Tyrex (Java Transaction Service or JTA). The ExoLab Group is financially sponsored by Intalio, Inc., which aids in the development and vision of the project and develops commercial servers based on the open source software. All of the ExoLab projects are governed under a BSD-like license.

OpenEJB's lead architect is Richard Monson-Haefel. The mission of the project is to create a unique EJB 2.0 container system that outperforms all other available implementations. It is including support for both session and entity beans. The container system is currently under development and is not ready to begin testing for production.

OpenJMS is an implementation of J2EE JMS. It is currently in development phase and the community is expecting version 1.0 release in the first half of 2001. The goal of the project is to create a fully compliant JMS implementation with broad database support.

OpenORB is an implementation of the CORBA 3.0 specification that is designed to be a customizable and modular object request broker. OpenORB currently provides 8 of the 15 services in CORBA including transactionality, persistence, and security. The goal of the project is to provide CORBA services without the bulk of features found in many complicated CORBA implementations. OpenORB is in the later stages of development phases and is nearing rigorous testing for production.

Tyrex is an implementation of the JTS. It provides services for local and distributed transactions, resource pooling, security, and transaction process monitoring. The community describes the software as "probably one of the most boring open source projects on earth" because it functions as a behind-the-scenes system to connect EJB, JMS, and Servlet implementations. Although no one can see the system directly in action, its services are important. Tyrex is in the later stages of development and is expected to be production ready in the early part of 2001.

The Exolab group, although not as mature as projects like Enhydra and Open3, represents a significant and growing contribution to open source J2EE software. Its backing by the commercial company, Intalio, provides a basis for third-party support for e-business initiatives. Look for Exolab to be production-ready in 2001 for many of the key components of the J2EE platform.

Zope

Zope is a Web application server based on the Python programming language. Zope provides a multi-user platform for the development of dynamic online applications, like community portals and e-commerce Web sites. Zope has grown rapidly in popularity since its release in November 1998 and has over 10,000 members registered at Zope.org. The platform is a strong open source competitor against similar proprietary systems like Allaire Cold Fusion and Microsoft Active Server Pages.

The basic functionality in Zope that enables the creation of sophisticated Web applications is its ability to present dynamic content. Dynamic content, as opposed to static HTML pages, enables a customized and interactive Web site. Zope has built in features like the ability to access major database systems, site search, and user personalization to create an active and dynamic application. Zope provides e-business with the ability to build and deploy quality Web sites quickly.

Zope applications are built through the assistance of a Web-based interface. Zope uses the concept of folders that contain objects. These objects, shown in Figure 4.6, construct the Zope application. There are three basic types of Zope objects: content/data, business logic, and presentation. Content/data objects contain text-based and binary data like documents and

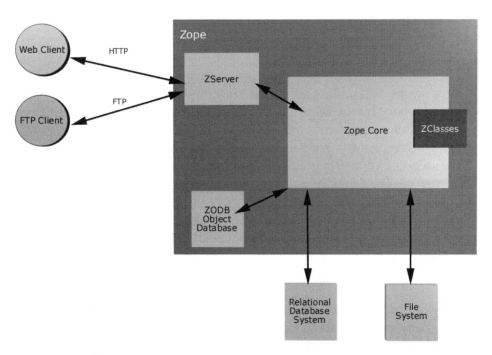

Figure 4.6 Zope environment.

graphics files. Business logic objects contain algorithms and perform database interaction. These objects are generally coded in Python or SQL. The third type of object, presentation, utilizes the Document Template Markup Language (DTML). DTML provides tags or methods to access and manipulate dynamic content.

The platform provides a robust user role and security system for collaborative development. Various users, such as site developers, content developers, site designers, and administrators are all assigned access to specific portions of a project. This is a significant advantage to project managers who face the difficult task of coordinating the various roles of users on a project. Various resources of the site, like the site pages, can be labeled as public or as restricted. When a particular user accesses a restricted resource, that user is verified against an authentication list to permit or deny entry. For example, Zope has three default roles: Anonymous, Owner, and Administrator. Anonymous users are permitted access to public resources. Owners are assigned access to objects that they create. Managers can access administrative functions of the site. New roles can be easily defined. This system provides a highly effective way to manage security and effective collaboration for a Web application.

Zope enables basic content integration by supporting access to relational databases, file systems, and through protocols like HTTP and FTP. This feature provides content to be scattered in diverse locations and brought together on the Web application.

Zope supports a remote accessible component model. The functionality of a component can be accessed from a remote site and used locally. Zope enables this support through the SOAP and XML-RPC protocols, through which a component is accessed through a URL. The ability to access the components of a site provides a point of integration. The component model also provides the capacity to create a Web site that is a conglomeration of various components from other sites. Thus, functionality is reused and Web applications may be built more quickly. For example, a component may be built that downloads weather reports and can generate a five-day forecast based on input of a particular geographic region. Once the component is built, other sites, such as a skiing portal, can utilize it.

Zope is a mature product that continues to grow in feature set and ease of use. Zope provides for a rapid learning curve and flexible application development. Zope is a strong contender in the open source space and provides the quality demanded for e-business Web applications.

Zend

Zend is a suite of products primarily developed by the commercial company Zend Technologies. Zend generally refers to the Zend Engine, an open source application server that supports the PHP scripting language. PHP provides rapid application development of enterprise-class Web applications. Its strong feature set has enabled PHP's popularity to explode since its initial development in 1995. The PHP Group, the open source community for the PHP language, announced in early 2001 that there are over 5 million Web sites based on PHP, according to findings from the research firm Netcraft. Driving this growth of PHP is the Zend Engine, which provides the processing and execution of PHP code.

Andi Gutmans and Zeev Suraski originally developed the Zend Engine. The Zend engine has grown in popularity, performance, and feature set since its inception. Dramatic improvements in execution speed for the Zend Engine from version 3.0 to version 4.0 has moved the Zend/PHP combination from limited use in the enterprise to acceptance by enterprise development for e-business. Released in mid-2000, the Zend Engine 4.0 switched from an execute-while-parsing architecture to one that compiled before execution. The result was a performance boost of several magnitudes and broader acceptance by the performance-driven development community.

Through Zend, PHP supports a broad range of platforms including Linux, Unix, and Microsoft Windows. PHP frequently operates with Apache Web Server. The PHP module is one of the most popular modules for the Web server. PHP can also execute as an ISAPI extension for the Microsoft Internet Information Server on Windows platforms. Beyond operating systems and Web servers, Zend also supports connectivity to all major database systems. This includes proprietary systems like Oracle and Sybase and major open source databases like MySQL and PostgreSQL. Zend also connects with external utilities that perform functions like parsing and building XML and generation of Adobe Acrobat PDF documents.

The Zend Engine is released under the Q Public License. This license provides the general freedoms that are found in other open source licenses such as access to the source code and ability to modify the code and redistribute it. The open source nature of PHP and the Zend Engine has been instrumental in its broad acceptance. Look for Zend/PHP to continue to deliver a solid platform for building dynamic Web applications for the enterprise.

ArsDigita

The ArsDigita Community System is an open source software platform for the rapid development of sophisticated Web applications. It is particularly suited toward B2C and community-oriented sites but also has several components to aid in B2B Web application development. ArsDigita's e-commerce, collaboration, and personalization features make it a strong open source alternative to commercial products from BroadVision and Art Technology Group (ATG).

The ArsDigita Community System revels in solid support from the open source and business community. Its enterprise-class software is deployed in major corporations like the World Bank and Siemens. The software was originally provided in the Tcl programming language but version 4 also offers a system developed in Java. Since Java has wide adoption in the business world, ArsDigita is receiving even broader support and market penetration than with its previous versions. The dual programming language deployment also permits greater flexibility to the enterprise's IT department. Either Tcl or Java expertise may be utilized to leverage the full capabilities of the system.

In the last couple of years, application software vendors have recognized the need for more sophisticated systems than those that just simply generate dynamic Web pages. Modern application servers are moving toward a Web application framework that contains many of the features found in enterprise applications. These include items such as customer relationship management (CRM) and marketing analysis. The added features enable a development team to quickly implement Web sites that not only display information but also provide functionality to support customers and business processes. ArsDigita is one of the early adopters in delivering this robust functionality for Web applications.

ArsDigita's feature set solves many of the issues in implementing an effective e-business application for the Web. ArsDigita is crafted on a component-based architecture (see Figure 4.7). The system components include collaboration, personalization, marketing, e-commerce, and content management. Integration of these components permits each of the modules to work seamlessly together. The component-based architecture enables a high degree of customization while leveraging pre-built functionality for rapid application development. The components also expose an API that provides a way to integrate an ArsDigita application with other applications. However, ArsDigita does not provide an integration framework, such as a message bro-

Figure 4.7 ArsDigita architecture.

ker, to provide the connectivity to external enterprise or legacy applications. Open source software like Open3, JBoss/JBossMQ, or OpenJMS may be utilized to provide integration with external systems.

The collaboration component provides discussion boards, chat rooms, file sharing, community presentations, and scheduling features. Collaboration leverages the power of the connected Internet to allow employees, business partners, and customers to communicate with each other better. Collaboration enhances essential business processes such as efficiency between co-workers and customer service.

The personalization component enables a Web application to deliver a personal experience to a customer. Site content, promotions, and customer service can be tailored to each individual or group of individuals that interact with a site. Amazon.com employs an excellent personalization engine, recommending new book publications based on a customer's past purchases. Personalization permits a company to optimize its marketing effectiveness and deliver targeted information to an increasingly demanding customer base.

The commerce component provides a turnkey solution to e-commerce enabling a Web site. This includes features such as product cataloging, shopping carts, checkout, discounts, gift certificates, and payment processing. Utilizing these pre-built features enables the enterprise to quickly add e-commerce capabilities to their Web application.

The content management component solves many of the problems in creating, approving, aggregating, and delivering content to the end user. Content management is essential for Web sites that deliver any significant amount of information. ArsDigita also employs a useful workflow engine that assists in organizing the processes to bring content from idea to finished reality.

The last major component of the ArsDigita system is marketing and analysis. This system provides a way to analyze data such as customer traffic and purchases to create effective new site design and marketing campaigns. This analysis provides benefits like improved revenues and a more efficient marketing and sales operation.

The ArsDigita Community System is an impressive product. It provides a solid and comprehensive feature set for quickly building sophisticated Web sites. ArsDigita is a strong offering in the open source space and deserves a careful look when considering an application development system for a new Web project.

Summary

The solutions and projects examined in this chapter can be used to enhance or build the infrastructure within your enterprise. Many of these tools, including database systems, Web servers, communication servers, and integration servers, whether open source or proprietary, have become a requirement for most companies. Businesses simply can't operate within the current commercial environment without some core infrastructure components to assist in the day-to-day operations of the business. Many of the open source projects listed in this section have been created for just that reason—because they were needed. This need and the wide use of the solution sets have lead to the creation of robust, enterprise-class products that are often selected over proprietary solutions.

The third tier of applications often relevant in the current e-business environment includes enterprise applications. Enterprise applications are those applications that include functionality to manage a component or multiple components of the general operations of a company. These applications are typically large-scale deployments that are used throughout the company, such as an inventory or human resources system. The next chapter will explore these solutions and the current open source projects that are available. Properly layering enterprise applications onto the selected infrastructure solutions can help any company quickly grow.

Enterprise Applications

Enterprise applications (EAs) are the building blocks for e-business architecture. EAs automate business processes and facilitate communication throughout the business. Understanding how these applications fit into your business is essential for building an effective e-business strategy. EAs include customer relationship management (CRM), enterprise resource planning (ERP), inventory management, sales force automation (SFA), human resources management (HRM), and other software to transform all major business departments into e-business departments. Installing and effectively using EAs is crucial for success in today's modern economy. Open source software, although in the early phases of EA development, is enabling rapid innovation in this marketplace and can assist with constructing the EA architecture.

The following pages detail how EAs fit into the e-business strategy and how open source can be leveraged for part of this technology infrastructure. We'll examine the various EA categories and their connection to business departments like marketing, sales, manufacturing, and procurement. Open source enterprise applications like OpenSourceCRM, Akopia, and Relata are described for their usage as solutions in these business departments.

Open Source and Enterprise Applications

The EA infrastructure is one of the five main components of an e-business strategy (see Figure 5.1). EAs must be chosen that can deliver on business objectives and grow with new business demands. Solid technology is crucial to support the business processes that EAs replace and enhance. EAs can be either purchased as packaged systems or completely custom developed. Proprietary packages are generally difficult to change or extend, and this is often why businesses choose to develop custom solutions even though the cost to do this can be considerably higher. Open source EAs provide the instant out-of-the-box functionality of a packaged system with the freedom that is available from custom solutions. This makes open source software very attractive in the EA arena.

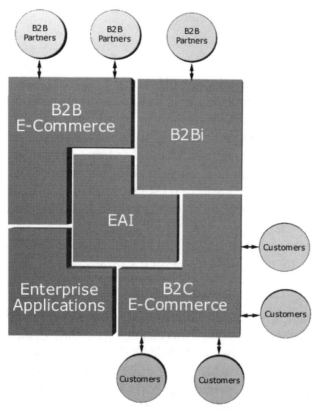

Figure 5.1 Enterprise applications are one of five components of e-business.

Unfortunately, the open source movement is just taking hold in this sector of the market and there are only a handful of available quality applications. Today, a business cannot rely simply on open source software for all of its enterprise application needs; it must look to proprietary software to fill the gaps. Fortunately, there is strong interest in developing open source EAs and there are dozens of projects in their early phases of development.

Will open source EAs consume all proprietary software in each of the categories? This is a difficult question to answer. Open source has seen development and success in the most popular types of software, such as OS, Web servers, and application servers. For open source software to succeed, it must have the backing of a community of developers, whether the developers assist for free (GNU/Linux) or whether they are paid to contribute (Red Hat Linux). It is much easier to find developers for a system that has 10,000 installations in the enterprise, like Linux, rather than a single installation, like an ERP system.

Due to their more limited usage, EA projects may have difficulty acquiring expert developers in the early phases. To deliver the quality and feature set found in many of today's proprietary EAs, software vendors must be able to succeed with an open source strategy. Strong development in the past two years from communities like Akopia and eGrail has been assisted by vendors pursuing a strategy on open source EAs. These vendors donate in-house resources to creating great software. They generate revenues through turnkey solutions and services. The open source software vendors are instrumental in launching these projects. Their success, spurring development toward an open source model, will make open source EAs a reality. This is good for the software world and great for the implementers of e-business.

Until universal open source EAs become available, the enterprise must rely in part on proprietary solutions. Wherever proprietary solutions are required, choose those that have open interfaces and are standards based. A standards-based system enables the business to move from vendor to vendor, without being locked into a single proprietary application. However, proprietary standards-based software doesn't allow you to access to the source code, making customization more difficult and even impossible.

In choosing a proprietary application, look to vendors who operate similarly to open source companies, ones who derive a bulk of their revenues by providing services rather than selling bits out of a box. These vendors are likely to be more cost effective and concerned with enabling solutions for the long-term. Also, evaluate the extensibility and ease of integrating the product into your enterprise. Does the application have interfaces or adapters to hook into enterprise-class integration systems? Optimally, choose solutions that interface to standards like XML or open source software like Open3.

Whether proprietary or open source, the types of enterprise applications your business chooses depends upon its EA strategy. The strategy formulates a roadmap to succeed in this fundamental area of e-business.

Developing an Enterprise Application Strategy

The first task in using these building blocks for e-business is to determine their business case and develop an EA strategy based on these business prerogatives. The strategy must include immediate and long-term requirements. Some of these needs may seem obvious, such as lowered costs or improved efficiencies. However, e-business opens new doors for strategies to compete in the modern era. One of these novel and crucial effects is the information age, whereby all information in the enterprise is available to all departments and potentially available to business partners and customers. An effective EA strategy reaps significant benefits like lowered costs, rapid completion of business processes, greater efficiency, higher quality, and the ability to tap into new revenue sources. Unfortunately, these rewards don't come simply or easily. There are six rules the enterprise must adhere to for an effective enterprise application strategy.

Rule 1

Internal business processes must translate to servicing customer's priorities.

Customers demand selection, value, and personalized attention. If your enterprise doesn't service your customer's priorities, one of your competitors will. Your enterprise must align its business processes and technology around the customer to succeed as a customer-centric company. Although some enterprise departments appear to be only internal, such as HRM or inventory management, they always directly or indirectly affect the customer. For example, HR software removes many of the mundane tasks for employees and allows them to concentrate on real business needs, such as better customer service. Inventory management software can accurately determine which items are in stock or when they will become available so that the customer knows exactly when they'll receive their purchases. The customer must always be considered when choosing EAs.

> *Open source advantage:* Open source helps to eliminate problems inherent in proprietary software like difficult licensing, high cost, and poorly customizable systems. All of these factors take away from what matters most, delighting your customers. The flexible and unrestrictive nature of open source software is the best technology foundation for a customer-centric e-business design.

Rule 2

Aligning and igniting corporate culture toward novel technology is essential for participation in the new economy.

Despite marketing hype from software vendors, there is no instantaneous success from installing a few EAs. The employees and corporate structure must adopt the applications into new models of workflow. Old habits are hard to break and sometimes getting people to adopt new technology is the largest roadblock. To be an e-business, your enterprise must dissolve this obstacle through training, awareness, and acceptance.

> *Open source advantage:* The users of open source software are also its developers. Therefore, open source software is market driven rather than marketing driven. This means that the software is developed to meet the needs of its users rather than developed to convince users that it meets their needs. This market-driven model makes open source software more easily accepted by your employees because it satisfies their demands. Often technology is not adopted because it is too difficult to use or does not do what it needs to do. Open source is the most effective software design to eliminate this hindrance.

Rule 3

Automate, automate, automate. The return on e-business investment is first realized when manual business processes become digital ones.

EAs digitize modern businesses. Automated processes that occur from this digital revolution not only reduce costs but also decrease the time to complete them. The fully automated enterprise can outmaneuver its competition and respond to customer demands before they occur. Processes must be automated wherever their long-term ROI is positive. Prioritizing and completing automation around customer demands is often the most effective e-business strategy.

> *Open source advantage:* No two businesses are the same. This makes it impossible to develop software that meets all of the automation needs for more than one business. Proprietary software packages attempt to be one-size-fits-all. Even if they provide avenues for customization, their black box nature makes them difficult to understand and extend upon fully. On the other hand, open source software is inherently customizable and configurable. There is no black box; all of the system's utilities and functions are laid bare for the highest degree of modification possible. Open source software allows the enterprise to automate processes not feasible with proprietary systems.

Rule 4

Capitalize on new possibilities that emerge from creating the digital enterprise.

Newly uncovered territories surface when a business becomes an e-business. The enterprise must realize that enterprise applications don't simply cut costs but also enable new revenue possibilities. For example, automation and integration along the supply chain may allow the business to manufacture according to customer specifications and enter new markets. Identifying novel ways to generate revenues is an essential component for the EA strategy.

> *Open source advantage:* The cost to install and maintain open source software is inherently less expensive than proprietary systems. This is obvious. Removal of license fees, publicly tested applications, and unhindered access to source code decrease the price of the IT infrastructure. What is less obvious is that open source can also lead your business to new revenue sources. For example, Linux is famously more reliable than one of its significant competitors, Windows NT. The enterprise that can depend on the uptime for its systems can create new revenue opportunities. For example, a bank, powering all of its customer transactions through a single, integrated, and reliable system can guarantee customers instantaneous and accurate access to account balances. Creating customer loyalty invents customers that come back more often and come back with friends. The reliability and security in great open source software ensures that your business has the basis to operate under the highest standards.

Rule 5

To participate in the information revolution, applications and data must be easily integrated and shared throughout the enterprise.

The fifth rule is one that many businesses are only beginning to realize. Stand-alone applications are not nearly as effective as integrated applications—those that can share their functionality and data. For example, integrating inventory management to CRM software enables a business to inform customers of the inventory availability of their purchase.

Integration is the cornerstone of an effective EA strategy. A business' needs extend beyond departmental requirements to those of the entire enterprise. Unfortunately, many EAs do not have simple interfaces to connect to one another, so in choosing these applications a business must also decide from the onset on an EA integration strategy (see Chapter 6, "Enterprise Application Integration"). To reach Tier 3, your business must effectively utilize integrated EAs.

> *Open source advantage:* It's a reality; software has been developed to lock customers into a particular vendor. Look at the incomprehensible file formats found in some legacy systems or Microsoft's heavy hand with the Windows platform. This highly proprietary nature of software makes it incredibly difficult to provide integrated solutions. Wonder why the e-business integration marketplace generated $1.5 billion in revenues in 2000 and is expected to grow 75 percent per year for the next several years? It's due in part to the difficulty to integrate with proprietary software. Once again, open source comes to the rescue through unlocked applications. Full view of the source code guarantees that your applications and their underlying data can be integrated.

Rule 6

The enterprise must recognize that technology changes quickly and must plan for revolutions in the future.

Many of today's large corporations, dependent upon 30-year-old outdated legacy systems, are finding it difficult to adapt to new technology. Much of this problem stems from proprietary software that is difficult to update. Choosing technology that your enterprise can grow with is essential. Anchors are for boats, not modern businesses.

> *Open source advantage:* There are two reasons corporations don't change with technology: cost and the technical infeasibility to do so.

Proprietary software vendors constantly charge customers through upgrade churn and lock them into systems that they can't easily escape from. Additionally, proprietary solutions may not grow to meet new needs by the enterprise. Open source solves these problems. Upgrades occur on a constant basis and new features are added as quickly as the market demands. Open source is highly maintainable and easier for IT employees to become experts with the system. Leveraging an EA strategy based on open source enables businesses to prepare for continuous technological change.

Enter Enterprise Applications

Managers, realizing the amount of time and money invested in their legacy systems, are often reluctant to change to newer and better applications. Much of this lack of enthusiasm is due to personnel training and how enmeshed outdated systems are into the lifeblood of the business. Some of this unwillingness stems from fear to go with another vendor's proprietary solution. Even vendors with standards-based solutions incorporate their own proprietary add-ons, which defeats the purpose of standards.

Open source eliminates the problems of proprietary systems through lowered cost and timely software. Open source, developed by the public and for the public, embraces change as fast as the market demands. Your enterprise, based on open source, will better be able to enter technological revolutions because of lowered cost to upgrade, better availability of IT talent, and the inherent flexible nature of the software.

Aligning your strategy based on the six rules for an effective strategy will help your enterprise more effectively leverage enterprise applications. Once your business has determined customer priorities, primed corporate personnel, developed an automation game plan, prepared for new revenue potential, integrated enterprise-wide, and designed for future changes, it can then begin to leverage EAs to reap the rewards promised by e-business.

Whether open source or not, EAs are essential to the e-business strategy. There are several different categories of EAs. Many of the categories are aligned to specific business departments, such as HRM and sales force management, but others cross departmental lines, including ERP and supply chain automation. Although open source software is not available in every one of these categories, all major categories are presented. Understanding the functions of enterprise applications in and throughout various business departments is essential in transforming your business into an e-business.

Human Resources Management

HRM software automates the administration of employees. The core part of HRM software is to direct payroll and benefits but may also include components such as managing recruitment, hiring processes, taxes, worker's compensation, insurance, training, expense reporting, project management, and more. There are dozens of proprietary HRM applications provided by companies like Oracle and Extensity, and many HRM functions are available in enterprise resource planning suites. This category lacks any comprehensive open source applications, with the phpGroupWare project developing one of the first set of applications for open source HRM software.

HRM enterprise software is most useful in medium and large companies. Businesses with less than 50 employees will find many of the features in a full-scale HRM application suite as extraneous. HRM software is designed to eliminate administrative manual processes and to ease time-consuming tasks that add to an employee's workload.

phpGroupWare

phpGroupWare (www.phpgroupware.org) is a suite of Web-based applications written in PHP for group information management. It includes features like email and group calendaring. phpGroupWare also contains an API for developing add-on applications, and there are active projects for inventory management, resource booking, trouble ticket management, and human resources. These applications are all in a developmental stage and are not ready for enterprise use. If your business is utilizing PHP-based software then this project may present some early stage programs for further refinement into your enterprise.

Procurement Automation

Procurement is the various processes involved in the acquisition of products. This includes product cataloging, authorization, shipment, warehousing, receiving, and payment. There are two types of procurement: production and non-production. Production procurement is the acquisition of products, such as raw materials and components, used in the manufacture of goods or services. Non-production procurement is the acquirement of goods and services used for the day-to-day operations of the business. Typical large corporations spend upwards of 10 percent of their revenues on the procurement of non-production goods like office equipment, software, and supplies.

Procurement traditionally represents a significant expenditure of resources. Procurement involves a group of employees known as purchasing agents, or employees who spend a significant amount of time in purchasing activities rather than their real work, to siphon through hundreds of suppliers to acquire the highest quality products at the lowest prices. Before a purchase order is generated, management must approve purchases. Huge bureaucracies exist in larger companies where procurement must be approved by several layers of management. Once authorization is finally acquired, shipping and receiving must handle delivery and accounting must direct payments for the goods.

In the past, procurement practice involved mounds of paperwork. Procurement automation or e-procurement ends these inefficiencies by automating the exchange between buyer and seller. Software technology has focused on bringing non-production procurement to the desktops of employees. This allows individual employees to purchase goods and services from their computer. Approval for their purchases may be automatic, based on the employee profile and their spending allowance. For example, John Employee may have a $500 yearly spending allowance for basic office supplies. The system automatically checks the balance on the spending allowance before authorizing the approval. Approval for larger items, or items not normally utilized by the employee, are electronically routed to appropriate management. This happens in real-time, without paperwork, and streamlines the process.

The application of choice by employees for desktop purchasing is a Web-based intranet. This allows for employees using different computing platforms and those connecting from remote locations on wireless platforms to access the same system. Accepted products for purchase are cataloged on the Intranet, either by employees within the company or through catalog services made available by suppliers. Employees may be presented with only those products that fit their profile. For example, Jane Employee in marketing may be able to purchase color printing services but not mainframe computer systems.

Once products are selected and approval is generated, the fully automated e-procurement system must connect with suppliers to deliver purchase orders. The system must be intelligent enough to recognize when a particular supplier cannot fill a critical order and be able to route that order to someone who can fill it within the time demanded.

The electronic procurement space has several proprietary vendors such as SAP, Oracle, and SupplyWorks. There are currently no open source projects that have made significant inroads in this area.

Manufacturing Planning

Manufacturing planning software assists with sourcing of materials, optimized workflow for the creation of goods, and quality control. Manufacturing planning either replaces or works with procurement, workflow, and inventory management systems. Manufacturing planning benefits the enterprise by optimizing the production process. The automated procurement of production materials ensures that a business has the materials it needs to meet its manufacturing demands. Data entry along the assembly line helps managers to monitor worker and workflow efficiencies and to implement changes to improve productivity. Quality Assurance (QA) management records and analyzes the quality of goods and can assist with the enlightenment of the manufacturing line to improve production processes.

This category of software is often highly specialized to a specific industry, such as electronic component assembly or auto parts manufacturing. There are no current open source software projects that are enterprise-ready or even in strong development for manufacturing planning.

Inventory Management

Businesses that manufacture and/or sell goods maintain inventory. Inventory management is a significant activity that is closely tied to the success of the enterprise. Modern businesses must be able to work in distributed and global environments. Single, tightly controlled warehouses are becoming more rare in an environment where items are maintained in disparate locations that may or may not be controlled by the company. Outsourcing of inventory is growing in popularity. A striking example of this is Amazon .com that sells toys through its Web site, but the stock is maintained by Toys 'R' Us. Outsourcing inventory allows a business to have backup items in stock and sell more items than it has the physical space to contain. Multiple sales channels, warehouses, business partners, and shipping possibilities create challenges for the enterprise to control what's in stock and what's being sold on a real-time basis.

Inventory management software aids in the complexities of administering goods that come in and out of the enterprise. It usually contains or is tied to a sales management interface that allows salespersons to access information about the availability of particular items. Inventory management is essential for businesses that maintain all but the simplest selection of goods. There are many proprietary vendors of inventory systems, including large companies like SAP and Baan, and many smaller vendors that specialize in a particular vertical market. There are two Open Source applications with inventory management software ready for the enterprise, Akopia and Zelerate.

Akopia Interchange

Akopia Interchange (www.akopia.com) is a full e-commerce package for setting up and running an online storefront. The Akopia open source software is part of Red Hat's Linux platform offering. The software includes features like catalog management, shopping cart, checkout, marketing management, and e-commerce administration. The package is developed in the Perl programming language and supports a variety of web servers and SQL relational database systems.

Of significant concern to e-commerce development is the ability to tie the Web application into legacy systems and other enterprise applications. The Akopia package supports an architecture for point-to-point integration but does not have an adapter module or integration system for enterprise-class integration. Several open source integration systems are available that can provide the bridge from Akopia to external applications. These integration systems are detailed in Chapter 6.

The main benefits to using the Akopia package are rapid application development and unlimited customizability. E-commerce applications, founded on the business strategy of generating revenues, must be implemented quickly. Akopia provides a reliable platform to reduce the time and effort in a B2B or B2C e-commerce implementation. Additionally, it's open source foundation permits developers with the ability to customize and extend the application. Akopia Interchange is very mature product and a solid competitor in the e-commerce application development space.

Zelerate AllCommerce

Zelerate (www.zelerate.org) is a set of e-commerce modules to enable a brick-and-mortar business to move toward online operations. The Web-based suite contains modules for building and running an e-commerce site. There are two main application areas to the package, the storefront and the backend administration system. Since the Zelerate package is primarily an e-commerce package, it is more closely detailed in Chapter 8, "E-Commerce Applications." However, there are three modules contained in the backend administration system that are of interest for enterprise applications, the Inventory Manager, Warehouse Manager, and Order Manager.

The Inventory Manager allows the enterprise to maintain detailed inventory information that is accessed through an online interface. Goods are tracked with a stock count, status on their availability, pricing options, brand name, and shipping weight. The interface contains a search function that enables the administrator to find inventory items by ID or keywords. Products are tailored for display to a custom page type, providing the capability of distinct user interface styling based on product category or brand.

The Warehouse Manager maintains a listing of warehouses for shipping and receiving. It works in tandem with the Order Manager to review order tracking from a single warehouse or across multiple distribution centers in disparate geographic areas. Orders can be tracked by warehouse, order ID, order date, and order status. Each Order contains detailed information such as the bill of sale, shipping method, and ship to and bill to addresses.

These Zelerate modules provide a simple but effective system for storing and tracking inventory and orders. Use of these modules outside of the integrated package will require some work to connect into your custom solution. The package is also Wireless Application Protocol- (WAP) enabled to allow remote users on wireless platforms to interact with it. Zelerate is an attractive alternative to proprietary applications if your enterprise is looking for an uncomplicated Web-based system for inventory and order management.

Enterprise Information Warehousing

Enterprise information warehousing (EIW), also known as data warehousing and data mining, collects, analyzes, and administers information throughout the enterprise. EIW, often working in tandem with enterprise application integration software, pulls data from disparate information sources including databases, applications, and communication sources into a single system. This unified system of data enables the business to analyze historical trends, pool information to gain insight, and provide a cohesive knowledgebase from which to determine future business strategy.

Apache Jetspeed

Apache Jetspeed (www.apache.org) is an enterprise information portal (EIP) based on the J2EE platform for connecting information from various Internet and communication formats, such as XML and SMTP. Jetspeed provides for the development of a portal that is available as a Web application and through wireless devices utilizing wireless markup language (WML).

Channels of content, known as syndication, provide for the sharing of data inside and outside the enterprise. Jetspeed supports syndication through Open Content Syndication (OCS). OCS was created by Internet-Alchemy (www.internetalchemy.org) to support a listing of syndications spread out over multiple sites with content in multiple formats. Each channel of syndication may be composed of several formats that are customized by language, content type such as plain text or XML, and the frequency of content update. Content that may be syndicated in an enterprise include press releases, internal memos, project updates, contract statuses and more.

Syndicated information content is made available to various groups of users through security roles. Therefore, certain parties, such as general employees, have access to different content than that available to the board of directors or the general public. Jetspeed also nicely utilizes XSL to provide customized content formatting. Therefore, a particular group of users may be presented with the same information but in a different visual layout from another group of users.

Jetspeed is working toward the goal of providing an organized portal for employees, business partners, and customers to access various parts of a business' information. The Jetspeed project is still in its infancy and is not production ready. Apache has consistently produced enterprise quality applications and look to Jetspeed in the near future as a viable contender in the EIP space.

Content Management

The proliferation of users on the Internet and the strategy to empower customers with information requires the substantial production and organization of multimedia material. The Web provides a medium for the delivery of content in textual, graphical, audio, and video forms. Large Web sites like Amazon.com or Yahoo.com must effectively manage and deliver trillions of bytes of data. Even small Web sites see their content base grow to billions of bytes. The combination of the varied content types, massive amounts of data, and the constant update of information requires a strong organizational solution. This solution is content management software. Such software provides an automated way to manage workflow and create the infrastructure necessary to support information creation and presentation on the Internet.

Content management software is similar to EIW as both facilitate the storage and organization of content. Content management differs from EIW in a couple of ways. First, EIW employs statistical and other analytical features to assist primarily with internal business decision-making. Content management software does not implement these features. Secondly, content management focuses on the workflow and processes to create, edit, approve, and display content to the end user, and therefore utilizes tools not found in EIW packages.

ArsDigita provides an enterprise-class open source solution for content management. The ArsDigita Community System features a content management module. This module provides the infrastructure for organizing the business processes throughout the lifecycle of content management. As part of a larger application development platform, ArsDigita is discussed in more detail in Chapter 4, "Open Source Infrastructure."

Enterprise Resource Planning

Enterprise resource planning (ERP) software is an integrated suite of enterprise applications designed to revolutionize the enterprise (see Figure 5.2). If there is one turnkey solution for becoming an e-business, the ERP system is it. These suites are dominated by software juggernauts like SAP, Oracle, J.D. Edwards, and PeopleSoft. ERP systems carry hefty price tags, often several million U.S. dollars per installation. For this reason, ERP systems have seen a majority of use in only the largest of companies, primarily those in the Fortune 1000 and Global 2000. Today, there is interest by some of the major vendors and many of their smaller competitors to deliver cost-effective ERP systems for smaller companies.

ERP systems contain back office applications for human resources, procurement, manufacturing, financial, accounting, inventory, sales, distribution, and more. Installation of the ERP framework provides the business with an operational system that can communicate across corporate divisions. It has been marketed as the magic bullet for an enterprise application strategy and major companies like General Motors, Coca-Cola, and three-quarters of the Fortune 1000 have found it to be effective.

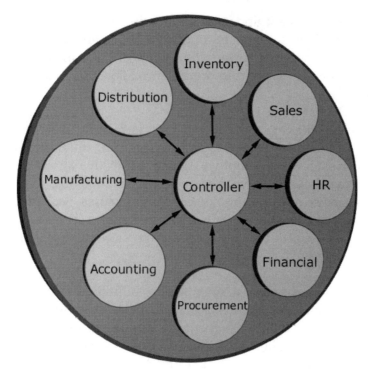

Figure 5.2 ERP is an integrated suite of enterprise applications.

In the past, many enterprise application solutions have been haphazard (see Figure 5.3). Businesses have custom developed and pieced together various systems to meet short-term needs without regards to long-term growth and maintainability. As a business installed more and more applications, it quickly realized that two of the systems needed to be integrated. Piecemeal point-to-point integration solutions would then be added. As more applications were added to meet immediate corporate demands, more bandages for integration were necessary. Soon the enterprise technology became a complicated, inefficient, and highly unmaintainable system.

ERP systems remove outdated and difficult solutions with a unified system. It provides the enterprise with benefits like better on-time delivery of orders, decreased manufacturing delays, and quicker processing of purchase orders. Some efficiencies gained decrease time and costs by as much as 90 percent. These are the rewards promised by e-business and leveraging an ERP system can bring the enterprise directly to Tier 3.

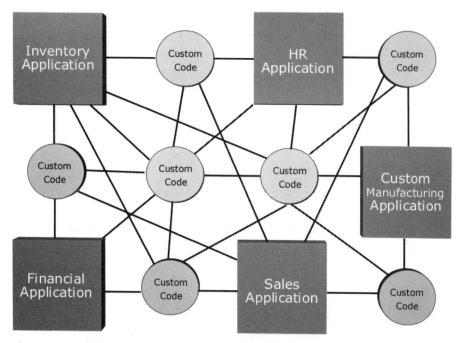

Figure 5.3 In the past, the enterprise application strategy was poorly designed.

There are significant benefits to ERP systems. However, there are a few disadvantages. The main complaint of the enterprise is that the ERP system isn't wholly tailored to their business. The enterprise must accept generic features common to major businesses or devote significant time and effort to customizing their ERP solution. Unfortunately, due to their proprietary nature, ERP systems can be difficult to customize to specific corporate needs. Another complaint is the ability to effectively integrate the ERP system with other enterprise applications like customer relationship management or an e-commerce Web site. Many of these systems require another integration solution to tie them together with other applications.

Some modern enterprises, instead of turning to generic ERP solutions, develop an enterprise application strategy based on enterprise integration. This enables the business to choose those applications that best satisfy their needs, rather than accept a dozen applications that may only fill some of the enterprise's requirements. This strategy also requires that an enterprise application integration platform be selected that can connect the various chosen applications. This strategy is initially more difficult to implement, but provides for a highly custom solution and prepares the business for future application integration scenarios.

ERP systems require considerable development effort. The Open Source world is just beginning to enter this sector of the market with the Sajix project.

Sajix

Sajix (www.OpenSourceERP.org) is a project aiming to deliver a completely Open Source ERP implementation that is competitive with leading vendors like SAP, PeopleSoft, and Baan. The project is in the early stages of planning and development. Considering the size and complexity of ERP systems, the community has considerable work before delivering on its goal of a competitive product with current proprietary systems.

Sajix's plan is to deliver a suite of integrated enterprise applications including sales management, inventory, human resources, manufacturing, accounting, and more. Each of these applications is being developed under the guidance of experts specific to the application domain. The broad and diverse expertise available to the community provides Sajix with a strategic advantage in developing a system that is superior to current proprietary offerings.

Sajix's technological architecture is based on Java with an API for integration with legacy applications and data. The design of the system includes database independence, multi-language support, robust security, email integration, and customizable modules. Sajix is also developing a migration toolkit for enterprise systems to move from their existing legacy applications to the open source system.

Sajix is an ambitious project that if realized, will be a welcome addition to the open source enterprise application toolkit. A completely open source ERP solution is especially attractive when considering that proprietary systems often carry price tags in the millions of U.S. dollars. If the project is successful, it will likely be late 2001 or early 2002 before enterprise-class applications begin to emerge from this project.

Customer Relationship Management

Customer relationship management (CRM) software, also known as front office applications (FOA) or enterprise relationship management (ERM), helps companies manage their customer relationships. This includes sales support, marketing, customer service, and more. The ultimate level of a CRM solution allows a business to keep track of customer data across all parts of the business. Therefore, customer data is shared and managed by the sales department, marketing department, customer service, order processing, and other associated departments.

A good CRM strategy enables a successful customer-centric business. A customer strategy is needed before a business can decide what CRM software to implement. This strategy determines the CRM software that the business requires to accomplish its customer-oriented goals.

An important purpose of CRM software is to integrate all of the information from the contact points. These are ways that a customer can contact a company. Whether the customer uses email, phones, writes, or speaks in person with a customer service representative, CRM keeps track of all these points of contact and makes sure that all sales people involved in the different points of contact have the same information.

CRM has an interesting relationship with enterprise resource planning (ERP). ERP deals with uniting data within the enterprise for more efficiency and CRM is a part of this overall strategy. Several ERP companies, like PeopleSoft, have modules for CRM that are integrated into the ERP suite. It's a recurring theme in e-business; integration is essential for most enterprise technology initiatives, and is especially evident in its ability to manage the diverse communication with customers.

For example, let's say a customer calls a ski equipment company (see Figure 5.4). He's interested in buying the new K2 skis. The sales representative (or customer service person) pulls up his file and notices that he has bought K2's before, and knows his size and performance capabilities. The representative then offers the customer the new K2 skis that fit his performance level. He has product information for the customer at his fingertips describing boots and bindings that go with the new K2 skis. He also knows that if the customer buys the K2 skis, and packages them with a ski jacket, he will get a certain discount.

Another example of how CRM is used is to predict what the customer wants and to offer customized products based on past purchases and demographics. Amazon.com and Netflix.com do this by having the customer rate which books or movies he or she likes, and then correlating that data with the data from other customers. This allows them to predict what other books or movies the customer may choose for future purchases.

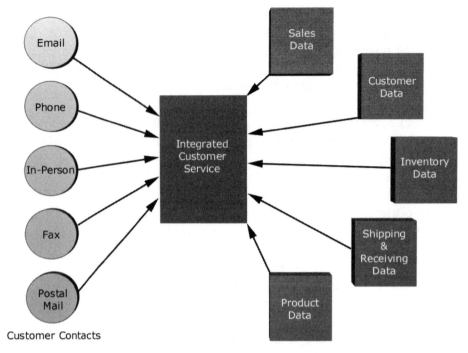

Figure 5.4   CRM provides an integrated view of customer data.

CRM is based on designing a business to meet the customer's wants and needs. CRM is a strategy that businesses adopt to better communicate with their customers. A successful CRM implementation improves profits through satisfied and return customers. All good businesses succeed by focusing on the customer. CRM aids a company in reaching this goal.

Open Source CRM Software

There have been many open source CRM projects initiated in the last two years. The most popular projects are OpenSourceCRM and Relata. These projects are in their initial versions of development and do not yet have all of the features of expensive proprietary CRM applications. They offer basic functionality, such as targeted email campaigns and are adding different modules as they develop and grow.

There are several reasons that open source CRM software is advantageous over proprietary software for e-business solutions. One reason is initial cost. The CRM software is free with an optional fee-based service for the configuration, installation, and support of the packages. This advantage is extended by not being locked into a proprietary system, and thus new versions of the software do not require paying new license fees. An important second reason is that the features of the system are determined by the demand in the industry due to the open source development model. This means that features become available as demanded, not when a company decides to provide them. Additionally, the overall stability of the good systems are superior proprietary ones, because the open source community that supports the projects will be quick to fix any bugs or performance issues.

OpenSourceCRM

OpensourceCRM (www.opensourcecrm.org) is an open source CRM software package that is backed by the company Anteil. OpenSourceCRM has a goal of developing a suite of CRM applications that are all open source. Currently, they have a product called KeyFactor, which is a Campaign Management solution. KeyFactor allows the user to manage email campaigns.

The proprietary competitors for OpensourceCRM are companies like IBM, Siebel, Clarify, Oracle CRM, Vantive Corp., SAP CRM, BaanFront-Office, and SalesForce.com (online CRM software).

Relata

Relata (www.relata.com) is another growing open source CRM package. It is sponsored by the public company, Stratabase. There is currently one completed package for the Relata product suite, called Relatamail. The open source community is developing all Relata products.

Relatamail is a Web-based software tool that has been developed for organizations with large-scale communications needs delivered via email. Relatamail can be used for several aspects of enterprise marketing automation, including outbound email-based communications and customer support.

The Relata components are written in PHP, Java, and XML, making its acceptance broad by the open source development community. Keeping other open source projects in mind, Relata is designed to work seamlessly with other open source technologies, like MySQL, Apache, Linux, and Sendmail. The Relata family of software is free of charge and released under the GNU GPL.

Summary

EAs form the foundation upon which to build an e-business strategy. Strategizing for customer satisfaction, adoption by employees, focusing on automation, realizing new revenue potential, implementing integration, and adapting for change are essential to the enterprise application framework. Developing this framework by utilizing open source software can enable lower cost, greater reliability, and more customizability for the enterprise.

Central to the deployment of enterprise applications is an integration strategy. Integration is the language that permits applications to communicate with one another. Just as communication is essential to your employees for conducting business, so is communication between your applications. Data that are unavailable or too difficult to interpret by all facets of the enterprise become wasted information. The efficient and profitable end-to-end e-business is made possible through integration, which we discuss in the next chapter.

CHAPTER

6

Enterprise Application Integration

Enterprise application integration (EAI) has received much press recently as being the next breakthrough in the computing industry. The majority of this praise can be attributed to the rapid growth of the Internet, but the truth is that integration within the enterprise has been around nearly as long as different computing platforms. Most of the new work in the integration industry has been centered on the creation of easier to use middleware solutions.

The need to compete requires companies to operate more efficiently and adapt more quickly to the changing business environment. To accomplish this task, companies need to share data across traditional corporate boundaries. Decisions can be made more quickly if the proper information is available to the people who need it. New information, or rather the combination of existing information, can lead to the recognition of previously unnoticed company patterns. By automating tasks and combining redundant business processes, efficiency can also be increased.

As integration needs have increased, so have the companies that provide integration solutions. This increase in competition has led vendors to create solutions that are smarter and easier to incorporate into the enterprise. Integration companies have developed advanced message brokers and easily configurable middleware packages.

ERPs and other packaged applications have also led to the advancement of integration solutions. As integration companies repeatedly solved the same solutions, they quickly found the need to create standardized solutions. This has led to better and easier integration platforms, some of which can be simply installed and configured to connect certain applications. These EAI platforms are evolving to be much closer to the "plug-and-play" capabilities of other types of programs.

Introduction to EAI

Before delving into exactly how to create and carry out an EAI solution, it is important to understand what EAI is. Many definitions exist for EAI and enterprise integration (EI) in general. Marketing and advertising campaigns have blurred the distinction between the various integration problems. The most basic definition of EAI is the integration of information systems in an effort to share the data and processes used by those systems. Although EAI is commonly used to refer to any integration effort undertaken by a company or group of companies, for discussion purposes this definition will be narrowed. To hold true to the *enterprise* in enterprise application integration, this chapter will focus on internal integration issues. Further discussion about external integration and Internet integration needs will be handled in later chapters.

Most current enterprise computing environments exist in chaos. They have been built from the ground up using a mixture of technologies and systems. They exist in the Tier 1 or Tier 2 categories outlined in the first chapter. Computing environments are often split between corporate organizational boundaries with little to no sharing between departments. For example, one department may have selected a Windows environment utilizing Windows tools and programming techniques, while another department may use only Unix platforms and tools.

As companies grow, they often must share the information between departments or different systems. In the past, companies integrated as the need arose. This has lead to the proliferation of many one-off integration solutions, or those that are only relevant to the situation at hand. The main problem with these solutions is that the next time an integration problem is found, it must be handled separately and essentially from scratch. Each solution would require costly design and development time. This is clearly not the method of choice for rapidly growing companies.

One of the barriers preventing the advancement beyond the Tier 2 category is the proper selection of a solution or group of solutions that is capable of providing the integration needs of a company. The selection should not only handle the current integration needs but also must be expandable and adaptable to handle future needs and changes in the computing industry. Selecting the right architecture allows a company to move toward a Tier 3 company and be on the right track to reaching a Tier 4 or Tier 5 status.

To accommodate these needs, the best integration environment is designed around open standards. Open standards are not controlled in a proprietary fashion by any single company. They are published and freely available. Companies utilize these open standards as a means to provide some type of common interface or common functionality within products. Open standards often provide the best of breed design principles. They have been created by many architects and developers to accommodate common problems within the computing industry. It is almost a necessity that the integration environment utilizes some type of open standard to allow the greatest number of problems to be integrated. By using integration solutions based on open standards, the various integration components become interchangeable. For example, if a different messaging component is needed, it can simply be plugged into the existing framework with little to no changes in the surrounding programming.

This design philosophy also exhibits the strength of a multi-tiered architecture. A multi-tiered architecture allows the enterprise environment to exist in several different levels each providing a different type of functionality. Each level essentially represents a different piece to the overall puzzle that makes up the computing environment, as shown in Figure 6.1. Multi-tiered designs allow the company to separate specific functionalities. When a problem arises, it is easier to focus on the section causing the problem. It also becomes easier to add new functionality or change a piece of the puzzle without affecting the surrounding pieces. Any integration solution should provide the ability to tap into any of the tiers within this design when required. Utilizing the appropriate integration design and products can also help to create the necessary levels.

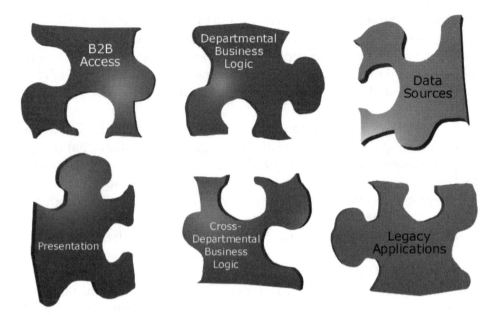

Figure 6.1 Multi-tiered environment puzzle.

So how does one begin the daunting task of overhauling the entire computing environment of a company? The simple answer is slowly. You should not throw out everything you have and implement a new environment from scratch. This is unrealistic and would most likely result in failure due to the size of the problem. Large projects often fail because they are too time consuming and difficult to implement while the company continues to operate. It is much better to select a solution that can be implemented as needed. Systems and programs can be tied together using a common solution when required. Small projects can be enacted to slowly replace or update the old systems. It is important to use what already exists inside an enterprise. The current environment can be molded into the preferred architecture.

EI is a difficult undertaking. Connecting various legacy systems, databases, and enterprise applications is a daunting task for most organizations. Typically companies don't have the in-house expertise to properly architect or fully implement a long-term and scalable solution. EI consultants are often brought in to provide the organization with the expertise it lacks.

However, a company should also not rely exclusively on outside help in the form of consultants or integration companies. Many of these companies do an excellent job at providing the necessary services and tools required for integration solutions, but because this help is relatively expensive, it is often cost prohibitive and unwise to allow any of these companies to implement the entire solution. The project should be understood and controlled internally. Outside help is used to provide a piece of the equation that is missing from in-house expertise. If the solution is not understood at completion, it will not be maintainable or upgradeable. Any changes will require that the consulting experts be called back in to make even basic adjustments.

It is also exceedingly difficult for any outside company to enact great change inside an enterprise without the support of the internal employees. For this reason, internal support must be garnered for integration projects before they are carried out. Since these projects often cross traditional corporate structures, it can be somewhat difficult to obtain this support. Input from affected departments should be considered since the end product must be usable by all involved. Only then can an integration project expect to succeed.

Most consulting companies rely on a lengthy and comprehensive methodology to carry out an integration task. While these methodologies do have their uses, companies often create the methodologies as deliverables for clients. Complicated methodologies confuse the integration task. It is best if a simple but effective approach is used to provide the framework for the overall project. Most of these methodologies can be simplified into four basic steps that are used in any computing project.

1. Research the enterprise.

2. Plan the implementation.

3. Implement the project.

4. Finalize the project.

This approach may seem oversimplified, however it allows you to understand what step you are in and when to advance to the next one. It is easier to get the most out of consultants when you understand what they are doing. By categorizing the tasks into these simple steps, no one step can be left unfinished before proceeding to the next.

Integration Tools

Many different forms of integration technology are available to assist in the integration process. Many of these tools and applications have been outlined in previous chapters, but this section will summarize their capabilities. Integration technologies can fall into several categories, but the main categories include messaging technologies, application servers, distributed environments, data replication, and other information source access tools.

Common messaging solutions include traditional message queuing software and the growing message brokering technologies. Messaging solutions provide a common communication medium, which allows the various applications to communicate. Applications are integrated by creating custom components that communicate with the application being integrated. This component will generally use an API associated with the messaging software to transmit messages to a message queue. Another component can then consume messages from the queue and process them accordingly. This approach often requires a great deal of custom coding, but does allow applications to communicate using a common communication medium or method.

While message queuing technologies can be somewhat invasive, often requiring changes to all applications involved, message brokers do much of this work less intrusively. Message brokers often use similar technology as standard message queuing software. They simply add a level of abstraction and processing logic that is unavailable with message queuing. Message brokers usually have adapters or connectors that can be configured to communicate with standard external EAs. If an adapter is not available, often a Software Development Kit (SDK) can be used to create the required connectivity component more easily.

Although these standard components are a great benefit to the new messaging technologies being created, it is not the only benefit. The real feature that distinguishes a message broker from the traditional messaging software is the ability to encapsulate certain business processes and transformation rules within the message broker. Most rules can often be added using a simple GUI-type interface. Not only does this reduce the complexity of the adapters, it also makes the end solution much more maintainable and manageable.

Application servers are similar to message brokers in what they provide. How they provide it, however, varies greatly. Application servers also offer adapters for certain applications although the adapter set for message brokers is often more abundant. Business components and message transformations can also be incorporated into the application server, but often these rules will require manual programming. The main distinction is the paradigm shift associated with the application server. Instead of sending and receiving asynchronous messages to a message broker to handle, application server components use synchronous requests to cause actions. Clients call application server components and then wait for the result or activity to be carried out.

The choice between these two unique situations depends on the present type of integration task and the enterprise environment. The messaging platforms provide a messaging medium more easily integrating a more disparate enterprise environment. Application servers are effective when writing custom applications to utilize various componentized application modules, especially if adapters are readily available for those modules.

Another relevant technology includes the various distributed environments that are now available including DCOM and CORBA. Distributed environments are similar to application server environments, without the tools and supporting server that make integration easier. These distributed environments provide the APIs and rules necessary to create component-based applications or environments. This architecture differs from application servers in that the component is required to handle nearly all the logic necessary to communicate to the client and the object being integrated. The application server, for example, will handle the management of multiple instances of the same object for multiple clients. With the distributed environment, these tasks may need to be handled by each component.

Although distributed environments are not necessarily designed specifically for integration purposes, they do provide a common framework that allows access to the process logic of an application or module. This framework is easy to integrate but is difficult to retrofit into an existing enterprise problem.

The majority of the other tools available all provide access to specific applications or information systems. Data replication tools, for example, provide the necessary procedures to integrate multiple databases, but are not directly able to integrate other technologies. Screen scraping technologies provide access at the user interface level to a specific set of applications. These tools access the user interface of certain application to autonomously communicate with the underlying application. Gateways and conversion tools are good for translating a specific type of information into another, but often other solutions must be used in conjunction with these limited information access tools.

Just as with any other job or project, the selection of the proper tool is of the utmost importance. Using the wrong tool or technology can cost time and resources. Many integration tools and techniques assist in the integration process, but each is good for its own purpose. There is no one technology that is the best at handling all problems. It is important to understand the available tools and technologies so an informed decision can be made for the specific problem encountered. It is also important to realize that often many technologies can be used together to provide the best possible solution.

Evaluating EAI Opportunities

The first step in any integration project, and often the most tedious, is research. Often portions of this research may already be done, but rarely is it done at the level that provides the maximum benefit to the company. Integration problems are usually first noticed because data or processes are needed where they currently do not exist. A company will already know what data or processes are to be accessed, and will have compiled information about those particular problems.

This initial compilation is only part of the overall problem. Before a solution can be implemented, the proper architecture and tools must be selected. A solution that is customizable, flexible, and expandable with the enterprise, and not a one-off, is needed. To select the proper approach to use within the enterprise, more background information must be obtained. The entire enterprise should be analyzed to note what is already available to work with. Only then can a company wide solution be chosen.

Enterprise-wide information modeling is required to proceed with integration scenarios that are not destined to be stand-alone scenarios. A company can proceed with this modeling internally or with external assistance through the use of consultants. In either case, it is often difficult to overcome the company boundaries that may exist. It is important that a valid and relevant picture of the enterprise be created to understand how to proceed with integration projects.

To ease this analysis process, the relevant enterprise information can be separated into three distinct classes of information: data modeling, process modeling, and integration points. *Data modeling* is the compilation of the available data sources within the enterprise. *Process modeling* examines the various business processes contained within the enterprise. *Integration points*, although often overlooked, determine the availability of the data and the methods that can be utilized to extract data and processes.

Data Modeling

The goal of enterprise data modeling is to produce a single reference view of the available enterprise data. Because integration often occurs at this level, it is important to understand the data before implementing a new use for that data. Even if the data are not being integrated directly, the underlying data model can provide insight into how the information is being used. It is not enough to simply know that the data are being moved around, but it is also important to understand exactly how the data are being used and by whom.

The end result of the data modeling phase will consist of two primary pieces: the logical view and the physical view. The *logical view* disregards where the data reside and only contains information about the data. The *physical view* outlines where the data are located and information about the various databases and associated computer networks. The information will often be scattered across the enterprise but must be culminated into a single source. This can be an intimidating task but must be done before proceeding with any integration duties.

When creating the logical view of the data, the properties of the data elements, including structure and layout, must be noted. This is the more important view of the data as it provides the bulk of information about the enterprise. An example of the logical view is outlined in Figure 6.2. The logical view should include the following information:

Schema information. Schema information includes the layout of the data. Such information as the name of the data, the type, and length is noted. Often this information is stored within the database and can be used to obtain the required details directly.

Integrity and relational issues. Data integrity and data relationships are relatively important aspects of data usage. Before data can be properly manipulated or added to, the constraints that are tied to the data must be understood. Many databases provide built-in integrity support that must be observed to insert, alter, or delete the stored data. Beyond the

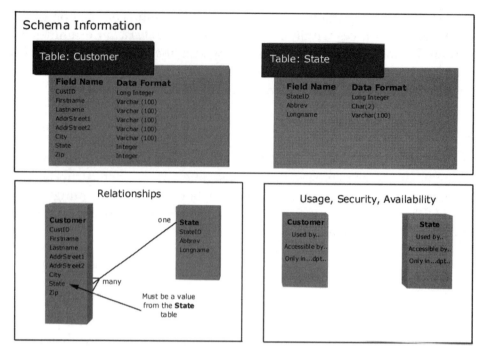

Figure 6.2   Data model (logical view).

standard integrity issues incorporated directly into the database, other relationship issues may exist. Often one data item cannot be altered without considering other associated information. Sometimes updates may also be tied into transactional units, which also must be respected.

Data usage. Details about what programs or applications currently utilize the data must be obtained. Since changes to the data may affect these programs directly, it is important to note how they will be influenced. Closely coupled applications may be difficult at the data level, since changes to the data may result in serious program errors. Data usage can also limit the latency allowed within the data flow. If the associated programs only use the data once a week, the data may not need to be updated in real time or near real time.

Security and availability. Security issues are always relevant when making data accessible to new sources. Not only should the database security access issues be considered, but also how visible the data are made to the rest of the enterprise. Availability of the data to the enterprise as a whole can create new problems. These issues along with ownership issues must be considered and addressed before embarking on an integration project.

The physical view of the data is much easier to create than the logical view. This view, as depicted in Figure 6.3, is used during the integration process to make decisions on how to access the data and where software components should physically reside. The various database makes, models, and capabilities should be determined. The type of database (relational or OO, for example) should also be noted as it could effect how the data is extracted. Network organization should be included in the physical view. If firewalls or other network obstacles prevent or restrict data flow, it is important that the limitations are known early in the integration process.

Once the final enterprise data model is created, it can immediately be used to optimize the enterprise data. Normally, data elements will be replicated across the enterprise, causing redundant data entries. These redundant elements can be found and the entire data model can be normalized. This normalization should, however, be done with care, since changes to the database can affect a great number of systems.

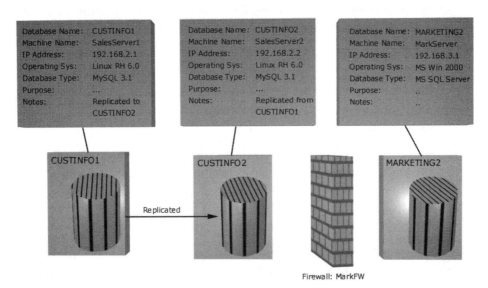

Figure 6.3 Data model (physical view).

The combination of the logical and physical views provides the starting point for integration projects. Although it is a relatively massive undertaking, once the data model exists, it can be easily updated to maintain a valid representation of the enterprise information. This model can then serve as the basis for all integration tasks.

Process Modeling

Just as data modeling provides insight into the company databases, process modeling provides information about the applications or modules within the enterprise. It helps to gain an enterprise view of the processes involved within the enterprise computing environment. This information is invaluable when performing integration at a level higher than direct database integration. The culmination of the process information can be used to create method level integration, which attempts to connect logical elements within the system rather than simply the underlying data.

The process of collecting and creating documentation for the business processes within any environment can be a cumbersome activity. It is often more difficult than data modeling because processes are much more diverse. However, like data modeling, the same information is sought after. Data, including the following items, should be recorded:

Process purpose. It is important to understand what each business process does. For example, why it was created and what problems it solves should be noted in summary form. This information can then be easily referenced during the integration decision-making phase.

Associated data and methods. It is easiest to document all the methods using an object oriented documentation approach. This approach looks at each process as a module with methods and data. These methods and associated data are documented to understand how the module works.

Actions and reactions. During the data culmination process, the specific actions and reactions of the various methods must be determined. This information will often take the form of pseudocode, data flow diagrams, and state diagrams. This information can be used to determine what results will occur when a specific enterprise process is utilized.

Technology utilization. Since the technology used by the different business processes can vary greatly, information about the technologies must also be gathered. This information can be useful during the actual integration phase to determine how to access or bundle the enterprise process. Items such as language and the required run-time environment should be considered.

Accessibility and performance. When integrating a component, it is important to understand how to access the module and what relevant performance factors may be present. A process that is written for use by an individual can cause unexpected problems when it is suddenly utilized by multiple systems simultaneously. Possible problematic issues must be discovered early in the integration phase before serious problems are created.

Security and availability. Security and availability issues involved with business processes are just as relevant for data level integration as they are with method level integration. Ownership issues may also exist for the various applications and components that will be integrated.

Although documenting these business processes within the enterprise can be difficult, the task becomes manageable by utilizing object oriented documentation methods. The most widely accepted of these documentation methods is the Unified Modeling Language (UML). UML is considered a third-generation modeling method created as a unification of the second-generation methods including Booch, Objectory, and the Object Modeling Technique (OMT). The UML methodology allows computer programs and even more general, non-computer related systems to be easily documented and visualized. Object properties, relationships, and interactions can all be described in a graphical format using UML. Companies like Rational Software Corporation offer many tools and process methodologies that can help during this documentation phase of the project.

It is also important during the documentation process that any information concerning business processes or software processes be analyzed. The original documentation about these processes should be located and used when available. When this information is not found it must be created. The use of UML diagrams and process models can be utilized to combine the information into a meaningful pictographic representation of the processes.

After the completion of the documentation process, the processes can be analyzed to reduce redundancies and possibly to add missing functionality that may improve the enterprise environment. Patterns can be gleaned from the information. This is used to reduce the number of processes, thereby reducing the possible points of failure within the overall system. This process is similar to normalizing the data model. When workflow management and documentation tools are also used, manual processes can be implemented, aided by the use of automated activities. The enterprise process model can help to find these weaknesses.

Method-level integration provides the highest payout but also has the greatest risk. Usually much work must be done to modularize the current business processes. Because of the advantage, it may be something to strive for depending on your current environment and future goals. If the entire enterprise were modularized, it would be easy to integrate at the process level. Each usable task within the enterprise would be bundled and easily accessible when needed.

Integration Points

The next step in the documentation and research phase of the integration process is to determine the possible integration points that exist within the enterprise. These integration points will vary, and often a particular application may have several different possible integration points. To determine the best means of integrating the data and applications within the enterprise, the means to access the information must be determined and documented.

Before describing exactly what to look for, it is helpful to discuss some basic principles of integration. There are five physical ways to tie into an application or application data. Though many of these integration points will overlap, it is important to categorize and classify the various methods. The goal of any integration task is the transfer of data or the activation of business processes. To this end, there are a limited number of ways to carry out this task. The five access points (see Figure 6.4) are data, protocol, environment, application, and user interface.

Data-level integration is available with most applications and provides direct access to the underlying application data. This data can be in the form of an actual database or in various stored files. If the data are stored in a database, it is relatively easy to access but can often be difficult to interpret. If the data are closely coupled to the application, the information can be rather cryptic and a single change can affect a multitude of activities within the original application. If the information is stored in files, the problem becomes more difficult. File system stored information will often be more cryptic than that of a database because the format of the file may not conform to a standard database view. The data in a file system may also

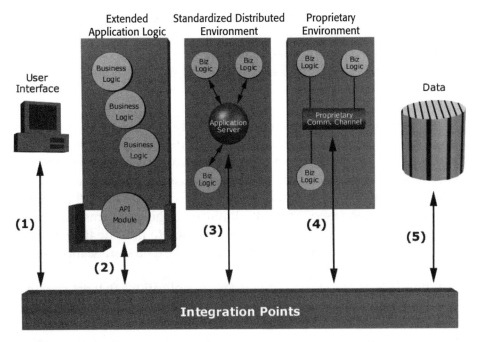

Figure 6.4   Five basic integration points.

be encoded using a proprietary scheme, making the information almost impossible to access. If other integration points exist, they may be the better option.

The second integration point is through the application communication layers or the through the protocol of the application. If the application is a multi-tiered application, it will often access the separated tiers through a communication medium that can be tapped. This again is difficult if the communication methods use proprietary and closed procedures. However, if the program utilizes an open communication standard, the communication channels can be used to transmit information to various components within the system. This is also not a preferred approach but is an option that may be considered.

The third possible integration point is through the application environment. Many applications have been written using modules or distributed components. These components can be accessed through some common distributed environment architecture. The components may be created to use such well-known platforms as DCOM, CORBA, or EJB. Utilizing some other means of integration, programs that weren't originally written to operate within a distributed environment can be wrapped and placed inside a distributed environment. Access to this level is often recommended if it is available.

Another common integration point directly accesses the application through an API or other functional libraries. Programs that offer APIs will often document those APIs and design them to be used by external programs. Internal programs that do not have APIs can be extended to create the necessary access methods for external applications. Once an API is created, the logic can be accessed, thereby eliminating the problems of directly manipulating the data. The program logic is used to provide the necessary integrity and data access principles required by the data storage mechanism.

User interface access is another option for applications that are designed to be used by an individual or group of individuals. Occasionally, a program will be so closed and proprietary that no other access point will exist. Although companies are quickly realizing that these types of applications should be avoided, many of them still exist in the current enterprise environment. For this reason, user interface integration is a less desirable option that can provide access to the necessary information and business processes bundled within the application.

These possible integration points must be documented before selecting the most viable option. If multiple options are apparent, the selection process will depend on many issues, including the amount of work required, any maintenance issues, and possibly the amount of risk involved. All of these factors must be weighed to determine the best approach for an integration project.

Data-Level Integration

Integration of enterprise data can be achieved in several ways. One approach to solving the problem of sharing information between applications and systems is to implement integration at the data level. In contrast to other integration approaches that focus on access to information via APIs or directly through the application user interface using screen scraping techniques, data-level integration focuses on bypassing applications and accessing information directly from a data repository (see Figure 6.5). These data are generally in the form of a database, such as a relational database, but may also exist within files stored directly in the file systems of various machines.

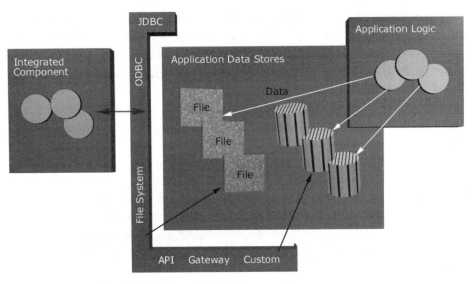

Figure 6.5   Data-level integration (direct data access).

The implementation of multi-tiered and client/server architectures in the modern enterprise often make this an attractive approach to EAI. The end goal of a data-level integration approach is to make heterogeneous data sources in an enterprise appear as one large database, where application data can be accessed via well defined and standard methods.

Unfortunately, various obstacles prevent implementing such a complete level of integration in the real world. The combination of many different databases within the enterprise has led to an increase in the various types of databases that must be integrated along with the varied access methods that are required to communicate with these databases. Other limitations that often prevent complete integration at the data level are poorly defined data source APIs, complicated data schemas, and closely coupled application logic.

Poorly defined access methods and APIs are a possible problem with any integration scenario, and data-level integration is not different. Client/server modeled applications that decouple data from business logic ease the difficulty, but problems will still exist if the underlying data store does not have a standard and well-defined interface for data access.

Most modern client/server applications use relational databases as an underlying repository for application metadata. As such, accessing a database is often made relatively simple by means of vendor provided tools and APIs. Still, developers must have a good understanding of the capabilities of a particular database, and especially of the relationships among the actual data contained in the database. This allows for the transfer and mapping of either all or a subset of data to a target database or application, while maintaining data integrity.

In some cases, application data are stored in flat-files or other formats. If the particular format is well specified by the application vendor, it is still possible to export the desired information from such a repository. On the other hand, it can be prohibitively expensive and unreliable to reverse engineer obscure and often proprietary file formats that may have been created for a specific application.

Even when the data sources provide clearly defined and well-documented access methods, data mapping problems can still exist. This is usually caused when two similar problems are solved by two different development efforts. This results in the teams creating slightly different data requirements. Even if both efforts selected a relational database, for example, the tables and data relationships may be different.

Integration between two such systems, after the fact, will often require some data conversions or data translation efforts. These conversions are outlined prior to the integration effort, to ensure the integration project will succeed. The conversion may be as simple as creating stored procedures or utilizing some data-mapping tool but can occasionally be more complicated. The conversion may include a process such as exporting a set of database tables into an intermediate set of database tables, performing any necessary transformations, and importing the result into the target database.

Mapping among data schemas can be further complicated if one set of data resides in a relational database, and the other data set exists in an object database. In this case, some type of brokering agent must be used to provide the necessary transformations between the two systems. This usually requires investment into various tools or a development effort.

Another difficulty arising in data-level integration involves the close coupling of application logic to the underlying data repository. Imagine an integration scenario with a CRM system and an inventory management system. Both systems rely on their own data store, but a mapping has been established between the data in the two systems. Both systems work well together until a bug is discovered in the inventory management system, and the vendor of the system provides a patch. Unfortunately, the patch affects how inventory data are stored in the database, and the resulting change breaks the CRM system. Closely coupled systems should be integrated through another integration point if possible.

Data-level integration is most useful where applications do not provide APIs that allow for a method-level integration approach, or where a screen scraping approach is too difficult to implement. Due to the risk factors involved with other solutions and the limitation of those additional solutions, the direct data access approach is often used in the integration industry.

Protocol-Level Integration

Protocol integration projects are designed to communicate directly on the communication layer of the application being integrated. Some protocol integration applications may already exist within the enterprise in one form or another. This type of integration can be used to either tap into some communication medium utilized by a specific set of applications or it can be used to translate one protocol into another protocol.

Integration at the protocol level is always an option when an application utilizes some means of communication to transmit information to other components utilizing the same or a similar protocol. A good example of this data transmission is in multi-tiered applications. They will normally utilize some communication method to send data between the various tiers within the application. Although many of these applications utilize some common framework or distributed architecture, which is normally integrated using environment-level integration some will use a proprietary communication medium that can be exploited to integrate the application.

Integration at the protocol level is often only done as a last resort. This is because other options exist that are easier and more robust solutions. In the example of multi-tiered applications, most of these applications utilize a distributed environment that is easier to integrate. Most open protocols already have APIs or translation software that provides the necessary protocol-level integration. These tools can then be use to integrate the application using some other form of integration.

Usually protocol integration is only relevant when a proprietary closed system presents limited means to access the data or processes locked inside its environment. Even in these instances, integrating at the protocol level can be risky if the application was not designed to handle this type of integration. For these cases, the problem becomes even harder because the protocol has probably not been documented well. Reverse engineering techniques are required to document and communicate using the proprietary protocol. Because this is an extremely costly and high-risk solution, others should first be considered.

Screen scraping technologies and user interface integration will often fall into the protocol integration arena. Because these technologies have techniques and principles that are unique, they have been included in a separate category. If a screen scraping solution must be done from scratch, however, it should be considered a protocol-level integration problem.

Gateways also utilize protocol integration techniques to turn one protocol or service into another. By converting the various protocols, a protocol that is available and necessary to be used from one application can be used to access another application or service that it otherwise would not be able to use. Gateways exist for several protocol-to-protocol conversions as well as service access. For example, SNA Gateways can be used to provide access to applications or services that were previously only accessible via direct SNA communications. The gateways will translate TCP/IP requests into SNA communications to carry out the specified activities. IBM also provides a DB/2 gateway that can be installed on certain Unix systems to provide access to a mainframe DB/2 system. An ODBC driver can then be used from a Windows platform to communicate with the gateway, which will relay the information to the mainframe application. Gateways are a useful tool that may be considered for certain integration projects.

Another example of protocol-level integration is demonstrated by work done in the Java programming language. Java presents the programmer with an API to access data sources and databases known as JDBC. JDBC, although the principles are similar, is not the same as ODBC. For this reason, several vendors, including Sun, provide bridges or translation classes that convert the JDBC method calls into their equivalent ODBC counterparts. This translation is protocol integration at work. A portion of code that converts one protocol into another.

One example of when protocol integration is a valid option is with the ERP package from SAP. Because data-level integration is extremely difficult and risky with SAP, due to its closely coupled logic and complicated data structures, protocol integration is often used. The SAP package presents many integration points, one of which is available by communicating with the SAP system through its communication channels. Originally this communication channel was designed and implemented to allow the various SAP components or systems to easily communicate with each other. The different components communicate by transmitting an Intermediate Document (IDOC). These IDOCs usually represent an activity or event in the system, but can also be used to transmit data elements. By essentially emulating an SAP component, as shown in Figure 6.6, an integration solution can use this protocol level communication to access functions in the SAP system and send and receive data.

Clearly there are times when protocol integration is relevant and even required, but it should be used with caution. The engineering and development effort required for protocol integration is often much higher than any other form of integration. This is especially true if the protocol

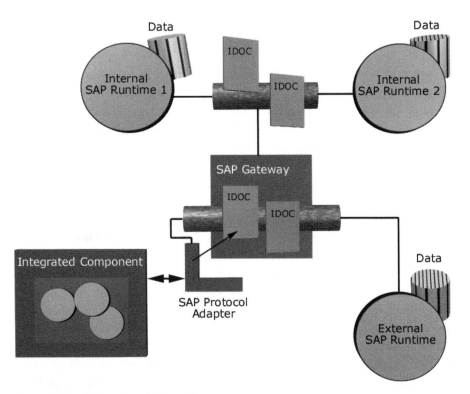

Figure 6.6   SAP protocol integration.

communication portions of the integration solution must be designed and written in house. Many tools and existing solutions are available and should be researched prior to embarking on a full development project.

Environment-Level Integration

Environment-level integration is the process of integrating with the environment used by an application or group of applications. This environment will contain the logical elements of the applications. The environment can take several forms, but if a distributed type of programming architecture does exist, it is usually the best choice to integrate various logical components.

Integration directly with an environment gives the integration developer access to all the logic that is available to the applications that use the environment. Most, if not all, of the logic elements are available through this architecture. Most of these architectures use open standards and are well documented. Even for the environments that do not utilize open standards, the underlying technology to create the environment will normally be well documented. The original application developers would have selected an architecture that was relatively easy to use, requiring the need for good documentation.

Although most of these environments will utilize a common API for communication purposes, they are placed in a separate category because the techniques of integrating with the environment differ slightly from those at the standard application, or API level. To integrate at the environment level, the environment must be well understood. Most distributed environments contain an elaborate architecture policy that must be adhered to and understood to communicate with other components.

Two main types of application environments exist that can easily be integrated. Applications will use either a standard distributed architecture, such as DCOM, CORBA, EJB, or a distributed environment will be created through the use of some middleware product. Both of these types share a common design, which is demonstrated in Figure 6.7. If a standard distributed architecture is used, developers should already be familiar with the environment and need only research the component. If the environment uses some middleware communication server technology to create a distributed environment, the integration may be more complicated. The integration architect may be required to learn a relatively proprietary architecture and research the component and various component interactions that may exist.

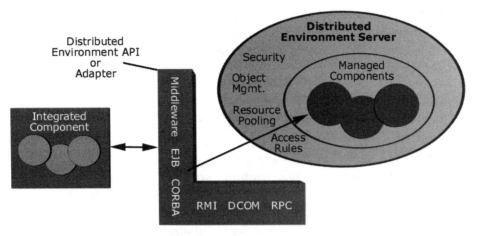

Figure 6.7   Typical distributed environment.

Componentized application modules are by far the easiest to integrate, but they are also the hardest and most time consuming to implement. Implementing a distributed environment from existing application components requires a large development effort. Not only do the original applications have to be fully understood, but often those components will need to be entirely rewritten to operate properly in the distributed environment. Even if the modules were written properly using OO design principles and can be easily adapted to the distributed architecture, all applications that previously used the module logic will have to be modified to access the component via the new distributed environment.

When a choice exists between re-implementing previously useable code for the purposes of integration and integrating the logic using a less invasive approach, the designer should almost always select the less invasive solution. This solution will require less development effort and much less testing. If, however, a distributed environment already exists within the enterprise, integrating with the environment is most likely the solution of choice.

Because integration solutions for these environments are relatively straightforward, several integration platforms come bundled with tools to access components within the various architectures. The Open3 E-Business Integration middleware solution, for example, provides an available DCOM/COM adapter to access components designed for that environment.

Other adapters also exist to access many different environments. Many of the commercial-grade application servers and Web servers also provide similar solutions to access distributed environments and middleware created architectures.

Beyond tools and servers, several programming languages provide a certain level of support for access to distributed environments. The Java language is arguably the best example of this capability. It has built-in methods to access RMI components, making them easy to locate and integrate. The J2EE platform also contains specifications for a distributed architecture (for example, EJB) and a messaging service, such as JMS. Because these are essentially designed into the language, applications using these environments become easy to integrate.

One of the best examples of applications that utilize a distributed environment is the entire Microsoft Windows platform. This environment is nearly entirely built with COM components. All of the standard applications used with Windows use COM to create modular program modules that can be used by any other application. For example, if an Excel spreadsheet contains information that must be integrated with another application, COM methods can be used to access the required information. Since this architecture is so deeply embedded into the design philosophy of the OS, it also means that many applications that are written for the Windows platform utilize this architecture to some extent. For Windows programs, COM or DCOM is often the preferred and expected integration method.

Because distributed environments provide an environment that is relatively easy to integrate, this will usually be the most viable option when it exists. Even if other options exist, integrating with the environment allows the programming logic to be modularized, leading to a better design. Access to the data or protocol level will bypass some of this logic, which can lead to integrity and performance problems. The use of modules allows programmers to bundle the data along with the methods to access the data and hide certain complexities from the integrating platform. For this reason, it is preferable to integrate directly with distributed environments when they exist.

Application-Level Integration

Application-level integration is accomplished by communicating through some application interface provided by the program developers.

An application interface exposes various services or callable methods within a self-contained application. This interface is known as an Application Programming Interface or API. An API provides the necessary interface to communicate with a program and access functions and data elements contained within the application. This integration point is one of the better choices since it is often designed to allow access from external systems.

In the past, APIs were done as an afterthought. They were added after the original application was completed and developers noticed the need to access various logical components embedded in the application. If the application was designed and written in house, it was not a major undertaking to modify the application to provide access to this functionality. If the application was purchased, the source code was normally not available, and the original vendor would need to be lobbied to create the necessary interface. This could be difficult since companies often saw this as "sharing" too much information and giving away technology.

This view has changed over the years as the need to make disparate applications and systems work together in a harmonious fashion has increased. The existence of a usable API is often a selling point with current packaged applications. Even the most guarded and highly proprietary systems have created APIs to allow some access to the underlying logic. Developers now design the API along with the application, making a much more stable and usable end product. These APIs provide the necessary integration point to allow access to the bundled program application hidden within the program.

Many of these program developers utilize one of the common or standard API methods that have been created and adopted over the years. Utilizing these APIs will make the process of integration much easier but can cause an application to be tied to a particular technology. Solutions that use COM, for example, are destined to operate within a Windows environment. They are also required to keep up with any changes that might occur to the COM architecture that could affect their product. Integration of programs that use this type of API, although it is a valid API architecture, fall under the category of environment-level integration, since integration projects must focus on the environment as much as the application being integrated. Once the environment of a distributed architecture is well understood, the problem may become similar to a custom API problem.

Because of the problems apparent with some of the distributed architectures and the changing computing environment associated with the various technologies, some companies opt to create a completely custom API solution. These types of APIs were also extremely common before the standard APIs existed, and so many custom APIs may exist within the enterprise environment. Often these APIs are completely custom and relevant only to the particular vendor supplying the application. Even individual vendors will often vary the type of API used between their different products. This type of API will normally come in the form of a callable library or even a custom RPC style call.

Given that APIs are created by developers, their functionality and usability can vary greatly. One of these variances includes the method of access. An application written using COBOL will probably provide a COBOL callable API. A program written in C or C++ will most likely provide a C/C++ library while Java products provide compiled Java classes. Some vendors place a great emphasis on the creation of APIs, so these products will normally have a diverse set of functions that will be available through the API, including possibly direct access to the data and internal services. Other vendors provide the API only because clients request it and therefore will limit the functionality that can be accessed.

The existence of an application interface of any kind can provide a viable integration point. If documentation exists for accessing the API and it provides the necessary functionality and access methods, the interface will normally provide the best method for access to the underlying program functionality. Since APIs provide access to the internal logic from an external source, they are often designed with that principle in mind. This makes the use of an API in an integration solution the least risky and possibly the most robust option.

Poor API documentation is one of the reasons that another integration option may be selected even when an API exists. APIs without documentation or with little documentation can occur for many reasons. One of the most common reasons is that proprietary APIs were created to only allow access to vendor products from the same vendor. These products may not supply the necessary information to use the API for customers or other third parties. This can complicate the use of the API in an integration scenario. The calling method may need to be researched to determine how to access the internal functions. Even the functionality may not be clearly understood, requiring much testing to determine the resulting actions of a particular function call. This can be a time consuming and costly process that may suggest the use of another integration option if it is available.

Integration with application APIs can be made easier by using integration products and tools that are already written to use the API. For many of the enterprise-grade packaged applications, message brokers offer adapters or connectors to communicate with the applications. Beyond message brokering technologies, products also exist that essentially provide a bridge between a distributed environment and the custom API. A product can, for example, wrap the API and expose it within the distributed architecture allowing the use of a common distributed environment integration solution.

PeopleSoft is one example of an enterprise-grade application that utilizes a common and well-documented API. The entire PeopleSoft architecture uses an underlying communication layer to create a distributed architecture. PeopleSoft relies on BEA's Tuxedo product as its underlying messaging platform. This platform is used to create a distributed architecture allowing all the components of the PeopleSoft application to communicate and transfer information. At first glance, this would seem like a valid environment-level integration point for the PeopleSoft product. It is true that this is a possibility, but PeopleSoft does not recommend this type of solution. As shown in Figure 6.8, their product also has several well-documented APIs that they recommend for integration purposes. This is partially due to support and control issues within the product, more than the best possible integration point. Using an API, PeopleSoft is able to control the integration point more easily and, thereby, limit the type of logical modules that can be accessed. This makes managing the support issues that arise from integrating a product much more controllable. Since it is recommended by PeopleSoft, integration with their product should almost always be done through the API, even though other options exist.

In the realm of enterprise integration, APIs offer one of the best options for the integration specialist. They provide normally well-documented and useable access methods, thereby making the integration tasks much easier. Vendor suppliers also often offer support for API access while the other integration points may not be supported directly by the vendor. APIs also provide access at the business logic contained within the application, possibly reducing the amount of logic that must be incorporated into the integration solution. Clearly, when an API is available, well supported, and it provides all the necessary features required by the integration project, it should be used.

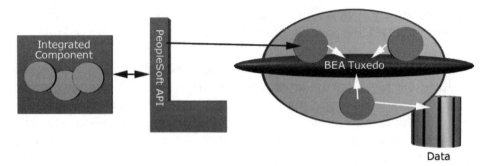

Figure 6.8 PeopleSoft API integration example.

User Interface-Level Integration

Almost any application that is accessible via a user interface can be accessed using some form of user interface integration. User interface-level integration takes the place of the user. A program or script can issue commands, extract information from the user interface, and provide input. This form of application access is commonly referred to as screen scraping or application automation. User interface integration normally relies on some other form of integration, such as protocol integration, but the end result is something much different. Applications that can be integrated by no other means suddenly become accessible.

Most forms of screen scraping utilize protocol integration techniques to create a user interface solution. Screen scraping will often access the underlying protocol of some terminal communication procedure to emulate the existence and activities of a user. This user interface access technique is demonstrated in Figure 6.9. For most mainframe green screen applications, the terminal protocol is either a VT3270 or VT5250 terminal communication method. The screen scraping program will access the application by tapping into these standardized communication mediums. It will use this communication channel to transmit and receive information that normally is used to present the user interface to the user. Data can be sent and received allowing the screen scraping program to insert data, extract information, or simply carry out some activity.

Many different forms of screen scraping exist with varied architectures. If a commercial screen scraping package is used, it will often create an

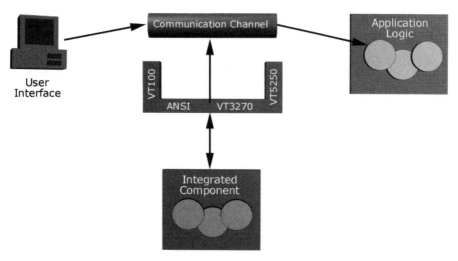

Figure 6.9 Screen scraping.

architecture that will modularize the mainframe applications. These packages will essentially perform the necessary integration and communication with the user interface to create a solution that still needs to be integrated with the remaining enterprise. This further integration will then fall under the veil of either environment level integration, if the package uses a distributed architecture, or application level integration, if the package presents or creates an API to access the information.

Windows-based products also exist to communicate through the user interface of Microsoft Windows applications. These programs normally do not use protocol integration techniques; instead, they utilize the Microsoft environment to communicate with the application. These types of programs are normally referred to as automation or macro programs. They allow a user to essentially record or define a set of steps including mouse clicks and data entry to communicate with a program. Just as with screen scraping techniques, the exchange of data can be used to integrate the application.

The integration industry has introduced several problems that customers associate with user interface integration tools. Some of them are well founded, but many are myths that can be overcome through a good design and the use of the proper technology. It is important to thoroughly test any user interface solutions, as they are more prone to problems than most other integration techniques.

Because user interfaces are designed to be used by people, problems can often arise as soon as a program starts accessing the information. Error conditions and GUI intricacies are better interpreted by a person rather than a program. For this reason, the user interface access tool must be well designed and thoroughly tested before it placed into a production environment. A good user interface integration specialist with the right tools can create a robust solution, but it requires work.

Another problem that is common with user interface integration issues is the limited number of accesses and simultaneous access problems. Some applications simply can't handle the increased load that arises from the integration usage. The removal of the physical user can cause the application to be executed at its very limits, often pushing the program to failure. These problems must be determined early in the integration process, so they can be properly handled. One solution is to limit the number of simultaneous accesses and otherwise reduce the number of communications transmitted to the application. This can be done through the use of connection pooling and information caching. Many user interface tools now use such techniques to reduce the occurrences of these performance problems.

User interface integration also has benefits. It can often provide a solution where no other form of integration can be used. Even if other options exist, occasionally they are not cost effective to create. User interface integration can be relatively simple for some problems and applications, thereby providing a rapid development solution for the integration project. Legacy green screen applications can usually be extended to create new user access screens much easier than creating a new API.

Legacy mainframe applications are the best example of when the user interface solution provides the most benefits. If an enterprise relies on a legacy mainframe application, currently accessed by users through a terminal. Quite possibly the developers do not exist to modify the original application or the costs associated with any major modifications are relatively high. The original application probably had no API or other means to access the program logic. The database may be accessible, but the application may be closely coupled with that data making the data difficult to use correctly. The most suited solution for this situation is through the user interface. Many tools exist to access standard mainframe applications through the terminal interface. This solution can be implemented without changes to the original applications, creating a usable integration point.

User interface integration is often considered a last resort for the integration project. Although it may not be the first choice, it does have its place in the integration world. Commonly, applications exist that present no other integration points or those integration points are cost prohibitive to use. For these situations, or when the user interface solution is simply easier, it should be considered. Through thorough testing and the proper application of technology, a usable and robust user interface integration solution can be created.

Planning EAI Projects

The planning phase of any project is often the most crucial step. Because most projects are rushed to meet market demands, it is important not to forget about thorough planning even under tightened timelines. Poor planning will inevitably force a project to an unsuccessful ending. The planning phase relies on information obtained during the research phase to outline and create the integration projects that should occur within an enterprise. In its simplest form, planning for an integration task requires the selection of the items to be integrated, the development of requirements and various project plans to accomplish the integration, and plans to put the completed project to use.

The first step in the planning phase is to select your integration opportunities. Utilizing information obtained during the research phase, various integration projects can be created. You should not decide to integrate everything. This is too large of a task to be accomplished in one project and foreshadows failure. The selection process involves measuring the relative costs of implementing each solution against the expected benefit of the integration process. It is often easy to lose sight of the fact that an integration project must be completed with a clearly outlined benefit that is worthy of achievement.

This is easy to say but is much harder to actually measure. The cost, in time and resources, and the development effort involved require justification. The reason must be more than simply, "it is what everyone else is doing" or "it is the wave of the future." The "coolness" factor, although it may seem compelling, does not justify such a massive undertaking. Outlining some criteria or measurable benefits that are expected from any integration project is important.

This is best demonstrated by an example. Assume that a company has a sales department and a separate collection or accounts receivable department. Both these departments utilize different computer systems to manage and maintain their respective information. To offer customer targeted payment plans and various pricing options, the sales department needs information about the timeliness and payment methods used by existing customers. The integration of the accounts receivable data into the sales and marketing computer systems allows this to occur. The sales department is able to estimate the increase in sales that are achieved by this integration process. Notice that even with this example, other possible sales opportunities could be found by having access to these data. Accounts receivables may even benefit since the sales department is offering payment options that are designed for the customer. If these measurable business benefits are greater than the expected cost of the integration project, then the project is viable. If the perceived gains are not high enough, and no other benefits of the project can be found, then the project should not be undertaken.

Most integration projects are initiated due to some specific integration need. Using the metrics and information obtained during the research phase of the integration work, it can now be determined if the project is worth doing or if another option is available. Occasionally, it is cheaper to rewrite the original applications or duplicate information rather than tackle an integration issue. When considering these other alternatives, it is wise to factor in the maintenance and future upgrade costs of any solution. Although duplicating information may seem like the cheapest choice originally, the future maintenance of such a solution can quickly cause the overall price to increase.

Effort must be put forth to determine the measurable benefits of any integration project. Only then can true integration opportunities be found. If a project was not originally envisioned at the outset of the integration tasks, a feasible project may be selected using the discovered criteria. These metrics can also be used upon project completion to determine the successfulness of an integration solution. It is hard to determine if a solution meets expectations if those expectations are not outlined prior to project completion.

Another key factor in the problem selection process is the scope and size of the problem. To limit the risk of the project, integration tasks are completed in small pieces. This is especially true if a new product, technology set, or solution provider is being used to integrate the selected items. Problems can always occur with unused or unfamiliar technology. Even if the solution set has been used, project sizes are best limited to manageable sizes to reduce the risk of any integration project.

Once the integration problems are selected, they are still only understood at a relatively high level. Specific requirements must be created and compiled into formal documents. Gathering requirements for an integration project is just like requirements gathering for any other development project. Problems may, however, be introduced because of the enterprisewide interactions that exist with most integration projects. Multiple departmental requests may have to be incorporated into a single agreeable requirements document. All parties involved must provide input and come to some agreement or the project could be impeded later.

The requirements document must also explicitly state any success factors that can be used to measure the outcome of the project. These include not only the key benefits outlined earlier but also performance considerations, including access and response times and the number of supported users or transactions. The requirements also contain the specific data mapping and transformation requirements of the integration project.

Once the requirements have been clearly outlined, they are not to be changed much after the implementation phase is started. Changing requirements are always a problem with integration tasks. People will find new tasks after the fact and add them to the list of things to be done. These "while you're in there" type of tasks can greatly increase the overall timeline of the project and quickly lead to cost overruns. As such, they are to be avoided whenever possible.

An initial test plan can also be developed during the planning phase of the integration project. The requirements can immediately be converted into test cases. These test cases will most likely be added to later in the development phase, but some effort should be exerted to create a solid test plan that will not need many additions. This will make the development and testing phases much easier.

The deliverables from the planning phase are the clearly defined objectives and project guidelines that will be used throughout the remaining phases of the integration project. These objectives and guidelines will be in the form of several common development documents including a completed requirements document, a viable project plan, and the start of a test plan. Upon completion of the planning phase, no unanswered question should exist as to how the integration is to proceed or what is to be integrated.

Implementing an EAI Solution

After all the documentation, planning, and research, you finally reach the most enjoyable part of the integration project—the actual work. The implementation phase involves all the work that is required to get the integration project operational. Once this work is completed, all that remains is the testing and project rollout. This section will outline some standard implementation techniques as well as specific techniques for each of the different integration points.

The implementation phase will normally begin within an isolated test environment or through the implementation of a prototype to test the theories of the outlined integration plan. The production environment is never used for development purposes. As shown in Figure 6.10, some projects may even have three or more environments depending on the internal enterprise computing environment. Typically, the enterprise will be separated into a production area and a test area. Occasionally, a development area will exist that is separated from the other two environments.

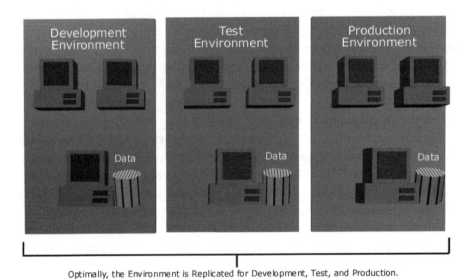

Optimally, the Environment is Replicated for Development, Test, and Production.

Project Development Timeline

Figure 6.10 Project development cycle.

The production area within a given enterprise project is often considered the go live environment. This area represents all the EAs and systems that are used on a daily basis by the company to conduct day-to-day business activities. For this reason, it is unwise to disrupt this environment. A project is moved to production only after it has been developed and thoroughly tested.

The development environment, or test environment if no development area exists, is used primarily for development purposes and to introduce new applications into the enterprise environment. The development environment will somewhat match the original production environment. Typically, it will contain copies of the applications and resources used in the production environment. Occasionally, even the data elements will be replicated to the development area on a weekly or daily basis. If a separate test environment does exist, projects should only use the test environment when the project reaches a stable point and is ready to be robustly tested. These environments present a safe area to develop and test new programs and integration projects.

If these separate environments do not currently exist within the enterprise, they must be established at least at a minimum level. The cost may seem high to support multiple environments, but the lost income caused by system downtime can be even higher. If the required system applications and components do not exist in a development or test environment, mock-ups should be created or a test set of data can be obtained. These temporary measures can be used to initially test the integration implementation before it is moved into an area that may cause damage and lost income.

Provided with an understanding of the environments available within the typical enterprise, the project begins by first testing the most important principles of the integration plan. The highest risk tasks are tackled first, not saved for last. For example, if it is unknown whether the API of a particular application will support the required number of users, this is tested first. The failure of these high-risk items can cause a project to be sent back to the drawing board. It is better if these problems are found early in the project, before great time and effort is exerted on a project that is not technically capable of successful completion.

While constructing the integration solution, the various development procedures and any developed code are documented for later reference. Not only is this information used for maintenance, but it may also be used for future projects to reduce the development time. The test plan is also modified to include any new test criteria that may be discovered during the development phase of the project. Also, remember to update the existing internal documentation for any systems that are altered during the development phase. This includes updating the enterprise data model and the process models if these areas are affected.

By following these basic techniques, the development process has the best possibility of being completed successfully without incident. Development activities always require at least a basic process and documentation. Adhere to the development process of the enterprise to limit the project risk factors and produce the necessary documentation for the enterprise.

Data-Level Integration

Implementing data-level projects is one of the easier integration tasks. Because of their wide use and common functionality, many integration tools exist for databases and various data storage platforms. Given this wide assortment of available integration tools, it is often difficult to select the proper technology for the project.

The tools and techniques used for data-level integration depend on what is being integrated with the system. If one database is integrating with another database system, simple replication tools can often be used. If several databases are being linked to create a single view of the enterprise data system, another approach may be the best option. Still another technology solution may be selected if a data source is being tied to another integration-level component or system.

The type of data source can also affect the tool set that may be used to integrate the various platforms. Because of their wide use, relational databases have the greatest number of options. Even though relational systems are the most common, other database types do exist and are in use within enterprise environments. Some of these database systems are growing in popularity. Common options to relational databases include hierarchical systems and object oriented databases. The existence of different data models within the enterprise can complicate the integration tasks.

Database-to-Database Integration

Database-to-database integration is roughly analogous to point-to-point integration using traditional message queuing software. In this case, a data schema contained in one database is mapped onto a database schema contained in another database (see Figure 6.11). In the simplest scenario of database-to-database integration, tables from one database are exported or imported using vendor provided tools to a different database format. To automate such a process, database vendor tools often support some form of batch-style processing. This processing can be set to run at a specific time to periodically update the data sources or it can be set to update when changes occur within the databases. Many of these database replication tools are currently available on the market, but the feature set can vary greatly.

One of the more important features of a replication tool is the supported platforms of the tool. Some of these tools are limited to a particular vendor's database, but other tools offer a wide range of support to provide cross-platform replication. The needs of the tool are dependent on the needs of the enterprise environment, but to maximize the investment, a tool should be selected that supports many platforms. Such tools can be found from third party vendors or from the open source community. This allows the enterprise to grow without being necessarily tied to a particular vendor.

Even more problems are introduced when the databases utilize different database models. Some vendors provide tools that cause one database to appear as another database. For example, an OO database can often be made

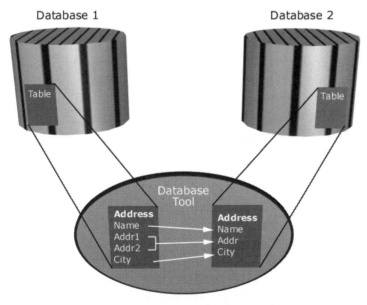

Figure 6.11   Data integration using database tools.

to look like a relational database. But even then it can be difficult to find a replication tool that allows data to be replicated across many diverse systems.

When a replication tool cannot be found, another form of data integration must be used. At this point the integrator has several options to solve the problem. The proper selection depends on the goals and environment of the enterprise. The choices include either a custom solution or some other form of integration that converts the database problem into an environment integration problem. The custom solution is only viable if the other choices are not cost effective. Any custom solution means spending time and resources developing features that quite possibly already exist.

Beyond a custom solution, the integrator can select another form of integration to tie the databases together. These additional integration tools include application servers and messaging software. Most application servers provide methods to attach to various databases. Some application servers also allow embedded processing rules of some form. These features can be used together to create an integration solution. For example, an EJB server has the capability to access several databases through JDBC. Processing logic can also be added in the form of beans to manipulate and access the database. Although this does allow a new form of database access to the enterprise, it can be somewhat limiting. Application servers aren't normally designed for this type of database-to-database integration and therefore may not support all the necessary features that are found in standard replication tools.

Messaging software provides another choice for the data source integration project. Standard message queuing software can be used to transmit the information from one database to another, but custom components may need to be written to communicate with the database and transform the data. The more advanced message brokering technology can provide all these features. Many of these tools provide some connection mechanism, similar to the application server, which attaches to the database automatically. They often offer a wider range of support for multiple databases, since they are required to integrate more systems. These message brokers also provide the ability to transform the data and create relatively complicated business logic to process the data.

The main problem with using a messaging platform for such a task is that it is often considered overkill. It is true that these solutions do provide many features beyond simple data replication, but when no other solution is available it should be considered. In the past, these tools would cost a large sum of money to use; unless the enterprise already owned one of the messaging tools, it was unlikely to be purchased for database replication purposes. Open source messaging packages are now available that offer feature sets that rival the proprietary products, so this should no longer be a barrier.

The right tool for the job depends on the enterprise doing the integration. The easiest solution for database-to-database integration is the data replication technology that has been available for years. This solution is limited by the fact that it only ties together databases; if that is the only problem that requires a solution, then it should be used. Other solutions are available, but the choice depends on what the enterprise goals are and what tools are available for the given scenario.

Database-to-Secondary Integration Point

Integration at the data level to other integration points takes a slightly different form than the database-to-database integration problem. This type of integration requires a different tool set. The data replication tools usually only offer data integration between similar data sources, and therefore they provide little help for more complicated situations. Application servers and messaging software offer the best alternative in these instances.

As previously mentioned, both application servers and messaging software provide viable options for most integration projects. They work relatively well for database integration when integrating with some other integration level. For example, when integrating at the application level using an API, the middleware component can be used to provide a common access point to the database, as shown in Figure 6.12. The use of message brokers can also provide benefits through the use of data translation and embedded business logic.

Beyond the common integration tools, another option may exist. Certain vendors now provide the ability to link multiple databases. These tools will make the data sources appear as one combined database. This approach to data-level integration aims to provide a homogeneous interface to various back-end data sources. The solution aims to smooth out the differences between data sources, and from an application perspective makes disparate data sources appear as one large database. Occasionally, data models can be mixed, although the final model will need to be consistent. For example, tools exist that can combine the information from an object-oriented database and a relational database, but the end result will have to be either relational or OO.

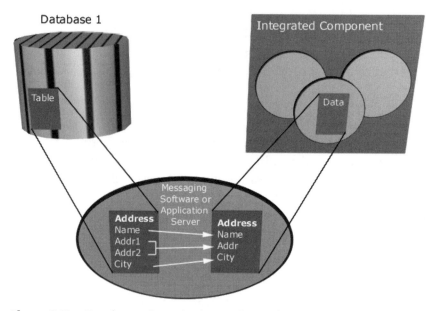

Figure 6.12 Data integration using integration tools.

These tools help to create a common enterprise data system, but often they only work with products from the same vendor.

This single data model can also be achieved through the use of application servers or message broker-style messaging software. Several data sources can be integrated with the application server or message broker and be made accessible through a common interface. Linking data sources can be complex, but the benefits can be great. By capturing the necessary logic to make the data sources appear as one in the message broker, the solution becomes much more maintainable. The logic is not contained in the multiple databases or at the integration point, but in a common server environment that can be altered as needed.

Integration solutions at the data level look similar to those that use the other integration points when not integrating directly with another data source. Since the same technology may be used, the same techniques can be applied to other integration problems. If the proper technology is selected, it can be used to easily integrate the remaining integration problems using a common solution.

Protocol-Level Integration

Protocol integration normally takes two forms—relatively easy and extremely difficult. There is usually no in between. Either the given protocol has tools associated with it or tools must be created from scratch. The creation of this type of program can be a difficult development effort and is only worth pursuing if it is necessary.

The main tool to handle protocol integration is a protocol gateway, depicted in Figure 6.13. The gateway will interpret the necessary calls and communications using the required protocol. Protocols such as SNA have gateways that can be used to communicate with components using TCP/IP. XML gateways are also being created to translate various communication protocols into an XML format. For example, gateways exist to translate the Lightweight Directory Access Protocol (LDAP) into XML messages. Several gateways exist for common protocols, but support for more obscure protocols can be hard to find.

If a true gateway does not exist for the necessary protocol translation, often a library or product will exist to help in the integration process. These

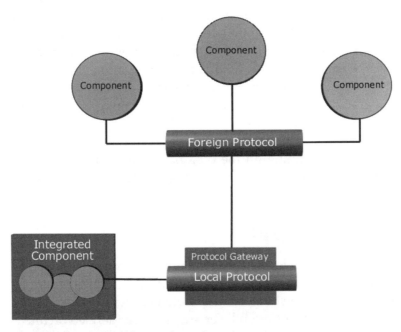

Figure 6.13   Protocol integration using gateway.

products essentially provide the translation capabilities of a gateway in a smaller package. They come in the form of a program or application extension that can be used by an integration component. These packages will often present an API that allows access to the given protocol and allows another program to communicate using the proper communication channel. This method abstracts the protocol specifics and makes it usable through an API or other access means. Occasionally, this functionality will also be built into a message broker or other middleware component.

If none of these options are available, the problem moves into the extremely difficult category. When all other options have been exhausted, a custom solution must be built to access the communication channel. The more obscure a protocol, the less information that is available for it. The decreased amount of information greatly increases the development effort and the risk of integration. If no documentation exists for the protocol, it may need to be reverse engineered. This is usually not as difficult as reverse engineering an entire program since the original protocol was developed to allow some form of communication, but it is still difficult. All the methods of the protocol must be understood and documented. Once the protocol is well understood, a translation or communication engine can be created to use in a standard integration scenario.

No matter the method, there is one problem that exists with nearly all protocol integration scenarios. The data translation procedures will often need to transform the original data into a format understood by the protocol being integrated. This means that the data goes through an extra translation that is not normally present with other integration points. The protocol is not the end component; it is an intermediary communication channel. The integrated application will need to receive this data and again interpret it. Gateways can suffer greatly from these problems since they usually translate every incoming and outgoing request without filtering or logical optimizations. Depending on the type of problem, this issue may not be a serious problem, but one that should be considered when creating the protocol integration solution.

Environment-Level Integration

Integration at the environment level involves communicating with the common environment that links an application's components. These environments often take the form of a standard distributed environment, but may also use a middleware communication layer and a clearly defined architecture. The key components that make a distributed computing environment usable are the clearly defined communication methods and a well-defined architecture or rule set that components must follow. These properties remove most of the problems that exist with other integration levels.

In the case of a standard distributed environment such as DCOM or CORBA, the rules and communication medium are built into the environment. For example, to use DCOM, a session must be established and a link to the object must be obtained. Once this object reference is obtained, it may be used just as if the component is part of the application accessing it. The environment defines where the object physically executes and how it starts and stops itself. As long as the basic rules in the environment are followed, all the components operate in a similar manner. These distributed environments clearly define the access methods and often provide the libraries or classes needed to access that environment, typically in the form of an API. The API is designed in such a manner that the module is allowed to extend or use it to offer various unique services. This means that all the modules use the same API but can provide unique functionality. The developer must then only learn the environment to understand how to access and communicate with all the application modules.

Some enterprise applications create their own rule sets and utilize a standard communication medium. This type of architecture does not directly subscribe to any of the main distributed environments but the same principles apply. The standard communication channel will typically be messaging software such as JMS or MQSeries. These packages normally provide libraries or classes to use the communication software to transmit information with the various components. Even distributed environments are often based on some other underlying communication technology. DCOM and CORBA, for example, use some form of RPC communication as their underlying technology. For custom environments, the application developers will have defined the rules separately from the communication channel, but they will still exist. Once these rules are understood, the problem becomes similar to the standard distributed environments normally used.

Integration with the environment level of an application is the preferred method if it exists. This is due to the principles that allow the distributed environment to work well for the original application. The clearly defined communication channel means that it is not a problem to talk with the environment. The defined architecture rules provide the means by which the environment operates. Each module represents an individual business logic component. This allows applications to be separated into operational modules or processing units. Linking to these components provides access directly to these logical components. This is quite powerful since it will use all the integrity and error checking capabilities that have already been designed into the original product. These features will not again have to be incorporated into the integration solution. This level of integration is often the most beneficial since it can utilize nearly all the logic that an application uses.

The environment itself can be used for integration purposes. New components can be built to access various applications and data sources to provide a common integration point for all the resources within an enterprise. The only problem with using the environment as an integration platform is the development effort surrounding these projects. Each newly integrated component will have to be designed, developed, and tested. Depending on the development projects already ongoing in an enterprise, this may not be a problem, but often the cost is too high for most businesses to incur.

For this reason, most integration platforms, like message brokers, provide automatic access to the common distributed environments. Most of these tools provide an adapter or connector that can communicate with the environment. Many environments provide the ability to use object reflection properties to explore the features offered by a particular component. This allows the integration platform to determine all the unique methods offered by an application module. The integration problem then is to define how those methods are used. This is done by providing certain data translations and business logic that can be embedded into the message broker platform. With the appropriate tools, these integration problems approach a simple point and click style of integration.

Application-Level Integration

Application-level integration communicates directly with the application, usually via an API. The API is provided by the application developer or vendor. Since no common framework or architecture is required, as provided by distributed environment architectures, the capabilities of a given API can vary greatly. This can make understanding and integrating with the given application slightly more difficult than accessing the application modules contained in a common distributed environment.

The first step in integration with any API is a complete understanding of the capabilities and limitations associated with the application interface. The application vendor or developer normally provides the required documentation, but occasionally this information will not exist. If it no information can be found about the API, the interface will need to be researched and tested. Reverse engineering techniques may be required to explore the functionality of some APIs, adding to the development cost of the project. Integration must not occur unless a thorough knowledge of the features available through the API is understood.

Most enterprise-grade integration tools provide support for the common EAs that allow application-level integration (see Figure 6.14). Since these solution providers encounter the problem often, these integration solutions have already been developed and refined. In these cases, the integration platform will either automatically integrate with the application or require only minor modifications for the particular purpose.

For more obscure applications, however, the integration specialist will need to create a custom solution for the application. This can be relatively costly, but it is manageable if the proper documentation has been made available. A custom adapter or connector can be built that links the application into an integration platform. The application can then be used as any other integrated component within the system.

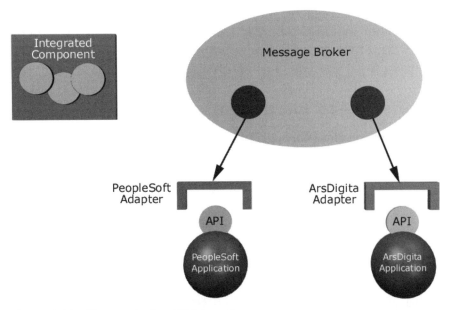

Figure 6.14   Message broker API integration.

If a custom solution is to be developed, the application can also be linked with a distributed environment or an application server. This method essentially wraps the application functionality presented by the API into a form that may be more accessible to other enterprise development efforts. The work required to do this is similar to the amount of work required to link the application through a standard messaging platform, either a message queuing package or message broker solution. The main benefit for using a message broker for such a task is the added translation and business logic components that can be added to the environment separate from the application adapter.

The end result of application integration can suffer from one glaring problem. Because these solutions require integrating directly with the application, the resulting solution will often be closely coupled to the application. This means if the application changes, or more specifically if the API changes, then the integration component will also need to be changed. This is normally not a major problem since application developers do not alter APIs without good reason, but it is something to consider when designing the integration solution.

For application-level problems, many methods of integration are available. If a solution already exists for the problem, for example with a message broker adapter, then it must be considered. If a custom solution is to be developed, then more option may exist. The proper selection depends on the enterprise environment. If the enterprise already uses a distributed environment, then that method must be maintained. If a messaging product exists, then it may be used. The solutions set should match the tools and products already used by the enterprise.

User Interface-Level Integration

Accessing a user interface through programmatic means requires the use of a third-party tool. These third-party tools allow the user interface to be abstracted and accessed through some other interface, such as an API. Tools exist for nearly any accessible user interface including mainframes, Microsoft Windows, and Unix applications. All the tools differ somewhat, but they all have one thing in common. The program emulates a user by interacting with the user interface to obtain the necessary data and carry out the required activities.

Normally these tools utilize a session recording mechanism so that they may be initially recorded by allowing a user to interact with the program and record that interaction. Scripts are then created that can be edited and fine-tuned to interact with the application. These tools differ on how they allow data to be transmitted and obtained, but typically several functions are established that can be called through some common means, such as an API. These functions will take several data elements that are used during the program interaction and then certain data elements may be extracted from the user screen. These elements are returned as the result of the function call. Although the methods of data exchange may vary, a tool should be found that does allow both data transmission and data reception.

During the tool selection process, a tool must be found that properly interacts with the required application. This means that the tool should be tested to ensure proper data transmission and reception. Tests are also carried out to ensure that exceptions are properly handled. Exception handling is the major downfall of most user interface integration projects. The tool must be capable of handling situations that aren't necessarily expected. Some tools can become confused and will hang the application or cause it to crash. This can be a major problem if it is not found until the integration solution is being used.

After the tool has been properly set up and all the scripts or user interface interactions have been defined, the problem becomes a standard integration problem. If the tool being used allows access via an API, then application level integration methods are recommended. If the tool automatically wraps the solution into some distributed environment, then the remaining solution requires environment level integration techniques. If all this sounds too difficult, certain integration tools do come bundled with screen scraping or application automation technology. Many message brokers and application servers provide this functionality. Some third-party tools are written to be used with various integration platforms.

The most difficult part of user interaction is the selection of a proper tool. Great effort should be spent testing and selecting the screen scraping or automation tool that will be used in the integration project. Many tools come bundled with integration software, but others may provide better support. The most important thing to remember when setting up a user interface integration solution is the exception handling. It is easy to establish scripts that simply interpret a user screen, transmit data, and then return results. It is much more difficult to properly handle problematic situations that may occur during this interaction.

Implementation Using Open Source Technologies

The open source community has begun to create tools and environments to assist in the integration tasks required in today's enterprise. Many of these tools are approaching the complexity and feature sets of the proprietary tools being sold for several thousands of dollars. Two main classes of open source tools exist to support enterprise integration including application servers and messaging platforms.

The majority of tools available in either class also rely on the power of the XML language to some extent. Most of the open source organizations have incorporated its use into their product offerings. XML provides the common language that has been missing in the past. If used properly it can increase the portability and usefulness of most integration platforms. The portability, maintainability, and ease of use far outweigh any performance loss that may be associated with the language.

Application Servers

Of the application server types of technologies that exist within the open source community, the most prevalent server type uses the Java EJB architecture. EJB implementations are available from Enhydra, JBoss, and the ExoLab Group (described in more detail in Chapter 4, "Open Source Infrastructure"). It is important to research each project since they vary in feature sets, goals, and J2EE compliance.

A compliant EJB server implements the EJB specification from Java. The EJB architecture provides a common framework for modularizing functionality into a distributed environment much like other distributed environments, like DCOM or CORBA. Components are written as individual objects or programming modules. Each component normally represents a logical business unit or process. Existing EAs can have wrappers or adapters written to present the application in the EJB environment.

The main distinction between EJB and other distributed environments is in the added features provided by the EJB environment. EJB servers manage much of the common functionality of a distributed architecture, leaving the component code to deal with the actual programming problem, not the environment. Common tasks such as data persistence, transactionality, and resource pooling are all managed by the server. The server is also tasked with handling client connections and starting, stopping, and managing various components on behalf of the client. Because the server manages these issues, the EJB architecture scales relatively well.

For integration purposes, the most important aspect of an open source application server may be the added toolsets and features that are provided with the server. An application server with no integration tools is simply another development architecture requiring a great deal of coding effort to integrate the typical enterprise. Enhydra arguably provides the most abundant tools and associated products to go with the EJB implementation it offers. The Enhydra server currently provides a Servlet environment that uses XML to separate the presentation layer more clearly from the business logic layer. With the soon to be released Enhydra Enterprise server, it will incorporate in the ability to further utilize the multitiered architecture by adding full EJB support to separate out the data extraction or application interface layer as well.

Although the Enhydra architecture may be useful for certain integration tasks, it is more relevant to Web applications. Other open source application server models, such as Zope, do exist that do not use the EJB architecture. These also, however, are primarily designed to handle Web site deployment. As such, these servers will be covered in more detail in Chapter 7, "Business-to-Business Integration." The other open source EJB-based architectures only provide the standard J2EE tools. For now, they require a great deal of programming to facilitate the integration projects required within the typical enterprise.

Messaging Platforms

Just as with application servers, various open source messaging platforms also exist. Again, the most common platforms utilize another J2EE technology, the JMS. The JMS architecture provides a relatively sophisticated representation of the traditional messaging platforms. A great deal of effort was put forth during the creation of the JMS specification to create a messaging platform that incorporated the "best of breed" of the messaging technologies that had come before. Because of this, products that implement the JMS specification provide a feature rich messaging platform.

JMS provides not only the standard message queuing paradigm, it also allows for a publish-and-subscribe messaging style. Message queuing involves a client sending a message to a particular message queue. Another client or component will wait at the other end of the queue to pull messages off or consume them from the queue. The publish-and-subscribe method uses topics rather than queues. Multiple clients can be subscribed to a topic. When a single client sends or publishes a message to the topic, all registrants will receive it.

JMS also defines certain reliability and persistence standards that must be handled by each vendor. Various message transmissions modes, or acknowledge modes, exist to handle levels of guaranteed message delivery. These transmissions modes along with the persistence options can be used to create an environment where no message should be lost. If these features are not required, they may be turned off on a case-by-case basis for faster delivery.

The availability of two standard messaging methods along with the additional JMS features provides a relatively sophisticated messaging environment for any enterprise. By itself, however, it is still just a messaging platform that requires a great amount of custom code to be made useful. Certain open source projects do exist that are expanding this basic messaging platform. One such community, the Open3.org community, uses JMS as the underlying messaging platform for its message broker product. This product uses an XML-based implementation of the JMS specification to create a message broker environment.

The Open3 architecture, shown in Figure 6.15, uses JMS, EJB, and XML to create a full-featured message broker. JMS provides the messaging layer while EJB provides the business component repository. Standard JMS features are used for basic message filtering, while XSL provides the means for message transformation and more complicated message filtering. Complicated business rules or processes can be created and embedded in the EJB environment to handle even more complicated message processing.

This environment makes the overall system more maintainable by encapsulating the sophisticated message processing and routing within the server environment. The adapter or client is only then required to handle communicating with the external entity for which it is servicing. If a software component is to be a message source, an adapter component can be written to essentially handle only the communication with the external software component. Once the information was extracted, the adapter could relay the data to the server without the need to transform or otherwise manipulate the information.

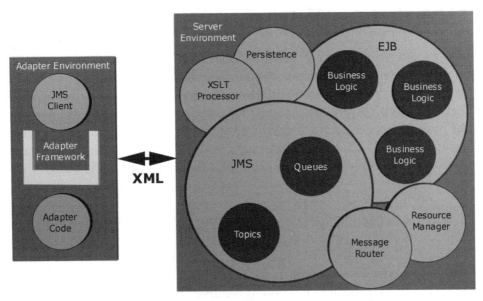

Figure 6.15 Open3 E-Business Integration Server architecture.

The Open3 integration server design allows for several standard adapters or connectors to be written for the Open3 environment. If a standard adapter exists for a particular purpose, it would not need to be customized. Various settings and configuration properties can be defined in XML documents. Rules and transformations would be tailored for the particular problem and handled by the server upon message transmission. If a custom adapter is required, it is much easier to create since it does not need to manipulate the data it sends or receives.

The choice of an open source product offering using open standards is the best possible scenario where integration tasks are concerned. It is risky to install yet another proprietary and closed software integration platform to integrate your existing proprietary products. This not only locks you into the original product that you will be integrating but also the vendor's platform doing the integration. At the very least, a product based on open standards should be selected. This reduces the reliance on any single company for something as important as your enterprise-computing environment. Remember, this is not just another application; it has the potential to interact with every system within the enterprise.

EAI Project Completion

The project completion phase must be properly planned and logically enacted to ensure the final success of the integration project. Project completion involves tying up all the loose ends. The solution must be thoroughly tested. The potential users of the end solution must be trained and the integration project moved into production. Some of these tasks can be done in parallel with the implementation to speed the process, however, no step should be left out or the project may fail when it costs the most, as it is being used.

The first step in the final phase of the project is the testing of the integration solution. The various environments available within the enterprise will determine the testing procedure. If the enterprise has a development, test, and production environment, then the solution must be considered *nearly* ready for production before it is moved to the test environment. The test environment can then be used for final testing and load testing. It may also be used for training purposes prior to project rollout. If only a test and production environments are available, the system must be tested as much as possible prior to moving into production. Possibly a trial in the production environment can be done before the solution is finally released.

The test cases are best developed throughout the integration process. The initial test document is created from the requirements for the project. This includes performance issues and any general goals that the project was attempting to solve. Test cases may also have been added during the development phase as more information was obtained about the specific implementation issues of the project. Prior to testing, the development team may sort the test cases by importance to ensure the most relevant feature set is tested first. Failure of these high priority items could send the project back to the development phase.

Beyond the basic functionality tests that have been extracted from the requirements and during the implementation phase, certain load tests should also be created. These load tests are designed to load or stress the selected implementation. Load tests typically emulate multiple concurrent users or clients, each operating as quickly as possible to determine how the system operates in extreme usage scenarios. For example, if a messaging platform is used, multiple clients can be created that send as many messages as possible to the messaging server.

Load tests can be a weak point for certain implementations, but they ensure that the solution has room to grow along with the enterprise. They also ensure that the solution is capable of solving the current integration problem even during peak usage periods. Most enterprise-grade applications provide statistics or other reassuring documentation to assist early on in the technology selection process. Even with this information, it is always important to test and tune each unique solution for the given implementation.

Once a sufficient number of passing results are obtained from the testing effort, the project solution is ready for production. This, however, does not mean it is placed immediately into production. Any potential users or affected departmental personnel must be trained. Training and user involvement are important for a successful project. You can't just move it to production and assume it will be used properly. A training plan must be developed and enacted to allow the company personnel a chance to learn about the new project. Since key personnel were included during the requirements development, they will be receptive to the training programs.

Beyond the potential users of the solution, maintenance plans must also be created and personnel trained. These maintenance documents describe the any potential upkeep required by the solution. It must also document any potential exception handling that is required. For example, if the solution utilizes a messaging software package, this software may maintain a log and place unhandled messages in a database. This log may need to be reviewed to ensure proper processing or may be used to provide an audit trail for the integration solution. The unhandled messages may also require a specific procedure to deliver the potentially lost information properly. These maintenance documents along with any development information can then be used to maintain and modify the existing solution throughout the lifetime of the project.

After all of these activities are carried out, the move into production should go smoothly. The enterprise will be provided with an enterprise data model, process model, integration point documentation, solution and development documentation, trained personnel, maintenance information, and of course a working solution. The process outlined in this chapter involves several steps. These steps can at times be potentially complicated and time consuming, but when this basic methodology is followed, the integration project becomes manageable and ensures a successful outcome.

Summary

Enhancing your e-business infrastructure to allow your software to easily communicate and share data throughout the enterprise requires sophisticated integration solutions. The techniques and methodology outlined in this chapter can be used to simplify this process. Often help will still be required from consultants, but the company will eventually be left with the solution and must ensure that it is documented and understood. Through a basic process of analysis, planning, implementation, and testing any business can find and implement the necessary integration solutions.

This chapter examined the key principles necessary to understand internal integration projects. Whether open source, proprietary, or a mix of technologies is used, the methodology and techniques remain the same. Properly implementing enterprise-wide EAI solutions will move a company into a Tier 3 status, just two levels from total e-business integration.

To further move up the e-business ladder, a business will need to also implement B2B and B2C type solutions. The information included here, specifically the methodology, can be used for these tasks also. Certain technological solutions capable of handling internal integration can also be used for external integration tasks, but the paradigm shifts slightly. The following two chapters will look at these differences, along with additional software solutions and techniques specifically designed for B2B and B2C problems.

CHAPTER 7

Business-to-Business Integration

Business-to-Business integration (B2Bi), or inter-business integration, digitally links applications and data between business partners. B2Bi connects an enterprise's externally facing applications to marketplaces, suppliers, and business partners over the Internet or private networks. B2Bi provides the foundation for electronic commerce between various enterprises. Most economic experts predict that integration and e-commerce between businesses will become the most important piece of the new economy. It will allow businesses to achieve incredible efficiencies, cost savings, and to tap into a global supply and selling-chain.

Executive management is faced with the pressure to adapt to changing business environments rapidly. Business partners increasingly utilize technology to collaborate more accurately and efficiently. The technology enables the enterprise to engage in previously impossible or at least extremely difficult global business exchanges. For example, a B2Bi-enabled corporation headquartered in the United States may contract third-party manufacturers in Mexico, Singapore, and India to produce products. It may then utilize a German company to fabricate packaging, a U.K. business for marketing, and leverage various selling channels in France, Spain, Canada, and Brazil. The enterprise must be able to accomplish these inter-business relationships with minimal time delay and low overhead. Companies that ignore B2Bi will lose emerging opportunities in new markets. Automated B2Bi eliminates human errors, dramatically speeds processing times for business transactions, and delivers a real-time view to critical factors such as material supply, inventory levels, and sales results across business boundaries.

B2Bi provides the technology and business processes to open the global doors for businesses anywhere and of any size. Even the smallest companies have the opportunity to access the low-cost Internet for B2B integration. Software technologies like XML and open business frameworks are providing a common language for communication. Many of these technologies have sprouted from open source initiatives. In the following chapter, we'll investigate the business strategy behind B2Bi, the underlying technologies that make it possible, and how B2Bi forms an essential component of the modern e-business construct.

B2Bi in E-Business

B2Bi and B2B e-commerce are the two main components of B2B. B2Bi creates an infrastructure to connect an enterprise to the external trading world. B2B e-commerce takes this infrastructure and creates applications, such as an auction portal for raw materials, which create the actual business exchange between partners. B2Bi and B2B e-commerce are dependent upon one another for an effective B2B solution. B2Bi, as the underlying component of B2B, must be implemented before commerce transactions can be initiated.

B2Bi is an extension of EAI (discussed in Chapter 6, "Enterprise Application Integration") and presents new business and technical challenges to integration. EAI permits a greater amount of control and tighter coupling than B2Bi. The success of EAI relies solely within the enterprise. However, B2Bi relies on disparate trading partners cooperating with the enterprise. For B2Bi to succeed, businesses must form the appropriate relationships with other businesses and cooperate in choosing and building the technical infrastructure. The technology of B2Bi requires a well-defined and mutually agreeable interface for the communication of data. B2Bi must also address additional security, scalability, and reliability considerations. Due to the complexity of B2Bi, careful planning of business strategy and technical implementation will ensure that the benefits exceed the expenditure.

The trend of B2Bi is to move applications and data that interact with business partners, such as inventory management or procurement systems, from an enterprise-centric model to a collaborative one (see Figure 7.1). The partner-collaborative model opens information and enables real-time order processing, instant view of stock availability, and timely order fulfillment.

The technology of B2Bi may be designed as a *partner-to-partner* or a *partner-to-hub* solution (see Figure 7.2). The enterprise engaged in transforming its processes into e-processes requires both B2Bi solutions. Partner-to-partner is similar to point-to-point integration in an EAI scenario, in that it links one entity to another entity. Unlike point-to-point EAI, a partner-to-partner solution may be designed to add new partners easily. Partner-to-partner integration usually results from close business partnerships and supply chain integration, such as between a preferred supplier and manufacturer. The two partners require a customized or sophisticated integration solution that can't be provided generically with a hub. Partner-to-hub integration connects the enterprise to a B2B hub or portal. The B2B hub connects to several businesses, usually in the same market or vertical, and provides a common interface of communication for all partners.

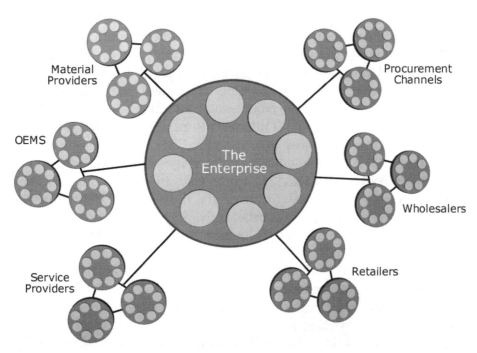

Figure 7.1   B2Bi is the move from enterprise-centric to a partner-collaborative model.

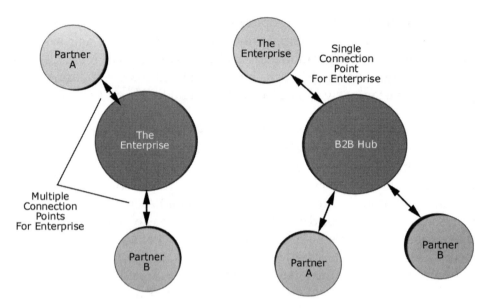

Figure 7.2   Partner-to-partner and partner-to-hub B2Bi.

B2Bi requires an organized exchange of data. Traditionally business-to-business communication and commerce have been conducted through Electronic Data Interchange (EDI). EDI is a complex and highly structured formatting of data that is communicated through a Value-Added Network (VAN). A VAN manages the transactions of data and charges a substantial fee for this service. Due to the complexities and high cost, the benefits of B2B communication through EDI have only benefited the largest companies. Although there is interest in broadening EDI communication through the Internet, EDI is gradually being replaced by secure XML communication over the Web. XML provides a highly flexible and easily translated data format. XML primarily utilizes the Internet as communication medium, thus making it highly cost effective. There is finally a basic infrastructure for the rest of the business world to engage in B2B transactions.

Many of the world's largest companies, those in the Fortune 1000 and Global 2000, have invested significant amounts of time and resources into EDI implementations. Due to their investment, these companies won't quickly move their existing infrastructure to the XML/Internet duo. Therefore, companies utilizing XML in B2B communication may be required to integrate with EDI. Fortunately, the inherent simplicity of XML makes it highly viable to connect with EDI. Open source tools like the Apache Xalan processor can be utilized to convert XML to other document formats. The nonprofit XML/EDI Group (www.xmledi.com) is coordinating the integration of EDI and XML.

The other key component of B2Bi is the supporting middleware and applications that facilitate the exchange. The wide acceptance of XML inter-business communication will depend upon quality and low cost software applications. One of the largest barriers facing B2B is enablement for all companies along the supply and selling chain. Enablement is the integration and the extension of the IT infrastructure to prepare the enterprise for B2B exchanges. There are more than 1,000 B2B trading exchanges, but several have few or no participants. Small and mid-size companies (crucial business entities in the world economy) face daunting price tags when looking at the cost for enablement. These smaller companies must have low-cost solutions to participate in B2B. Open source, by lowering the cost barriers of entry, has strong potential to be the foundation of enablement.

Modern and effective B2Bi solutions are being built on XML and enterprise messaging systems (see Figure 7.3). B2B messaging systems may be simple message queuing middleware or more sophisticated message brokers that are built into integration frameworks. They may also be built on object request brokers, implementation of remote procedure calls, and transaction processing monitors. Partner-to-partner integration solutions typically leverage generic message queuing or brokering software while B2B hubs employ an integration framework. These B2B frameworks include proprietary or commercially controlled systems like BizTalk and Ariba and open consortium-developed systems like RosettaNet and OASIS ebXML.

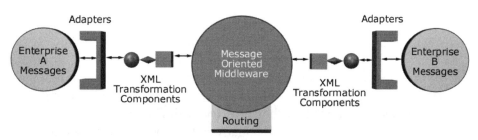

Figure 7.3   The modern technology of B2Bi.

B2Bi, like EAI, is a complicated technological effort and requires sophisticated software to be successful. Most B2B integration software revolves around EDI. The modern era of B2Bi, transformed by the Internet and XML, is creating a revolution in the software marketplace. B2Bi software is in its infancy, and proprietary companies like Ariba, Commerce One, and WebMethods are attempting to define standards for how to implement it. Their implementations, although potentially based on open consortium frameworks, are closed source and proprietary. Unfortunately, these proprietary systems are costly and limited in their customizability. Open standards and open source software permit entities from various organizations to contribute. This widespread collaboration provides for these technologies to have the best opportunity to emerge as implementation standards. Open source enables small and medium sized businesses and emerging countries to engage modern B2B. Business partners are more willing to accept software technology that is cost effective. Also, the added security and reliability in strong open source projects are especially suited for B2B.

In this chapter, we'll investigate how open frameworks like ebXML and RosettaNet compare to proprietary systems like BizTalk and Ariba cXML. We'll also take a look at how open source enterprise messaging software, such as Enhydra, Open3, JBoss, Exolab, and others provide a basis for B2Bi.

Planning for B2Bi

All e-business projects require careful and planned organization to flourish. B2Bi is one of the most difficult components of e-business to implement. Your enterprise and your partners must work together seamlessly. Smooth operation inside the enterprise is a difficult task; extending this to other businesses is even more arduous. A successful B2Bi solution requires a systemized implementation that all parties conform to. There are four basic steps for the enterprise and its partners to follow in planning and carrying out a B2Bi solution:

1. *Recognize long-term need to connect the enterprise.* Fundamental to all e-business design is the business case for the strategy. The rallying cry for e-business is "do or die!" However, there must be reality in the die before considering the do. Peer or competitive pressures to implement B2B may lead your business to make wrong decisions in its strategy. Reacting with business sense rather than business fear will enable your enterprise to make the most of its e-business initiatives. To recognize the long-term need to connect your enterprise, you must have a comprehensive picture of the

current business landscape and be able to make informed decisions on how this landscape is changing.

Some businesses may require an aggressive B2B strategy to survive, others may be best served to implement it at a more gradual pace. B2B strategies accomplish goals like just-in-time inventory management, efficient order processing, accountable procurement, accurate sourcing, and rapid order fulfillment. Your business must recognize its goals, prioritize these goals, and then determine the feasibility of accomplishing them. B2B is important to the modern enterprise, but wasting time and monetary resources on rushed or ill-conceived implementation will reduce the success of the initiative.

2. *Discuss B2Bi with potential partners.* Be proactive. While this is a great motto of major businesses, it can be a lot of hoopla if discussed but never actually achieved. To be proactive in B2B means to recognize both immediate and long-term needs and to develop a game plan to accomplish them. The proactive enterprise leads its partners to tap into the cost-savings, efficiencies, and new revenue possibilities that are viable through B2B. Your partners must adopt your B2B strategy or it will fail.

To begin the process of formulating a B2Bi strategy with your partners, first create a list of those businesses based on your prioritized goals in step one. If your prerogative is to lower costs by reducing the amount of excess inventory in your enterprise, you'll need to work with your suppliers to enable views into their inventory systems and implement timely order processing. If your top priority is to reduce procurement costs through a corporate buying extranet for your employees, then you'll need to work with suppliers to enable commerce exchange through a digital catalog.

Strategizing with partners may seem like a daunting task. For large enterprises with thousands of partners, this may be an impossible feat. Trading hubs and e-marketplaces exist to make a fundamental strategy, such as sourcing of materials, a simplified process. However, most businesses won't be able to develop a comprehensive strategy based on these massive trading hubs alone. Special customization will often be required with your most active partners.

Your partners must recognize that it is in their best interest to invest in B2Bi technology to integrate with your enterprise. A savvy partner will accept those initiatives that are most flexible for their needs, such as the ability to connect with additional partners through the same infrastructure. If your company is large and wields significant power with its partners, you may be able to coerce them into your proposed solutions, but often you'll need to make a persuasive argument for agreement by all parties. You're negotiating with partners who may not understand the need or reason for B2Bi, may be fearful of it, or may have failed with initiatives in the past. A well thought-out plan on your side is a great tool to bring to the table.

3. *Standardize on technology for all partners.* Fundamental to the strategy is the business case, and fundamental to implementing the strategy is the technology. Your business partners must accept technology that your business can integrate. This is what makes the Internet/XML combination so attractive. The Internet is worldwide and XML makes it fundamentally easy to communicate data. However, these two technologies don't enable all the pieces necessary to accomplish B2Bi. You and your partners must choose application platforms that can change with dynamic and demanding business environments.

   You and your partners may have invested heavily in legacy integration frameworks like EDI and VANs and be reluctant to change to emerging standards. The business case is strong for Internet/XML, but can you and your partners successfully implement it? Do your employees have the expertise to develop and maintain the system? Are you willing to pay for training and/or outside consulting services to acquire the expertise necessary to bring new systems online? These questions must be weighed against the benefits provided by the new technology.

   Beyond the Internet and XML is the application framework to support B2Bi. Choosing the right framework also creates new questions. What are the cost implications of proprietary systems versus open source ones? Do your enterprise and your partners want to invest heavily in proprietary systems? What if your proprietary vendor goes out of business? If I choose an open source system is there someone I can call for support? One striking reason to consider open source carefully is that the Internet and XML are creations of the open source movement. Many of the components of the Internet, such as the DNS, Perl programming language, and Apache Webserver are made possible by open source software. XML is an open standard governed by the WC3, an organization devoted to the open proliferation of software. The success of the Internet and XML for B2Bi makes a strong case for the continued use of open source-based systems for the application framework.

   It's advised that the technology platform your enterprise utilizes can be connected to those of your partners. If your business decides upon an EDI-based solution because it has considerable in-house expertise, then it must evaluate how much it will spend to integrate with XML-based systems. A simple rule for choosing the right technology may be to look at what standards are emerging in your industry. What are your potential partners using or implementing now? Are they successful with their implementations? How costly were their implementations? Are other industries using the same technology, and if not, what makes them different?

4. *Implement for growth and change.* Business changes. Technology changes. We compete in a dynamic world and the only thing that can be correctly anticipated is the unforeseeable. Your business strategy, B2B processes, and technology must be implemented to react swiftly to changing market conditions. This means that your B2B strategy must be based on business processes, workflow, and technology that is flexible. A significant portion of the ability to grow and change is dependent upon the technology. Today, major enterprises are struggling with the move from stand-alone legacy systems to integrated applications that can collaborate with partners. Fortunately, the trend in software and system design is to move from closed systems to open ones. By deploying a highly flexible technology infrastructure, your enterprise will be able to evolve as the market demands.

Supply Chain Management

The supply chain is the web of business processes and partnerships to source, research, develop, manufacture, pack, ship, and deliver goods and services. Every business participates in at least one node of the supply chain. Supply Chain Management (SCM) is the sophisticated discipline to coordinate the complicated process of working with tens, hundreds, and even thousands of businesses. SCM is especially critical to mid- and large-size companies. However, smaller companies are being pushed by its many benefits.

SCM coordinates the movement of physical goods, services, and information between businesses. The passage of goods involves the movement of raw materials to manufacturers, completed products to sales channels, and distribution to customers. The passage of services involves training of the personnel infrastructure, service tailoring, and execution of the service for customers. The passage of information includes the transmission of data like inventory availability, purchase orders, delivery notification, and financial data from its creation to its conveyance. B2Bi provides the infrastructure for the automation of information movement.

B2Bi's data exchange automation is revolutionizing the supply chain. Lowered distribution costs, reduced time to market, and just in time inventory management are enabled by utilizing integration technology. Dell's build-to-order supply chain would not be possible without sophisticated technology to support inter-business communication. Integration must work in tandem with business process management, governed by the workflow of the communication.

Workflow

Workflow is the organized completion of tasks to fulfill a business process. In B2B integration and e-commerce, workflow outlines the various stages of communication that must take place to complete a business transaction. The stages of workflow, or tasks to be accomplished, may be modeled in several ways. *Event-driven modeling* triggers a stage based on a particular event, such as: When inventory levels for product X become less than 1,000, then initiate a purchase order to supplier Y. *Address-driven modeling* is similar to addressing email, where a stage is assigned to a particular person, for example "route the customer service request to Bob in Toledo." *Decision-driven modeling* defines a stage as something to accomplish with an associated decision to be made, such as "validate the procurement order for employee X, then either accept or reject the order."

There are four possible routing mechanisms for modeled workflow: sequential, parallel dependent, parallel independent, and conditional stages (see Figure 7.4). *Sequential routing* is the simplest mechanism—do A, then do B, then do C. *Parallel dependent stages* allow two or more tasks to be performed concurrently, but the processes are dependent upon each other to complete before moving to the next stage. For example, do A and B, then do C if and only if A and B have been completed. On the flip side, *parallel independent stages* allow tasks to be completed concurrently but are not dependent upon each of these concurrent tasks to complete before moving to the next stage. For example, do A and B, then do C when either A or B is completed. Finally, *conditional stages* choose between moving to new tasks based on a decision made in the current task. For example, do A, if A is this then do B, else if A is that then do C.

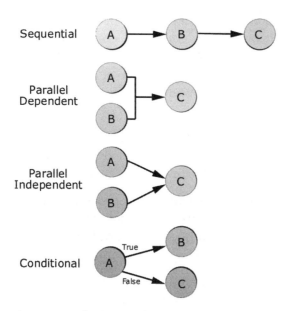

Figure 7.4 The four workflow routing mechanisms.

These routing mechanisms form a basis for all workflow in the enterprise, including B2Bi. XML and EDI support data definition and data content in B2Bi. Workflow provides the complex and organized routing of XML and EDI documents. Only the simplest of B2B communication is possible without workflow. Therefore, complex trading exchanges with hundreds of partners are not possible without workflow. B2B frameworks provide the mechanism to implement workflow with business communication.

B2Bi Technology Levels

The technology levels of B2Bi frameworks form an integral component of many B2B initiatives. These levels provide a roadmap for describing the communication format, business workflow, and messaging to implement a B2Bi solution. The levels descend from macro-B2B to micro-B2B technology. These layers are generally common among all complete B2B frameworks and provide an overview of the components that compose the typical framework.

Trading exchange. The trading exchange may consist of a simple two-way exchange or a hub that provides a connected environment for trading partners to route documents and conduct business. The marketplace creates an environment friendly to the participants by facilitating transactions and relationships between the system users.

Process repository. The process repository is a collection of data that contains commercial information about product lists, inventory levels, customer information, contracts, and other knowledge utilized to facilitate the business workflow in the trading partner agreement.

Trading partner agreement. The trading partner agreement describes a contract of documents that must pass between partners to complete a business transaction. The agreement defines the workflow between two or more companies.

Metadata. Metadata is high-level information that defines the data type of the document that is transferred between partners. There are many formats for data. XML is the most popular format being implemented today. EDI is the most widely used but is losing market share to XML. Other formats, such as delimited or binary files, may be used but not widely. Metadata may be part of the document or defined externally.

Schema. The schema of a B2B document is similar to a schema of database, and outlines the field names and field contents of a document. XML defines two types of schema entities: the document type definition (DTD) and the XML schema. DTDs are more common but are being replaced by XML schemas, since the latter is defined by XML while DTDs are not. There are many XML DTD or schema repositories, such as XML.org, Biztalk, and RosettaNet. These schemas are generally organized around industry groups such as agriculture, health care, or finance.

EDI's schemas are X12 transaction sets and United Nations Electronic Data Interchange For Administration, Commerce, and Transport (UN/EDIFACT) messages that define the tables, loops, segments, and elements of the EDI data structure. X12, part of the ANSI standards, and UN/EDIFACT, are standards for communication of EDI data. Transaction sets and messages are organized by number in repositories, such as the Purchase Order transaction set for X12 (#850).

Message envelope. The message envelope is the header of the message and contains protocol, routing, and tracking information for the message. The message envelope may be defined in the same format as the data of the document or in a different format. An example of a mes-

Figure 7.5   A JMS message envelope and message data.

sage envelope that is different from the data format is a Java Message Service (JMS) message. The header information is contained within attributes of a Java object, while the data may be an XML text message (see Figure 7.5).

Message body. The message body encapsulates the data of the business document. The message body may be composed of textual and/or binary data. XML data is stored in human-readable format, while EDI is not. The message body is also known as the payload of the document.

The following is a sample simplified message body for an XML purchase order:

```
<purchase_order>
    <company>
        <name>XYZ Technologies</name>
        <address>123 North St.</address>
        <city>New York</city>
        <state>NY</state>
        <zip>12345</zip>
        <vendor_id>ABC123</vendor_id>
    </company>
    <order_list>
        <order number="1">
            <sku>BCD234</sku>
            <quantity>12</quantity>
        </order>
```

```
<order number="2">
    <sku>CDE345</sku>
    <quantity>6</quantity>
</order>
        </order_list>
    </purchase_order>
```

B2B Frameworks

B2B frameworks provide a packaged solution to implement both B2B integration and B2B e-commerce. They incorporate the functional levels of B2Bi and provide a mechanism for the communication format, document structure, and workflow between trading partners. B2B frameworks may target vertical markets and/or provide a broad horizontal foundation for general business. *Vertical frameworks* concentrate on specific industries, such as RosettaNet for the IT business. Their technology levels are tailored to the vertical markets that they serve. *Horizontal frameworks*, like OAGIS or ebXML, provide a basis for all business transactions. Horizontal frameworks serve a larger market and may be customized to fit the nuances of specific industries.

Some B2B frameworks are dominated by commercial entities, like Microsoft's BizTalk, and others are developed by open consortiums of businesses and individuals, like OAGIS or ebXML. The open systems, due to their democratized development process, have the best chance to become standards for B2B frameworks. This is evidenced by the ebXML project, which has been in existence for less than 2 years but is already garnering strong attention among major business leaders. Open source software will follow the open B2B frameworks, providing quality software at low cost to the enterprise. The adoption of B2B by businesses worldwide will depend upon the lowered barriers created by open source software.

Open Applications Group Integration Specification

The Open Applications Group Integration Specification (www.open-applications.org) is a nonprofit group composed of various software vendors of enterprise applications, application servers, and integration servers. The mission of OAGIS is "to define and encourage the adoption of a unifying standard for eBusiness and Application Software interoperability that reduces customer cost and time to deploy solutions". OAGIS is an

XML framework for both EAI and B2Bi. OAGIS supports loosely coupled integration for enterprise applications like ERP and CRM, which extends to business partners. The specification has the distinction of providing a single integrated network internal and external to the enterprise.

An OAGIS-compliant middleware server provides standard integration functions like message queuing, message routing, guaranteed delivery, and directory services. The OAGIS server transports messages in a Business Object Document (BOD) container. A BOD contains data in XML format for communication between a sender and a recipient. There are BOD specifications to interface between various enterprise application areas like human resources, customer relationship management (CRM), financials, and manufacturing.

The BOD provides the architecture to communicate messages. Understanding the BOD is essential to comprehending the architecture. A BOD document includes a Control Area and Business Document Area contained in <BOD></BOD> XML tags. A Globally Unique Identifier (GUID) is created in the control area that uniquely identifies messages. The GUID is composed of a Business Service Request, a Sender, and Date/Time stamp. A GUID is an essential component for messaging in B2Bi. The GUID supports the workflow routing of messages and error handling.

The Business Service Request in the Control Area provides a noun/verb/revision syntax that informs the receiving application what action the sender requires it to perform. The noun refers to an object name, the verb to an object method, and the revision to the version number of the service request. This syntax enables software vendors to use BODs as a wrapper to functionality in their respective underlying applications. Therefore enterprise implementers of OAGIS-compatible systems have flexibility in plugging in and out the application engine.

The Sender in the Control Area provides information that relates to the application that sent the message. The sender contains eight fields: LogicalID, Component, Task, ReferenceID, Confirmation, Language, CodePage, and AuthID:

LogicalID. This may include information such as a DNS address or IP Address/Port that defines the location of the sending application or server. The DNS method is preferred as it abstracts the name from the physical location. Therefore, if the physical location moves, the physical reference must be updated in one location, the DNS, rather than in several parts of the application. Utilizing a DNS creates a more maintainable system.

Component. The Component refers by name to the sender. The name is indicative of the type of application sending the message such as "CRM-001" or "FINANCIALS".

Task. The Task names the specific business event to be adjusted such as "PURCHASE" or "RETURN".

ReferenceID. The ReferenceID is used for auditing purposes. It provides a reference back to the originator of an event.

Confirmation. The sender may require a confirmation to be sent back from the receiver of the document. This provides a layer of guaranteed messaging that may be tied to or works independently of the integration server.

Language. The Language field contains a three-letter code conforming to ISO standards specifying the human language of the data. This is an important component when transacting business on a global scale.

CodePage. The CodePage refers to the character set of the document specified by ISO 8859.

AuthID. The AuthorizationID describes the application used to generate the BOD. Assignment of this ID provides the ability for the receiving application to authenticate the sender of the message.

These fields in the Control Area provide the essential message header components for transacting intra- and inter-business documents. In addition to the control area, the other critical piece of the BOD is the Business Data Area. This piece contains data header information and the data. There may be one or more Business Data Areas in a document. For example, if the document is utilized by the enterprise procuring supplies, the data area will contain a purchase order. OAGIS supports the notion that multiple purchase orders may be made to the same supplier, potentially for different departments, and therefore the enterprise may send several orders in a single document. This flexibility supports a diverse range of business processes and does not force the enterprise to mold its operation to the underlying technology.

The BOD forms the core message of the OAGIS framework. The ability to support multiple languages, handle confirmation to enable guaranteed message delivery, provide authentication, and to assign tasks to recipients makes the OAGIS BOD architecture a solid framework for the enterprise. OAGIS-compliant application vendors may employ a variety of communication mechanisms for BODs, such as the DCOM, CORBA, and the JMS. OAGIS is designed to be neutral to communication transport mechanisms. Implementers of OAGIS must utilize the same transport mechanism or have translators or adapters that interface different systems.

ebXML

Electronic business XML (ebXML) is a framework to standardize electronic business data exchange in XML. The mission statement of the project is "to provide an open XML-based infrastructure enabling the global use of electronic business information in an interoperable, secure, and consistent manner by all parties." The framework, through open collaboration and ease of use, is intended to lower the barrier of entry to electronic business for small and medium-sized companies worldwide.

ebXML is a collaborative effort between OASIS and UN/CEFACT. OASIS is an international non-profit consortium for industry groups and organizations to develop XML specifications. Companies like IBM, Sun Microsystems, Hewlett Packard, and SAP are sponsors of the project. UN/CEFACT is the United Nations body for Trade Facilitation and Electronic Business, which mandates international trade policy as it applies to electronic business. UN/CEFACT has been instrumental in the development of business exchanges based on EDI through the international EDI standard UN/EDIFACT. Together, OASIS and UN/CEFACT are creating one of the best open frameworks for business-to-business transactions.

EDI has not provided the intended vision of a global e-commerce Web for all businesses. Only the largest businesses have benefited. The smaller enterprises that have invested in EDI have done so only at the insistence of their larger trading partner. Often these smaller enterprises must adopt the proprietary integration approach utilized by the larger partner, which limits their ability to connect with other businesses. ebXML provides a open standards-based solution that is accessible to smaller businesses but also compatible with existing B2B systems. ebXML recognizes the reality that many of these large companies have invested heavily in EDI with some success and will be reluctant to rebuild on an XML-based architecture. Therefore, ebXML's framework allows for the current EDI architecture to remain intact but to also extend it through XML.

The target implementer of ebXML is the business with 100 to 1,000 employees. However, small businesses and even those in the Global 2000 will find use in the framework. The intention is that small businesses will be able to acquire ebXML compliant applications at low cost. Many small businesses (50 employees or fewer) may not have a need to engage in an ebXML framework, however, those that do will have a cost accessible solution. On the flip side, the largest companies in the world have already invested heavily in EDI-based technology. However, this is often in only a few parts of the company. ebXML can provide completion of the B2Bi infrastructure at a price significantly less than that of EDI. ebXML has the opportunity to become the pervasive glue that binds B2B worldwide.

ebXML is not simply a mechanism for moving bits of data between business partners. The framework provides intelligent error control systems to account for difficulties that may arise from automated B2B. Manual B2B, carried out by phone, fax, email, or postal mail have human checkpoints at each end. These human checkpoints are a filter for duplicated or improper transactions. For example, take a small company with 20 people. They make an incorrect 100-million-dollar purchase order that was actually only supposed to be 100,000 dollars. A human operator who receives this purchase order will have the capacity to recognize that it is incorrect. A simple automated system will pass the order right through, creating a nightmare for both trading partners. Therefore, ebXML provides a mechanism to validate all transactions coming through the system.

The ebXML technical architecture is composed of the following items:

Business process definition. A business process is a unit of exchange between trading partners. For example, a business process may be a purchase agreement between a trading partner that is the buyer and another trading partner that is the seller.

Collaboration protocol profile. A trading partner's collaboration protocol profile (CPP) documents describe their supported business processes and their interface requirements. The interface requirements provide other trading partners a mechanism for exchanging business documentation. The CPP references the roles in the business processes. The CPP is registered and stored in an ebXML Registry. The following trading partner information is recorded in the CPP as its Business Profile Information:

- Supporting business processes

- Supporting business service interfaces

- The business messages that are transmitted between business service interfaces

- Technical configuration of communication and security protocols

Trading partner search. The framework provides the functionality to search for a trading partner in an ebXML Registry.

Trading partner information retrieval. Other trading partners through the ebXML Registry may query the trading partner's information contained in the CPP.

Business arrangement execution. This defines the workflow based on the trading partner information.

Messaging service framework. This is a standardized system that provides for the secure and reliable communication of messages between trading partners.

Collaboration protocol agreement. The collaboration protocol agreement (CPA) is derived from the collaboration of two trading partners and their respective CPP. The CPA defines how messages are communicated based upon the workflow defined in the business arrangement. The CPA may be stored in the ebXML registry, but it is not required.

Business processes are created through the use of the UN/CEFACT Modeling Methodology. The UMM utilizes reusable components that contain object classes. The object classes are based on discrete business practices and are known as Business Information Objects. For example, an object may define the sales tax calculation on a purchase order. Creation of a library of these objects is designed to permit the rapid development of interoperable ebXML applications.

Summary

The automated exchange of information between businesses is one of the most important endeavors in an enterprise's e-business strategy. To participate in the global economy, businesses must recognize the need to be extroverted. Businesses can no longer be completely self-sufficient and independent. The nodes of the supply Web stretch across the globe. A business based in one country may have sourcing, manufacturing, sales, marketing, and distribution on the opposite side of the planet. Leveraging a global economy means getting the best price and service for your business.

To become a business connected in this emerging supply web requires sophisticated technology and management. The utilization of the Internet and XML provides a cost-effective buy-in for most companies. B2B frameworks provide the core infrastructure to architect your solution. The enterprise must also exercise integration technology, like messaging middleware and application adapters, and be able to connect to disparate platforms like ERP and EDI systems. Open source languages and tools like XML, XSLT, and integration software can be exercised for a highly flexible and cost-effective B2Bi infrastructure.

Building from the integration between businesses is the ability for e-commerce. B2B and B2C e-commerce form the last major component of the e-business strategy. E-commerce provides a digital salesperson at the point of sale, enabling customers to make informed buying decisions. E-commerce is in its infancy and is expected to mature into a mainstay of the modern economy. The next chapter investigates how the enterprise can leverage open source software for various e-commerce initiatives over the wired and wireless Internet.

CHAPTER 8

E-Commerce Applications

The rise of the Internet has fueled the tremendous growth in e-commerce. A global network of computers connected to businesses, schools, and homes enables a radically new means for commerce. E-commerce is the buying and selling of products through digital communication channels, mainly through the Internet. Geographic boundaries have been stripped away, opening the local business to a worldwide market. The revenue generated from e-commerce transactions in 2000 was an estimated $233 billion (eMarketer.com), doubling in revenues from 1999. Strong growth in e-commerce is predicted for several more years, with the bulk (80+ percent) of the revenues to be derived from business-to-business transactions. The impressive escalation of e-commerce cannot be ignored. The modern enterprise must build e-commerce strategies into their business models to survive and grow.

This chapter presents the e-commerce business strategy and associated technology solutions for the enterprise. E-commerce is a challenging undertaking that forms a core component in the broader e-business strategy. We'll investigate how effective e-commerce initiatives must focus on the customer and deliver to the bottom line for the enterprise. We'll also detail how open source software can be leveraged to provide a secure, reliable, and cost-effective basis for the IT e-commerce infrastructure.

E-Commerce Initiatives

E-commerce can be broadly divided into two categories: business-to-business (B2B), and business-to-consumer (B2C). B2B e-commerce is commerce transactions between two or more businesses, and B2C is between a business and the end customer. The Internet has enabled the creation of online e-commerce businesses like Amazon.com and Buy.com. Traditional brick-and-mortar businesses, like Best Buy or Gap, are becoming click-and-mortar enterprises with e-commerce Web presence. Increasingly, these traditional enterprises are exploring new ways to reduce costs, improve revenues, and satisfy customers.

Many e-commerce models have emerged recently. Some of these models are simply old systems with a Web face-lift, and others are radically new systems taking good business from the past and applying the best in modern technology. The models that leverage the power of the Internet and e-business to their fullest extent have the best chance to succeed. Those that take something from the old economy and put it online, for example the retailer that puts its wares up on a Web site because everyone else is doing it, will likely learn an expensive lesson in how not to do e-commerce. Prime examples are rampant from the culling of companies in 2000, online retailers like Pets.com and eToys.com, had business models that didn't justify their valuation and they saw huge drops (90+ percent) in their stock prices. Many of these types on online retail companies have either gone out of business or are teetering on the edge of bankruptcy. To justify e-commerce in the enterprise, it requires a strong business case that is followed through by great technology and fantastic implementation.

Putting up a Web site to sell goods online is not rocket science. The challenge arises when attempting to create a Web site that functions across broad platforms, like wireless devices, making it scaleable, secure, reliable, and seamlessly integrated with back-end systems. Technology is a key component of every e-commerce strategy. It is the enabler of cost savings and revenue generation but it can also be a significant source of expenditure. Reducing cost for design, implementation, and maintenance of technology is a high priority in many modern enterprises. Open source software delivers these cost savings. The savings are obvious in the price tag of the software. However, the longer-term savings of reliability, security, easier maintenance and enhancement inherent in strong open source software outweigh its free licensing cost.

Customer-Centric E-Commerce

Customer-centric is probably the most important phrase to consider when developing an e-commerce strategy. It's a buzzword that's frequently used but difficult to implement in reality. Technology is crucial in the e-commerce initiative and must solve complex tasks. However, the technology that faces the customer, like the e-commerce Web site, must be simple and effective. Software developers often delight in creating complex interfaces to applications, like ESC-SHIFT+Z-SHIFT+Z to save a file in the Unix editor vi. These complex interfaces work for computer gurus but not for the average Web user. Customer-centric means developing applications for the user who doesn't really care about the complexity behind the system and has a greater appreciation for its simplicity.

There are five basic objectives to consider when designing a customer-centric blueprint for e-commerce: personalized service; right, rapid service; self-service; wide-selection tailored to your customer audience; and convenience.

Personalized Service

Personalized service is what shoppers expect when they enter a small neighborhood restaurant. The manager knows them by name, the hostess seats them in their favorite place, the waiter knows what they like, and the chef prepares their food to their liking. When shoppers enter a mega-superstore, like Home Depot or Wal-Mart, the size of the business and the number of people that come through it in one day make it almost impossible for personalized service. Shoppers have come to expect less customer service when they shop in larger stores. However, the customer who shops online should receive the same personalized attention from a small shop, no matter how big the business is on the back end. Technology is the enabler for personalization for Web-based companies.

Amazon.com is a great example of a gigantic company that delivers fantastic personal attention. As the shopper browses Amazon.com, the system remembers what they've looked at and creates a page of recommendations for them. Amazon.com encourages repeat business. The shopper is introduced to specials and new items based on past purchases. The shopper can place a watch on a book or other item so that an email is sent to them when it becomes available. These features make a shopper feel like they're "being taken care of." The beauty of the system is that it is done with technology. Amazon.com's front end, the Web site, is tied to its various back-end systems like customer relationship management (CRM) software and inventory databases. There aren't millions of customer service representatives watching over the customers at Amazon.com, just millions of bits.

There are many ways to deliver personal service to customers. Your personalization strategy will depend on who your customers are. If your enterprise is participating in a B2B e-commerce scenario, then the customers and businesses may expect a generic system that gets the job done. Frilly personalization may waste time for these customers. However, in B2C e-commerce, the customer is often more demanding. The personalized service may involve product offerings tailored to customer preferences, information customized to prior purchases, email updates during order fulfillment, and dedicated customer support. If your customer base expects personal attention, your business must deliver it.

Right, Rapid Service

Shoppers hate to wait in lines. We live in a busy world and people don't want to spend their precious free time standing in line. Recognizing that impatience is part of the psychology of the modern consumer is essential to your e-commerce strategy. Impatience is cured by *right, rapid service*. Right means that the customer gets what they want, and rapid means that they get it quickly. Right, rapid service is essential for e-commerce Web sites.

Online toy retailers in the Christmas 1999 season received $1.5 million in fines from the U.S. Federal Trade Commission because they failed in right, rapid service. Thousands of customers got the wrong products and/or got them late. Just over a year later in 2001, eToys.com, one of the most popular online toy retailers, is struggling to stay in business. Failure to meet this required component of the customer-centric model will crash the enterprise.

Right, rapid service is important because shoppers face two crucial uncertainties when they shop online. First, they don't actually handle the products they're buying so they don't know if the seller will give them quality merchandise and the correct merchandise. Second, shoppers don't receive the product immediately upon purchase and must wait for it to be shipped to them. Right, rapid service mitigates these uncertainties.

Constructing right, rapid service for the e-commerce strategy requires significant planning and work (see Figure 8.1). First, customers must be quickly able to find and make their purchases. *Click work* is the number of clicks, or page loads, starting when customers hit the home page and ending when they're finished with checkout. The lower the number, the lesser the click work is. Many customers still access the Internet through dial-up connections. Web pages generally take 15–60 seconds to load. Reducing click work by 20 clicks will, on average, save the customer ten minutes. There is much attention given to interface design to make finding and buying products a painless process. Features like Amazon's one click shopping, although patented and a hindrance to other sites wishing to employ it, is an excellent example of site design for rapid service.

Even more significant and time consuming than good interface design is to make the fulfillment system efficient. This means integration with back-end systems like inventory and supply-chain management, so that when customers order products, they'll have an accurate estimation of the availability of their products. It also requires workflow and organization to route orders from the Web site to order fulfillment and to be able to pull and pack the purchase accurately. Therefore, efficient partnerships must be created with shipping companies like UPS, USPS, and FedEx. The shipping

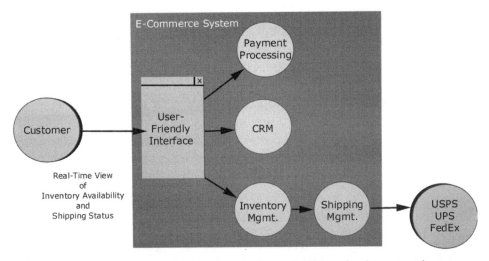

Figure 8.1 Deploying right, rapid service requires a significant, but important, investment of resources.

and receiving portion of your business must be able to work seamlessly with these companies. All of these activities must be done without delay.

Self Service

The shopper who frequents physical stores has attendants to call on for help. Customers in cyberspace do not. Online shoppers shop year-round, every day of the week, and every hour of the day. They must be able to find the products they need without human assistance. This means that a new level of self-service must be implemented for e-commerce Web sites.

Fortunately the Web provides a fantastic medium to empower customers. Information and products can be organized into intuitive and easily accessible ways. The search box, the ultimate in simple yet effective design, is a great tool to find products. Many of us wish we had a search box while wandering through a superstore looking for a particular product. Customers must not wander around aimlessly within your Web site. If they do, they won't last long, for another URL is just a few keystrokes away.

The key to empowering customers is to understand the type of products you sell and be able to provide the information that customers require when making a purchasing decision. This job is difficult if your Web site sells "everything to everyone". Know the products you sell and then convey that knowledge to your customers. What goes through the mind of someone making a purchase for a particular item on your Web site? What size or colors does it come in? Will it fit into or work with my existing product? How bulky or heavy is the item and how much will it cost to ship it? Your enterprise is best served to design a list of these questions that customers will ask about your products. Then you must answer all of the questions in detail for every product and post this on the site in an intelligible format.

Investing in customer self-service has a long-term ROI. Customers that can service themselves don't require handholding from human representatives. These self-serving customers become highly profitable assets to your enterprise. Once customers learn they can find the information they need from a Web site and easily buy their products, they'll return time and again.

Wide Selection Tailored to Customers

Superstores have emerged in the last couple of decades to offer an enormous selection of products. For example, Home Depot has been one of the largest growing retailers in the United States in the past five years. Its numerous aisles are packed with building materials, hardware, home fixtures, garden equipment, and more. Its selection is tailored to the do-it-yourselfer and small general contractor for home improvement. Its ability to provide wide selection that is customized to a particular customer market is the main factor for its success.

In the online world, customers have come to expect great selection. Amazon.com stocks about a 1.5 million books, which is ten times greater than the number stocked by the brick-and-mortar book superstores. It has enormous warehouses and fulfillment centers across the United States to complete its orders. However, this does not mean that every enterprise must invest millions in new infrastructure to deliver a wider selection. Technology integration with key partners can enable the e-business to leverage their partners' inventory as their own. This requires a coupling between inventory and fulfillment systems, part of a B2Bi initiative.

Providing millions of products is not a necessity for e-commerce. The necessity is to provide choice, one-stop shopping, and expertise for your market base. If your business sells parts for automobile engines, should you carry parts on your Web site for other components of the car, like brakes or the transmission? Potentially yes and no. You must ask yourself if the particular demographic will want to purchase brake pads with a new set of pistons. Your enterprise must also consider its expertise in these additional parts and its ability to stock and ship them (either physically or virtually). Carrying the extra product lines increase the opportunity for more revenue, but will it decrease the profit? In forming a customer-centric business, you must also break down your customer segment. This research will provide insight to the selection that your average customer will demand.

Convenience

Trade stocks while lying in bed. Order groceries while watching television. Order books over donuts and coffee. Purchase exercise equipment when you realize that you've been spending too much time in front of the computer. Convenience has been redefined in the Internet era. Convenience allows customers to make their purchase quickly and easily. To achieve convenience means accomplishing personalized, right, rapid, and self-service with selection that provides choice and value. Convenience is what emerges when the other four objectives have been accomplished. Your enterprise can gauge the success of its customer-centric e-commerce endeavor by measuring how convenient the service is.

These objectives look good on paper and even better in reality. Customer-centric should not be scorned as just a buzzword but as the epitome of successful e-business. Central to your e-commerce strategy must be the customer. Technology is important in serving your customers. It must be reliable, integrated, complex but simple to use, secure, and grow to meet the customer's needs. Open Source software can provide much of this technology infrastructure at a fraction of the cost of proprietary systems. Which is better for your bottom line and for your customer's. To begin to investigate the technological underpinnings of e-commerce, the enterprise must identify which e-commerce categories it will participate in.

E-Commerce Categories

Adding items to a cart and paying for them is just one form of e-commerce. There are numerous other ways to conduct business digitally such as auctions, catalog aggregation, business hubs, seller-driven exchanges, and more. Many of these categories apply to B2B and B2C initiatives. Every e-commerce strategy must define the appropriate e-commerce categories that it will participate in. Some forms of e-commerce, such as auctions compared to traditional one-price sales, may present a wider buying audience, more dedicated customers, and a better return on investment.

The major categories of e-commerce include:

Online fixed pricing. The Web site that sells products at a preset price.

Portal and content aggregation. The Web site that aggregates content and services to drive revenues through advertising and fee-based services.

Catalog aggregation. The specialized portal for the sale of products.

Electronic auctions. Electronic auctions (e-auctions) that leverage the power of the Internet to drive a critical mass of buyers and sellers. Sellers bid competitively on items.

Reverse-auctions. Auctions where the buyer posts a bid and sellers bid against each other to provide the lowest price.

Hubs and trading exchanges. Hubs are central destinations for multiple participants, often composed of several sellers and buyers.

Digital product e-commerce. Digital products exist only in electronic form, such as software, digital music, and electronic documents. The sale of digital products engenders a unique e-commerce strategy.

Hosting and management services. Hosting and management services provide the backbone for connectivity to the Internet and other networks and may also actively maintain and monitor Web sites, enterprise applications, and more.

Application service providers. Application service providers (ASPs) are highly specialized digital product purveyors which supply rentable software through a managed hosting model.

Online Fixed Pricing

This is the most common form of e-commerce. The online booksellers, such as Amazon.com, BarnesandNoble.com, and Fatbrain.com are good examples of fixed pricing. Products are placed on a Web page, usually arranged into categories by product type or manufacturer. Each product has a specific price and is commonly accompanied by a picture and detailed information. Customers browse products and place them into a virtual shopping cart. Once all of the items are selected, the customer proceeds through checkout. The checkout process involves entering personal and payment information. After completing the order, the products are shipped to the customer. Anyone who has bought online has probably gone through a similar process.

Traditional businesses are adopting an online fixed pricing strategy to move from a brick-and-mortar business model to a click-and-mortar model. These businesses are generally retailers for the B2C market and to a lesser extent, wholesalers or other middlemen for the B2B market. Fixed pricing Web sites don't meld well with businesses that have flexible pricing structures, such as those who sell to customers at variable prices. However, those businesses that operate like many large retailers may find a fixed pricing strategy the optimal choice.

Revenues are typically generated through product sales. Online sellers often derive additional revenues through advertisements and product placement. Advertising is generally bought by manufacturers of the products that are sold on the Web site. Online product placement is similar to that in stores, products are placed on highly visible pages (like the home page) and are given more space. The business may operate virtually and not actually stock and ship the goods it sells. This scenario requires expenditure for outsourcing but also permits the business to concentrate on the sales and marketing aspect rather than fulfillment.

Open source projects like Akopia and Zelerate AllCommerce provide instant storefronts. Their open source nature makes them highly customizable. ArsDigita, Zope, Enhydra, Zend/PHP, and Apache Tomcat are development environments that can be leveraged to build online storefronts. Also, open source programming languages like Perl and Python have formed the mainstay of many Web businesses and are options for those seeking to custom design a commerce solution.

Portal and Content Aggregation

A portal is a provider that aggregates content and services into a single offering. A portal generates revenues directly from the sale of these services or indirectly through advertising or tie-in to fee-based offerings. The portal strategy tailors its aggregated offering to a receptive customer base. Yahoo! is probably the best and most successful example of the broad portal strategy, and businesses like E*Trade offer more specialized services. The portal strategy may be simply a middleman initiative, positioning itself between suppliers and customers. It may also take a hybrid approach by developing some of its own content and partnering with suppliers that provide information and services that it cannot.

Yahoo!'s portal offerings are astounding. At its basis is a search engine, once developed by its founders Jerry Yang and David Filo, which is now powered by Google. The search engine provides the foundation for a powerful portal offering. Extending from the search engine is content, such as feeds from news services, stock quotes, financial information, music, movies, and more. Then there are services like Yellow Pages, MAPQuest mapping, Yahoo! Mail, Yahoo! Stores, and Yahoo! Auctions. In just over five years, Yahoo! has grown from a dorm room project to a major new economy company. The power of the Internet can be astounding.

As Yahoo! has grown and evolved, its emphasis has been to move from a simple aggregator of eyeballs to an e-commerce powerhouse. It provides many of its services free of charge and leverages that traffic to drive revenues not just from advertising but also from fee-based services. For example, Yahoo! Mail is free, but if you want a large mailbox to hold hundreds of emails, then you're advised to spend $20 for more space. In addition to upgrading to fee-based services, Yahoo! ties free content with revenue generating capability. For example, a person can research information for free about travel and foreign destinations. If that person decides to take a trip, they can buy their airline tickets, hotel reservation, and car rental online through Yahoo! Travel. Each purchase earns Yahoo! a commission. Substantial revenues are reaped with over 30 million visitors to the site.

The opportunity in the mega-portal space is nil. Competing against the likes of Yahoo!, MSN, or AOL is a difficult challenge. The opportunity for portals is with niche audiences. An example of a niche portal is CelebrateLife.com, a Web site that enables individuals to build custom Web sites and collaborate with family and friends during special occasions like graduations or weddings. On the surface it may seem similar to GeoCities, but the site attracts its audience through strategic partnerships with nonprofit organizations. The nonprofit organizations drive traffic toward the site and in return receive a commission and donations made by members. CelebrateLife.com is unique and a model for niche portals and is growing its technology infrastructure on a move to open source applications.

If your enterprise is considering a portal strategy, it must leverage its current customer base by delivering content and services targeted to it. The portal strategy is being employed more often as an indirect generator of the revenues. This includes providing information and customer service through the offering. These features drive sales through other channels and provide a convenient access point for customers with service requirements.

Catalog Aggregation

Catalog or product aggregation is the integration of product information from various sources. A catalog aggregator is a specialized portal provider. Often catalog aggregators specialize in tying together various product lines from disparate sources to deliver a comprehensive offering. For example, a catalog aggregator may offer a one-stop shop for small businesses. Product lines might include law services to setup the company, leasing services to find a business location, office equipment, printing services, interior design services, and more. The offering makes it simple for the customer to find everything they need in one place.

Catalog aggregators generally work with retailers or B2B suppliers and, to a lesser extent, with manufacturers. Their revenues are derived from a commission on each product sold, usually 1 to 3 percent of the total purchase price. The catalog aggregator generally does not carry the inventory it sells, or at least not everything that it sells. Fulfillment is usually outsourced, including packaging, shipping, delivery, and customer returns, but portions of the fulfillment system may be done in house to generate additional revenues.

Catalog aggregation is an attractive e-business model for emerging companies who can tap into a customer base that demands a comprehensive product line. It becomes especially attractive when this can't be done with the manual logistics of traditional business. It's quite difficult to aggregate 20 catalogs, provide this information in a printed list, and be able to update it constantly. It's much simpler when the aggregator has real-time automated connection to each supplier and can instantly update the product list on a Web site. E-business and the Internet make all-inclusive aggregation possible.

Catalog aggregation may also be a strategy for the existing business for growth. For example, take a company that sells tennis rackets. It may aggregate with other tennis equipment suppliers, apparel and shoe providers, tennis instructors, health and fitness providers, and even local tennis facilities. It becomes the one-stop shop for everything tennis and is able to reach a broader and more dedicated audience (see Figure 8.2).

Catalog aggregation is not a simple task. This is good and bad for the business implementing it as a part of its e-business strategy. The downside

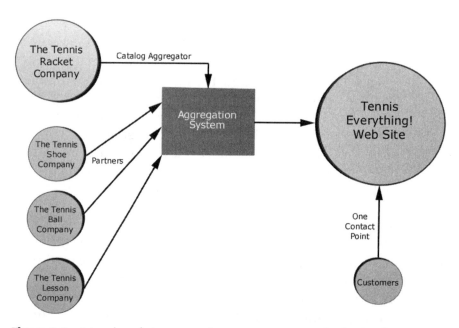

Figure 8.2 A tennis racket company becomes a one-stop destination for tennis through catalog aggregation.

is that a business must expend a significant amount of planning and resources to make it possible. Cost is major factor in whether the strategy will succeed or fail. Utilizing Open Source software can cut the cost for the project significantly. The upside to the difficulty in catalog aggregation is that it presents a barrier of entry for competition. Once your systems are integrated with your partners, those partners are more willing to devote their time and effort to your cause.

Catalog aggregation is technology intensive and requires a strong integration backbone to be successful. Systems ranging from legacy inventory management to modern fulfillment engines often need to be connected to the catalog aggregator. Catalog aggregation presents both EAI and B2B integration scenarios (see Figure 8.3). Open source message queuing products like Joram, Enhdyra/ObjectCube JMS, OpenJMS, and the Open3 e-business integration platform can provide a basis for connecting these disparate systems. In addition to the integration challenges, the catalog aggregator must also build the interface, generally a Web-based storefront, for their system. Catalog aggregators may work under an application service provider model and OEM their offering to other businesses. This requires the interface to be easily rebranded. Open source technologies like Enhydra's XMLC, Apache Cocoon, and Apache XSLT rival commercial technologies in creating Web interfaces that can be easily changed.

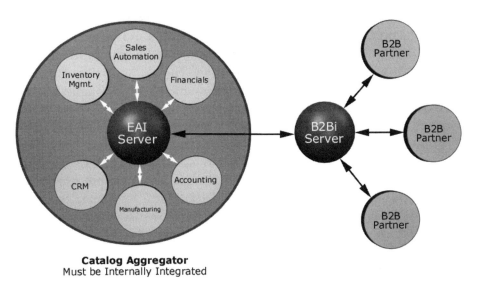

Catalog Aggregator
Must be Internally Integrated

Figure 8.3 The technology-intensive architecture of catalog aggregation.

E-Auctions

Traditional auctions allow multiple buyers to competitively bid on products. E-auctions may be traditional auctions that leverage digital communication, generally the Internet, to do the product listing and bidding, or specialized auction systems that operate uniquely because of e-business. Popular examples like eBay or Yahoo Auctions specialize in C2C, uBid and EggHead.com/Onsale have strong exposure in the B2C space, while companies like TradeOut.com specialize in the B2B arena. Auction e-commerce includes many of the same features as a fixed price destination, but with the added auction engine function.

E-Auction strategies are utilized in two main ways. First is to extend an old-world auction-based business model to the digital age. Second is to create new e-commerce markets through an auction-based model. Brick-and-mortar businesses that currently sell or would like to sell products through an auction model can benefit strongly from the global audience of the Internet. Businesses that will profit are those who have a worldwide potential market but have only been able to tap into local or regional markets. Auctions require a multi-user audience to be successful. This may mean 5 bidders on an item, or 1,000 bidders, but auctions don't work if there is just a single bidder. Leveraging the Internet can provide the critical mass necessary to make auction e-commerce a reality.

The Internet is creating paradigm shifts in auction commerce. eBay is a powerful example. It's been called the worldwide garage sale of the Internet. eBay has more than a million members and averages over half a million auctions per day. It operates by allowing mainly individuals or small companies to sell goods based on an auction model. Individuals from broad geographic regions can bid on an item. This is especially attractive for niche products, like certain collectibles, which may not have a large market in a local area. A minimum or reserve price is set for each item, which is the price at which the highest bidder must meet to buy the item. Sellers pay a small fee of $2.00 or less to list items. If a product sells, then the seller is charged 1.25 to 5 percent commission of the sales price. The commission is higher for lower ticket items and less for more expensive purchases. This auction model has proved successful for eBay because it has reached the critical mass of users to be successful. eBay would not exist without the open door for e-commerce made possible by the Internet.

The types of products an enterprise sells and the types of target customers are influential in determining if the auction model is appropriate.

There are many types of products suitable for auction commerce. These items range from bulk and surplus materials to everyday retail goods. To be effective, the sale prices of auction items must be relatively large ticket items or small ticket items that are sold in bulk. Not too many people will spend the time and effort to bid on something that costs $5 other than those who bid for entertainment, such as those on eBay.

An auction strategy for e-commerce may be implemented as a tactic against competition. Auctions have a tendency to drive traffic to those individuals or businesses that are looking for discounts, used equipment, or niche products. The enterprise that serves these types of customers may achieve a significant edge over competitors who follow a fixed-pricing model.

Implementing the technology foundation behind auction-based e-commerce is a bit more challenging than simple fixed-price storefronts. An auction engine, functionality that manages the bidding process, must be added to the site. There are several open source projects for implementing an online auction, including EveryAuction and PHPAuction.

EveryAuction (www.everysoft.com) is a Perl-based auction package released under the GNU General Public License. EveryAuction is production ready. EveryAuction contains all features necessary for a basic auction package, plus an add-on database, that permits customization of the base package. EveryAuction is recommended if you are implementing Perl-based solutions.

PHPAuction (www.phpauction.org) is a PHP-based auction system released under the GNU General Public License. It is in early beta version and is progressing toward production availability. It contains many of the basic auction features plus nice enhancements like email notification of bid status. Look for this project to be production ready in mid-to-late 2001.

Reverse-Auction E-Commerce

Reverse auctions differ in two fundamental respects from regular auctions. First, the prices for items during the process go down, rather than up. Second, buyers post a maximum bid and sellers compete to deliver the lowest bid. The dynamics of reverse auctions require a somewhat different e-business implementation than regular auctions. Reverse auctions require more attention to be delivered to the sellers in the system, rather than the buyers. This is because the buyer can simply sit back, place a bid, and see who can deliver the lowest price. The buyer, on the other hand, must be constantly updated about potential and current bids. In a B2C model, this means that strong attention must be delivered to the business. To get businesses to buy into reverse auctions, the time and effort to respond to bids must cost less than the profit generated from the sale. This often requires that the auction system be integrated with these businesses to deliver real-time information into their systems.

A reverse-auction strategy is often used when there is significant endorsement from the seller community to participate in the business. Therefore, a B2C-based or B2B-based system has a better chance to reach critical mass if it has solid partnerships with other businesses. However, the buyer community cannot be ignored because without it, there is no reason for the sellers to participate.

The auction technology behind reverse auctions is very similar to regular auctions, except that the pricing engine needs to work in the opposite direction. The open source auction packages, because of their open code nature, can be easily switched to function in a reverse auction implementation. Additionally, an integration solution may be required to service the connection with businesses. Therefore, the technology implementation for reverse auctions has a tendency to be more complex.

Hubs and Trading Exchanges

Hubs, also known as trading exchanges, provide a central location for e-commerce transactions. Hubs are generally composed of multiple sellers providing the same or similar products and multiple buyers competing for the purchase of those products. A variety of different e-commerce sales techniques are employed, but auctions, reverse auctions, and bid-ask systems (similar to the stock market) are the most typical.

Commodity items and products which have fluctuating prices based upon market conditions are the standard fare for trading exchanges. These include items like food products, raw materials, precious metals, collectibles, chemicals, and natural resources. However, hub-based systems are not limited to these items. Any good or service that may have multiple sellers and multiple buyers can be bartered.

A hub strategy may be a system that your enterprise utilizes in conjunction with business partners. By providing a central location for buying and selling, trade can occur more rapidly and efficiently. Therefore, the hub becomes a part of the cost-saving tactic in e-business. The hub system may also be engaged as a revenue generating mechanism. Your enterprise may participate as the market maker or broker between buyers and sellers and earn a commission from each sale. This is the strategy applied by Cyber-Crop.com, a Web system that provides the trading infrastructure for agricultural products.

The typical Internet-based hub is composed of a Web site with registered participants that may act as buyers or sellers or both. There may be one or several transaction engines, such as auctions or bid-ask, which govern how products are sold. There may be significant integration demands that require automated connections for both parties. To facilitate this, a B2B framework (as discussed in Chapter 7, "Business-to-Business Integration") may be employed. Many of the required pieces to construct a hub are available as open source software, but no turnkey solutions are available. E-commerce products like Akopia and Zelerate can provide part of the solution, integration products like Open3 e-business integration, Enhydra JMS, or OpenJMS can provide a basis for connecting various partners. XML repositories like XML.org and open B2B frameworks like RosettaNet and ebXML provide a strong foundation for building the transactional portion of the system.

Digital Products

Digital products exist only in electronic space. These are items that have some informational or entertainment value to customers. Examples of digital products include financial analysis documents, MP3 music files, software, graphics, digital video, and news information. E-commerce reaches an amazing level of efficiency when using digital business to sell digital goods. The products are created, browsed, delivered, and utilized electronically. There are no packaging costs, virtually no shipping costs, and low expenditures to sell and utilize the products. The total time from when a person begins to shop for a digital product and begins to use it can be done in a manner of minutes.

The rise of digital products can be attributed to the mainstream move to the Internet. As access and bandwidth increase across the globe, digital products will become a significant portion of e-commerce. Electronic goods are already changing the physical world. Take the rise of Napster and its music delivery model that has attempted to turn the music industry on its head. Napster provides a locator service that allows a user to browse other user's collections of music and download files encoded in the MP3 format. Although legal issues cloud its rise, it is hugely popular. As the music industry scrambles to stop the proliferation of lost revenues, it is unable to deny that the distribution mechanism exemplified by Napster has been successful.

The music business is being forced to change its dynamics from a few high-priced albums by a limited number of artists, to lower-priced albums by many artists. Why? This is because the Internet provides an efficient mechanism for delivery of music. Look at the current way to sell music. It costs about fifty cents to burn a CD, and about $15 to get it to the end customer. The artist receives less than 10 percent of the final cost of the product. The recording company takes $5 to $10. Customers are paying a lot more than they should for the music.

Digital music can cut this cost by 50 percent or more. The packaging, distribution, and retail costs become negligible. The recording industry is no longer a necessary middleman between the music creator and the music. A Web-based aggregator of music, like MP3.com, becomes the central distributor of the music files. Artists, especially local and niche musicians, now have a platform for the sale of their music. Digital music expands the opportunity for more career musicians. Digital products are creating a dramatic paradigm shift in the music industry. Other businesses will see similar changes.

Digital products are growing rapidly in popularity. New opportunities for storage, search, and distribution are emerging. A digital product strategy may form the core part of an e-business initiative or simply another component of the endeavor. The digital products may drive revenue directly or indirectly. The main challenges in the direct sale of digital products are licensing and preventing piracy. The benefits of easy copy and distribution of digital media are also a hindrance in preventing the end customer from giving away the product to friends. There are technology initiatives under way to prevent piracy. It's difficult to say whether an effective technology will be developed to prevent digital theft. If digital products carry a low price tag, their customers may simply be more willing to pay for the goods rather than go to the trouble to acquire them illegally.

The indirect revenue model of digital product distribution may be a more viable avenue. This model provides digital content free to users. Revenues are generated through external advertising or by enhancing or extending products or services that cost money. The open source movement is a good example. Many companies in recent years have sponsored open source projects to deliver free software. These companies derive revenues through turnkey solutions, technical support, and consulting services. The software is an indirect sales tool that provides revenues for the company. Users get lower cost software but still receive the service and support they may require in an enterprise environment.

Open source software succeeds because it is a digital product. It leverages the connected power of the Internet to distribute itself and evolve. The freedom to use licensing policy and its no cost nature makes open source a successful product of the digital age. It's interesting that open source software, a prime example of electronic goods, can also be used to create, produce, sell, and distribute other electronic items. It's the digital era building upon itself, and the next generation of the Internet will be created from tools developed in this era.

Much of the Internet is powered by open source software. The Web has propagated at its rapid rate due in large part to software like Perl and Apache Web Server. Recognizing and understanding the success of open source has direct correlation to your enterprise. A digital media strategy may be essential to an optimal e-business initiative. Digital products are a highly effective mechanism to reach a wide and receptive audience. If your business is involved in the direct sale, indirect sale, or dissemination of information or media that can be encoded electronically, a digital product e-commerce strategy may be indispensable.

Digital products are all about technology. Technology must be applied to every step in the process, from digital product creation to utilization by the end customer. From an e-commerce perspective, concentration is focused upon creating the marketplace that drives direct or indirect sales.

Hosting and Management Services

Hosting and management services are e-commerce initiatives that provide the backbone for higher-level e-commerce endeavors. ISPs provide the connectivity and service to access and do business on the Internet. A generic service provider supplies an interface to the Internet, typically through dial-up, DSL, cable, or other connections. They also usually provide hosting services for Web sites. A new generation of these service providers is also enabling management services, such as a 360-degree view of customers visiting a Web site and administration of enterprise applications.

Application Service Provider

Application service providers (ASPs) are a unique combination of digital software products and managed services. The ASPs' target market is businesses and consumers who wish to utilize software but don't want to pay the price of buying, deploying, and maintaining the applications. The ASP hosts and administers various applications that are generally accessible by the customer through the Internet (see Figure 8.4). ASPs provide a wide variety of applications. Yahoo! Mail is a simple application service to receive and send email. PeopleSoft's online ERP implementation is a complex service that controls many parts of a business's activities.

The ASP model has become popular for many existing software vendors and a new generation of ASP-only businesses. Revenues are derived from recurring rental fees. The idea is that the ASP client outsources the headache of installing and maintaining the software and is able to avoid a substantial initial cost in licensing fees. By utilizing an ASP, the business is able to save time and money and does not have to maintain a comprehensive IT department. For many businesses faced with spiraling technology costs and difficulty in enticing quality IT talent, the ASP model is attractive.

However, there are some downsides to ASP. Buying into the ASP model requires that a business give up control of its enterprise applications (EAs). The business must rely on another entity to provide it with secure and reliable service. Additionally, the business loses much of the ability to customize

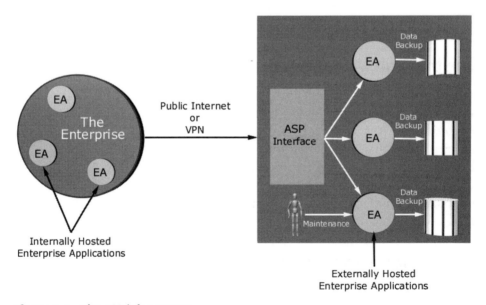

Figure 8.4   The ASP infrastructure.

the applications and must either rely on generic software or pay substantial fees to change it. Also, in the era of integration the business must rely on the ASP to provide the integration points and infrastructure to connect to disparate applications. Many ASPs don't adequately address integration between its applications and its client's applications.

The ASP approach may be a viable e-business strategy for companies that have a strong technological base and customers who will buy into the model. The enterprise must be technologically adept because it must be able to provide the support and infrastructure for the ASP applications. Therefore, companies like software vendors, IT consulting services, and other technology providers are best suited to adopt an ASP model as a part of their e-business strategy. Also of importance is the ability to sell the ASP software to the customer. Generally, in a B2B scenario, customers who are less savvy in technology will be more willing to accept outsourcing IT. Vulnerable clients are those who recognize technology as important but don't have the IT foundation to capture it. These companies would fit in the Tier 1 category.

Selling the ASP model to the end customer in a B2C scenario requires that the user replace a desktop application with a Web-based application. In this case, the ASP model has the best opportunity to succeed. The average Web user has a fair understanding of the high-level aspects of the Internet. They can enter URLs, navigate hyperlinks, and buy online. However, most don't understand how to diagnose problems with software. If 99 percent of the personnel in a company are composed of average computer users and the remaining 1 percent are solid at handling IT issues, then the corporation as a single entity can internally manage its applications. However, since the end customers are individuals and can't tap into the resources of a corporate infrastructure, they are more vulnerable to outsourcing their desktop applications. This may even hold true in the corporate environment, where the IT personnel are skilled with the EAs but don't have the resources to maintain hundreds of desktop applications.

Bandwidth will be the most crucial requirement for ASPs to succeed in overthrowing the desktop consumer market. An individual must be able to do online as fast and conveniently as they are able to do on their desktop. Therefore, bulky applications like office suites and graphics software won't survive under an ASP model until they can be quickly accessed.

The ASP model should be carefully considered if your enterprise is engaged in the technology arena. It's a model that has the potential to change the landscape of software from the sale of a product to the sale of a service. ASP companies are similar to open source companies in that they both generate their revenues by providing ease of service and working solutions rather than boxed licenses. The ASP may seem on the surface like a competing model with open source. The ASP design is about releasing control of IT, and open source is about taking full control. However, there's nothing to stop an ASP from open sourcing its applications and even providing the ability for their clients to tap into the codebase and remotely change the system. Open source in the ASP marketplace will also provide part of the solution to integration difficulties inherent in the ASP model.

These categories form the foundation for the majority of business models utilized in e-commerce. Determining which categories your enterprise fits into is essential to succeeding with the e-commerce portion of your e-business strategy. You must also consider what over what environment or environments that your e-commerce strategy will employ.

The E-Commerce Medium

There are three mediums to consider for e-commerce: the Internet, wireless, and custom solutions such as private networks. E-commerce and the Internet are often synonymous, and for good reason, but e-commerce is not confined to the Internet. The enterprise must investigate emerging environments like wireless and be prepared to engage them when the time is right. Beyond the public systems of the Internet and wireless communication are private networks that are leveraged to provide dedicated and highly customizable e-commerce solutions.

Internet E-Commerce

The Internet is redefining business. It is the birthplace of mainstream e-commerce. The modern day gold rush toward the Internet, although filled with lots of hype, is rooted in the reality of "be there or be out of the new economy." The two main benefits of an online sales presence are a lower cost of doing business and a customer base that spans the world. An e-commerce Web site's return on investment (ROI) depends upon its cost to implement and maintain versus the direct or indirect revenues that it generates. From a technical standpoint, success depends upon a well-architected and maintainable implementation. From a customer standpoint, success depends on attracting and keeping profitable business. To succeed with Internet e-commerce requires that the technical implementation support new levels of customer service.

Hundreds of Web-based e-commerce businesses have failed because the companies were unable to tap into the benefits that the Internet creates. Often their technological implementation was expensive, unmaintainable, and difficult to use. Their business planning and business case were traditional ways of selling, and failed to take advantage of new commerce possibilities leveraged by the Internet. Their customer service was mediocre at best and miserable in some cases. These companies have proved that doing business on the Web requires at least the business-savvy and customer-dedicated approach enlisted by traditional "brick-and-mortar" businesses.

The trend in e-business is adopt the new benefits of e-commerce on the Internet and apply this to the best components of the old models. There is a new economy emerging based on e-business, but it's not an instant on/off switch from old to new. The move in the next generation of the evolving new economy is toward hybrid click-and-mortar models (see Figure 8.5). Some pure-play Web-based companies will succeed, but it's the traditional businesses with rooted customers, brand image, and strong product lines that have a longer lever to move the e-commerce world. The Web becomes not just a channel for new sales, but a tool to engage partnerships and enhance customer relationship to new, and previously unattainable, standards.

Utilizing the Internet in e-commerce is undeniable. Whether it's a simple strategy to reduce costs through automated purchasing from suppliers or a

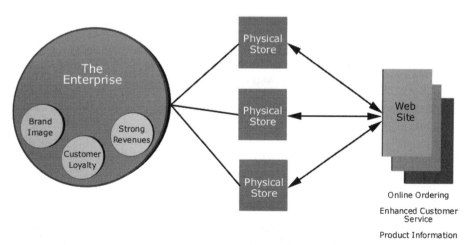

Figure 8.5 The click-and-mortar hybrid business model.

complex strategy of multiple channels for B2B and B2C, missing out on the opportunities for e-commerce on the Web will prove costly. The enterprise must also consider how the Internet is changing and be able to implement an e-commerce strategy that can evolve with it. One of these major changes is the move to communication over the wireless airwaves.

Technology for Internet E-Commerce

Enterprise-class Internet e-commerce requires a sophisticated technology infrastructure. A Web page that can accept credit card payments won't cut it. The application must support the customer-centric paradigm and integrate with back-end systems. B2B and B2C e-commerce solutions have several overlapping technologies, but there are some differing components. All systems have client-side and server-side application components. The client-side is the customer's view of the system, while the server handles the bulk of functionality. In general, the client-side application will require more effort in a B2C scenario whereas in B2B more attention is given to the server applications.

Since the enterprise-class e-commerce system is sophisticated, it requires substantial software technology. Purchasing high-priced proprietary applications can quickly become costly. For example, take the following proprietary recipe for an e-commerce Web system. Assume ten developers are working on the project with four QA personnel, and that the project follows good software engineering practices by having separate development, staging, and production environments.

- Art Technology Group Dynamo Server (J2EE Commerce and Content Management System) (one production license, one staging license, and ten developer licenses)

- Oracle 9 Database (one production license, one staging license, one development license)

- Windows 2000 and Internet Information Server (three licenses of the Server version, ten licenses of the Professional version)

- BEA Systems Tuxedo (e-business integration platform) (one production license, one staging license, one development license)

The estimated cost for the licenses in this system is $300,000 to $500,000. These licenses generally include support by phone and email. Now compare that estimate with the following similar open source system (licensing issues are not a concern):

- Enhydra Enterprise Application Server (J2EE server)
- eGrail Content Management System
- MySQL Database
- Apache Web Server
- SuSE Linux v 7.1 with Linux 2.4 kernel
- Open3 e-business integration system

Buy the packaged versions of the software to get printed documentation and minimal support for $500 to $1000. Purchase sophisticated support packages for the software for an additional $10,000 to $20,000. Your total price for the open source-based system with the same service and support as the proprietary software is 10,500 to $21,000. This is a savings of 93 to 98 percent from the cost of the proprietary system. Add in the long-term benefits of not being locked into version churn and costly upgrades and the savings go higher. It's hard to deny the benefits of open source to your corporate bottom line. Open source has one of the strongest offerings for the e-commerce portion of e-business. Take advantage of it.

The system described above is fairly standard architecture for e-commerce systems. It is composed of a browser on the client side and Web servers, application servers, middleware, databases, EAs, and business frameworks on the server side. Many technologies compose the system. Understanding which technologies are crucial for your e-commerce strategy is fundamental to the success of the Web site. Requirements will differ for client-side and server-side technologies, and awareness of the functionalities of these pieces is the first step in the architecture of an e-commerce solution.

The user browses a Web site with the Web browser, a client-side application. The basic foundation of technology in a Web page is HTML. HTML provides layout and formatting for text, graphics, input areas, and buttons. It's simple and sometimes not robust enough for more complex applications. However, the beauty in HTML is that with decent design, your application will likely have an interface that can be used by the masses. To provide more complex functionality in Web pages, JavaScript or ECMAScript is used. JavaScript provides a minimal programming language that allows the page to tap into its components as objects. More complex interface design, such as DHTML, can be leveraged with JavaScript. JavaScript is best used in an audience that is composed of users that use a variety of Web browsers such as Netscape Navigator or Internet Explorer. VBScript is an alternative to JavaScript for an Explorer-only audience. Flash may also be used to provide artistic flair in interface design. Additionally, Java can be used to build Java applets for applications that must closely resemble the interface of desktop applications.

The client-side technologies are produced by, or work in tandem with, server-side technologies (see Figure 8.6). At the foundation of the server side is the Web server. The hands-down winner of the Web server world is the Open Source Apache Web server. Interacting with the Web server are the other server side technologies that include open source programming languages like Perl, Python, and PHP. They include higher-level application servers like Apache Tomcat (Java Server Pages and Servlets), Enhydra (XMLC and J2EE components), and Zope (Python-based environment). Also on the server side are integration platforms like Open3. The server-side technologies provide the interface to back-end systems that include databases like MySQL, PostgreSQL, or Enprise and EAs.

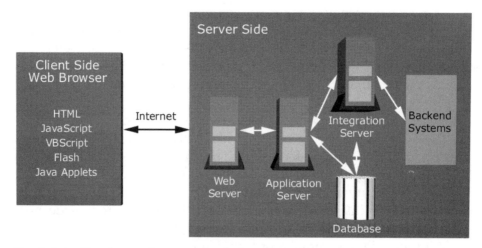

Figure 8.6   The client and server technologies of Internet e-commerce.

Open Source for Internet E-Commerce

Open source software is available in every major category of e-commerce. The enterprise may choose software built on technology with which it has experience. For example, if the enterprise has developer knowledge in Perl, it may choose Perl-based products like Akopia or Zelerate AllCommerce. This is especially important for application development systems like Zend, Zope, or Enhydra where the underlying language must be used to create the e-commerce system. It is not important with applications like Linux or Apache Web Server, unless there are plans to make changes to the code base.

Here's an overview of open source technologies that are utilized for e-commerce:

PROGRAMMING AND DATA LANGUAGES

NOTE Programming and data languages are covered further in Chapter 3, "The Foundation of Open Source Technology."

HTML. Basic language for Web page formatting.

XML. XML has several functions including content management, data warehousing, data and application integration, and a universal message format for e-commerce transactions.

XSLT. This language is primarily used in tandem with XML to enable output of data to any format. XSLT is especially useful to create dynamic interfaces, support multiple browser platforms, and for ASPs who rebrand and outsource their applications.

Perl. Perl is a popular language for building simple scripts to process requests and create Web pages. It may also be used for building complex object-oriented (OO) applications.

PHP. This language provides server-side logic for creating dynamic Web pages.

Python. Another language similar to Perl and PHP to build Web pages and scripting applications.

Java. Not open source, but it exists in the middle ground between open source and proprietary languages as a popular language for application development in the enterprise. Several open source applications utilize it and its J2EE architecture. Java and related technologies are used to build Web sites and complex OO applications.

OPERATING SYSTEMS

NOTE Operating systems are covered further in Chapter 3, "The Foundation of Open Source Technology."

Linux. The most publicly visible open source system, Linux has more than a 20 percent market share in the server industry. Known for its stability and reliability.

BSD. Operating systems built from BSD (FreeBSD and OpenBSD, for example) are known for their substantial security and reliability. Much lower market penetration than Linux but big names like Yahoo! build their multi-billion dollar infrastructure on the OS.

WEB SERVERS

NOTE Web servers are covered further in Chapter 4, "Open Source Infrastructure."

Apache Web Server. The ruler of the Web server world with an estimated 65 percent market share. It is a very reliable and robust system.

APPLICATION SERVERS

NOTE Application servers are covered further in Chapter 4, "Open Source Infrastructure."

Enhydra. A platform for developing Java-based applications utilizing a data and presentation separation system based on XMLC. Enhydra Enterprise is used for building J2EE applications and Web sites.

Exolab. A suite of Java J2EE application servers for building Java-based applications and Web sites.

JBoss. A Java J2EE application framework for Java-based applications and Web sites.

Open3. A suite of Java-based JMS-supported applications for e-business integration. In addition to the integration server, the system has several adapters to enable integration with other open source software applications.

DATABASES

> **NOTE** Databases are covered further in Chapter 4, "Open Source Infrastructure."

MySQL. A popular relational database system known for its speed and simplicity.

PostgreSQL. A solid relational database system developing a robust feature set.

Enprise. Borland's relational database system became open source in 2000. A strong asset to the Open Source database group.

BerkleyDB. A fast key-value database that is highly useful for quick access to information that is stored simply.

COMMUNICATION SYSTEMS

> **NOTE** Communication systems are covered further in Chapter 4, "Open Source Infrastructure."

Sendmail. The popular system for sending and receiving email, over 90 percent market share.

Queuemail. An alternative to sendmail for sending and receiving email.

Jabber. An instant messaging system that communicates with other IM systems like Yahoo, MSN, and AOL. Several Jabber IM clients are available for all major platforms.

ENTERPRISE APPLICATIONS

> **NOTE** Enterprise applications are covered further in Chapter 5, "Enterprise Applications."

Commerce

Akopia Interchange. A Perl-based commerce system to build online storefronts quickly. Has built-in functionality to integrate with major payment processing systems.

Zelerate AllCommerce. Another Perl-based commerce system that contains solid functionality for building the basics of an e-commerce Web site plus features for handling fulfillment across multiple locations.

EveryAuction. A Perl-based auction engine and modest infrastructure for building an e-commerce Web site.

Customer Relationship Management

OpenSourceCRM. This project currently contains one important component of CRM, Key Factor, an email campaign management package used for customer support, newsletters, and permission-based marketing.

Relata. Relata has a similar offering to OpenSourceCRM with an email management system named Relatamail, developed using PHP, Java, and XML.

Content Management

eGrail. eGrail Source is a content management system to handle digital assets like images and documents. It has built-in support for multiple users and multiple languages and is especially useful when serving content to an audience composed of a diverse and global audience.

Several of these open source software applications must be used together to build an e-commerce system. The challenge of the system, as in proprietary systems, is to have all of the components work together seamlessly. Many of the EAs like eGrail and Relata have built-in support for several databases. Open3 has several open source application adapters that will connect applications to one another through the Open3 server.

The open source community is working together to deliver comprehensive software solutions for Internet e-commerce. The benefits to the bottom line from utilizing open source software can't be ignored. These applications and several upcoming projects are changing the landscape for how e-commerce projects are implemented. Look for open source software to continue to be strong in the Internet e-commerce sector.

Wireless Mobile Commerce

Technology communication over the Internet is at the beginning of a transition. It is moving from interaction with a big box on one's desk to handheld, personal, and wireless devices that allow a person to leverage the power of the Internet anytime, anywhere. Millions of cell phones were sold in 2000 that allowed users to access the Web. Although not yet practical for anything but simple tasks, such as reading email or checking stock quotes, these phones are merging into personal digital assistants that will create a user-friendlier environment for the wireless Internet. As capable wireless devices proliferate, so will the potential for mobile commerce (m-commerce). M-commerce will lead the next generation in e-commerce.

M-commerce is more than e-commerce through a mobile device. It expands e-commerce to include initiatives tailored to a fast-paced world. For example, take MapQuest, a leading provider of geographic information on the Internet. MapQuest's most popular service is a mapping and locator service for over three million locations worldwide. A useful feature of this service is to access driving directions. The traditional way to utilize this feature is to log in through a computer at home or work, enter a starting address and destination address, and then print out the resulting map. It's quite useful, but its usefulness is being extended through wireless devices. Instead of having to remember to pregenerate a map for a trip, users can simply bring along their wireless device to assist with navigation while driving. Additionally, users can get instant information on traffic reports and nearby facilities like gas stations and restaurants. These new features provide a basis for m-commerce. For instance, users may be able to access a search engine of local advertisements that returns the best deals for shopping in their driving area.

Innovation in wireless technology will drive m-commerce. Take Bluetooth, a radio technology on an open and free wireless band that enables wireless local area networks. Devices that communicate through Bluetooth interact with one another as if physically connected together on a network. M-commerce has many possibilities with Bluetooth. For example, take the next generation retail store. When a person enters the store they use a keycard that plugs into a wireless shopping device. The keycard is similar to a credit card and contains account and payment information for the user. The user browses products through the store as usual, finding the location of specific products with their wireless device. Consumers no longer have to wander aimlessly around a store looking for assistance in helping them find a product. When they come across a product they're interested in, they scan in its UPC with their device and get more information about the product. To purchase the product, they touch a buy button on the screen and add the product to their shopping cart. When they're finished shopping, there's no waiting at the checkout line, they simply pass through a reader that validates their purchases. The wireless device records the total amount and the person is billed at a later date. The shopping experience is simplified and the store can operate more efficiently, providing items at a lower cost to the consumer.

Another use for wireless devices is to extend EAs in the enterprise for the supply and selling chain. For example, traveling personnel like salespeople and consultants can be empowered through mobile appliances. The real-time ability to access information can help manage customers and provide intelligence to enable correct decision-making while away from the home office. Instant availability of customer data, like order and pricing history, allows salespeople to tailor their approach to each specific customer while at the customer site. B2B m-commerce may entail ordering of materials or procurement of office goods while inspecting them at a source site. These examples are just the tip of the wireless iceberg in the enterprise.

Wireless and m-commerce are attractive for e-business. In the next five to ten years, wireless initiatives will become a standard part of e-business. The adoption of the technology hinges on the quality of handheld devices, applications for those devices, bandwidth, and the underlying protocols and gateways that make the communication possible.

Technology for Wireless

There are several systems that are attempting to emerge as the standard for wireless information. These include the Wireless Application Protocol (WAP) and its XML data language the WML, Japanese-based DoCoMo iMode, RIM/Blackberry (Waterloo), Palm Web Clipping, Short Message System (SMS), 3rd Generation mobile wireless (3G), and more. It's difficult to determine who will emerge victorious. However, WAP and iMode are receiving the majority of attention.

For open source projects, WAP is receiving the bulk of attention. WAP manages the communication between a wireless device and telecommunications server. WAP has been architected to work with the major world-wide networks including Code Division Multiple Access (CDMA), Time Division Multiple Access (TDMA), and the Global System for Mobile Computing (GSM). WAP is based on existing standards like the IP, Transport Layer Security (TLS), HTTP, and XML.

There are three components in the client/server architecture of WAP. The client is the mobile device and contains a WAP protocol stack and browser. The pages of a WAP-based application are cards. The cards are navigated through up and down buttons on the client device. TLS is used for basic encryption and authentication so that data and especially e-commerce transactions are transferred securely. The second component of the system is the WAP gateway, a proxy server that translates requests between HTTP and WAP. The WAP gateway also contains content encoders and decoders to transform Web content into a format that can be displayed by WAP-enabled devices. The third component of WAP, for access to content on the Internet, is the Web server.

It is important to comprehend the limitations of the client device when developing mobile applications. The most common WAP-enabled device is the wireless phone. The display on these phones is highly restricted, generally less than 100 pixels on the largest dimension. Therefore, the current generation of wireless devices will only support the simplest of applications. Fortunately, the current trend is pushing toward better resolution and more sophisticated hardware. It's predicted that in the next five to ten years, a multi-use pocket-sized device will become the norm. It will feature detachable handset for phone conversation, a foldout full-color screen for advanced computer applications, and instant access to the Internet.

Open Source for Wireless

The push toward wireless is garnering much attention in the technology world. This attention is fostering several open source projects. There are software communities like Kannel, Jwap, and Ophelia that are developing wireless application gateways. A strong open source software platform for developing wireless applications is Enhydra. The Open3 e-business integration system enables integrated data to be displayed to wireless devices. Additionally, products like Jabber IM and WAPUniverse have support for wireless systems like the Palm Pilot. The open source community is showing strong development effort in the wireless arena and can provide a basis for enterprise m-commerce initiatives.

Kannel

The name *kannel* comes from an ancient Finnish stringed instrument. This is quite different from its stringless, or wireless, software counterpart. The Kannel project (www.kannel.org) is developing Open Source software for a WAP / SMS gateway. Version 1.0 was released in January 2001, with documented support for GSM networks and designed, but untested, support for several other carrier standards. The software is written in the C language, is licensed under a BSD-style license, and is sponsored by the Finnish company, Wapit. The software currently runs on Linux, Unix, and Win32. Kannel was designed to be competitive with proprietary products by offering a fast data exchange through the WAP gateway. Kannel also operates as an SMS gateway for GSM networks.

Kannel represents a strong offering in the open source wireless community. Developers around the world are garnering attention to the project because it offers flexibility and performance that are comparable to commercial offerings. The performance is obtained through a multi-threaded architecture that supports both low-bandwidth HTTP connections and high bandwidth network connections. Kannel's goal is to emerge as the standard open source community for a WAP gateway. Its version 1.0 offering is a solid implementation for the enterprise.

Ophelia

Ophelia (www.3ui.com) is another open source project for a WAP gateway. It is in development and is progressing toward version 1.0 completion. Its 0.4 release offers a complete implementation of the WAP stack specifications 1.1, HTTP proxy server, HTTP basic authentication, and HTTP connection over SSL. It is written in the C language and supports Unix, Linux, and Win32 platforms. Its licensing is similar to BSD, but does not conform to a specific type. Ophelia has been designed to support platforms beyond WAP, such as third-generation (3G) mobile wireless and SMS.

Ophelia enables interactive Web-content over wireless devices. Its technology has budded from research at the Singapore Center for Wireless Communications. Ophelia is being delivered for implementation in the world's most populous country to the Chinese government for pushing information to wireless devices. The project is sponsored by Singapore-based 3ui Inc. (for Universal Ubiquitous Unfettered Internet). Ophelia, although still in development, offers a rich feature set and support from companies and governments in Asia, Europe, and Latin America. Its architecture to support platforms beyond WAP makes Ophelia an attractive solution for the enterprise. Look for Ophelia to emerge in 2001–2002 as a robust open source implementation for wireless gateways.

Jwap

The Java WAP gateway, Jwap (http://simplex.hemmet.chalmers.se/Jwap), is an open source implementation of a WAP gateway in Java. The project is the result of work by David Juran and Anders Mårtensson from Chalmers University of Technology in Göteborg, Sweden. Its Java-based foundation (supporting JDK V 1.1+) enables the software to run on dozens of platforms, including popular operating systems like Sun Solaris, HP UX, Linux, and Win32. Jwap is licensed under the GNU General Public License.

Jwap features connectionless WSP, a basic WML compiler, and is multi-threaded. Jwap can process simultaneous requests from clients. It currently does not support connection-oriented WSP and WML features like variables and WMLScripts. Jwap is an academic project that provides a good basis for building a Java-based WAP gateway. If your enterprise is interested in Java-based solutions, Jwap may be considered. It is not enterprise-class software, but with support from the open source community it has a strong likelihood of becoming a full-featured WAP gateway implementation.

WAPUniverse

WAPUniverse (www.wapuniverse.com) is a WAP browser for the Palm Pilot OS. The software is in development phase and is progressing toward beta availability. WAPUniverse supports a subset of WML tags, however it does not currently support WMLScripts. The goal of the project is to make the browser be WAP 1.2 compliant. The software is written in the C language and is licensed under the GNU General Public License. WAPUniverse represents a potential production offering for a customizable browser for the enterprise.

Private Network E-Commerce

E-commerce does not necessarily need to be conducted over the Internet. Private networks, like some corporate extranets, may leverage the technology of the Internet but not be physically connected to it. Other technologies, like virtual private networks (VPNs), employ the Internet through secure channels. The reasons for using a private network may include security considerations, the need for a highly reliable and dedicated connection, and the ability to customize the system.

Electronic Data Interchange (EDI) transactions are conducted over private value-added networks (VANs). Private networks may utilize the same features of the Internet, and therefore the software technology will be the same. The difference is in the underlying connections and hardware infrastructure of the system. Private networks may be used in a B2B system where a dedicated connection is given to highly important partners. The dedicated private network will not typically be used for B2C e-commerce. Private networks are to be considered when there are strong requirements for security, customization, and always-on and accessible reliability.

Technology Objectives for E-Commerce

Our purpose is to apply open source software to meet the technological demands of a robust e-commerce system. To architect enterprise-class e-commerce solutions based on open source requires that the following objectives be addressed:

- Customer centric and user-friendly
- Support for multiple platforms
- Dynamic and rebrandable interface
- Secure and reliable
- Integrated with other technology

Customer-Centric and User-Friendly

E-commerce applications must consider the five components of the customer-centric model: personalized service; right, rapid service; self-service; wide selection; and convenience. The trend in e-commerce applications is to embody these components into a user-friendly interface. The interface and platform of choice is the Web browser.

Putting all of these components together into a highly responsive system is necessary to be customer-centric. The obvious important objective is in the user interface, but this is the easiest part to get right. To deliver personalized service requires integration with technology that can manage user interaction on a one-on-one basis such as CRM software like OpenSource-CRM and Relata. To deliver right, rapid service requires that your Web application be integrated with inventory and fulfillment systems like Zelerate AllCommerce. Self-service is enabled through good design, great information, and expertise in the products sold by the enterprise. Content management systems like eGrail or Apache Jetspeed will assist in organizing and delivering information to the user. Wide selection is also dependent on the enterprise's ability to establish partnerships and integrate with business partners. Here an integration platform like Open3 or B2B frameworks like RosettaNet or ebXML provide the basis for connection to partners. Finally, convenience is enabled through the smooth working of all aspects of the system.

Chapter 9, "Open Source Technology Solutions for E-Business," provides a sample scenario for building a customer-centric e-commerce system.

Support for Multiple Platforms

In a world of diverse computing environments and a Web-based business that expands the globe, support for multiple platforms is essential. The Web browser is the application of choice for one important reason; it works on all major platforms. Windows, Mac, Linux, Unix, and several mobile platforms have Web browsers.

To reach the widest audience, Web application design must utilize technology supported by the majority of vendors. At the most basic level, this is simple plain text HTML. Full HTML and JavaScript pages will work on most wire-based platforms. To support many wireless platforms, the pages must be able to be converted to WML. Products like eGrail and XML/XSLT have the ability to output documents in all major formats. E-commerce applications will reach the broadest audience possible by planning for broad platform support in the early design of the system.

Dynamic and Rebrandable Interface

The interface is how the world interacts with your e-commerce application. A dynamic interface is one that can change without inordinate difficulty. There are several benefits to a dynamic interface. These benefits include the flexibility to support multiple platforms and to create applications with a novel look and feel that keep customers coming back. In particular, ASPs are well served to develop rebrandable interfaces. ASPs deliver specific applications to various businesses and consumers. Major customers, like Fortune 500 or Global 2000 companies, will often have specific requirements for the look and feel of the application. A rebrandable interface ensures that this will be a simple task.

The trend in e-commerce technology for dynamic interfaces is to separate data from presentation. Business logic, encapsulated in its own modules, creates data that are generally output in XML format. An XSLT stylesheet is then applied to the XML data to generate presentation in many possible formats, including HTML and WML. Therefore, if the system is designed with distinct data and presentation layers, multiple interfaces can be generated for multiple platforms. The initial investment in development time to create this system is higher than one built on an architecture without separate layers. However, the long-term savings from a more maintainable and flexible system far outweigh the initial expenditure.

Secure and Reliable

Despite millions of successful transactions, the number one fear of new Internet shoppers is using their credit card online. The SSL provides encryption and authentication between a user's Web browser and the Web server. Apache Web Server has strong support for secure communication. However, security must also be addressed on back-end systems and in B2B transactions. Encryption and authentication of all data accessible by the public is essential. The ability to mitigate shoppers' fears with solid technology is crucial to widening the acceptance of e-commerce.

Security ensures that those who should have access to information will be the only parties to handle it. Reliability ensures that those with proper permission do indeed have access. Reliability is essential along every point in the system. E-commerce is expected to run 24 hours a day, seven days a week—so must the hardware and software technology powering it.

Reliability and security are strong in solid open source software. The open nature of the software has the tendency to eliminate a higher percentage of the bugs and flaws. Proprietary software is tested in-house by a small quality assurance team. Some firms also have limited trials for field testing before shipping the software to the public. More often than not, proprietary systems ship without adequate testing for security and reliability. Open source begins field testing early in its development life-cycle and is constantly poked and prodded by the best developers around the world.

Integrated with Other Technology

Integration is a fundamental objective to deliver a customer-centric e-commerce system. Technology used to build the e-commerce software infrastructure must be able to communicate with each other and with back-end systems. Integrated solutions must be included in the system architecture from the moment of conception. Many of the Open Source applications, like their proprietary counterparts, have limited support for integration with other systems. The most frequently integrated application is the database. To support integration for all applications requires an integration middleware system. As described in Chapter 6, "Enterprise Application Integration," there are multiple ways to implement integration. Once integrated, the e-commerce system becomes a very robust tool for the enterprise.

Summary

Solid enterprise solutions for e-commerce can be built completely or primarily with open source software. Strong open source applications deliver the wide-feature set demanded by e-commerce. Its usage enables the enterprise to reap substantial benefits like cost savings in both the short term and long term, and more reliable, secure, and maintainable systems. A strategy based on strong technology that is combined with sound business acumen and customer-centric design will result in a successful e-commerce initiative. It makes business sense to pursue e-commerce and to pursue it with open source.

This chapter and previous chapters have detailed the five main components of an e-business: enterprise applications, enterprise application integration, B2B integration, B2B e-commerce, and B2C e-commerce. It is the goal of the modern enterprise to engage these components to its greatest advantage. However, construction of these components in the most effective manner is not a simple process. The following chapter presents a fictional case study that guides a company through its growth from a Tier 0 to Tier 5 enterprise. The case study is designed to provide an organized framework for all businesses in evaluating e-business strategy and the implementation of the underlying technology.

Open Source Technology Solutions for E-Business

E-business requires sophisticated planning and effort. These activities must include developing the business case, customer-centric focus, and a solid and robust technological solution. E-business must leverage the new frontiers that technology provides. These benefits include efficiency, real-time communication, partnerships without boundaries, and enhanced customer service. E-business is real business and an essential component for the modern enterprise.

There are five distinct, but interconnected, areas of e-business: enterprise applications (EAs), enterprise application integration (EAI), business-to-business integration (B2Bi), business-to-business (B2B) e-commerce, and business-to-consumer (B2C) e-commerce. In previous chapters, we presented each of these areas in detail and discussed how they fit into the total e-business solution. We also presented numerous open source software applications that can be utilized to build a secure, reliable, robust, and cost-effective technology infrastructure. This chapter provides a high-level formula for applying open source software to the five areas of e-business. To demonstrate the techniques more easily, sample scenarios are presented for each individual area.

Open Source at Its Best

Open source solutions within the traditional enterprise environment are growing. To demonstrate all the facets where open source products and platforms can assist within your computing environment, we will start with a small company and step through its growth. This company is fictional and provided for demonstration purposes to show the benefits that various open source solutions can provide. The company utilizes open source to build upon its enterprise software infrastructure. By no means should a company scrap everything with the hopes of re-implementing everything using open source technology. Unless the current software technology infrastructure is completely hopeless, it is more prudent to develop a roadmap to integrate open source software with existing technology.

Company Background

The company we're examining is called Smith Electrical Supply. This company manufactures and assembles various electrical components and sells them to distributors and retailers in the United States. It is a medium-size company with revenues under five million dollars a year. It has one office to handle the day-to-day operations of the business and a small assembly plant. The staff consists of about 40 plant personnel and an office staff of ten.

Just as with any business, Smith is required to interact with various external buyers and suppliers. The company purchases certain components and materials from several other companies. The office staff at Smith creates a 200-page catalog once a year. This catalog is dispersed to all of the distributors and retailers around the United States. These partners then phone, fax, or mail orders to the office.

Smith Electrical's current computer environment is fairly simple. It has standard desktop PCs for the office staff, a Microsoft Windows NT Server, and an IBM AS/400. All the desktop machines currently use the Microsoft Windows platform. A standard accounting application for the company is located on the NT server. The IBM server contains a custom created order processing system.

Smith Electrical has invested a great deal of money and effort into the creation of the order processing system. This custom application uses a DB2 database on the AS/400 (DB2/400). Plant personnel have access to orders from the order processing system, so they may package and send the requested items. This custom system has been tailored to the Smith business and the company has no desire to upgrade it at this time.

The average order requires a minimum of four days to process from the time the order is taken until the time the order can be shipped. Occasionally, the order can take up to thirty days before it may be shipped. The order is taken by hand as it is received. The accounting system is used to check the customer's account, to ensure it is not overdue and to obtain the shipping information. The order is entered into the order processing system where plant personnel can begin processing it. Currently, the inventory is not maintained or tracked by any formalized process or computer program. The plant managers maintain rough estimates, but occasionally things are forgotten. Once the ordered materials are available and assembled, the items are packaged and sent to the customer.

Smith's initial e-business initiatives are just beginning. As shown in Figure 9.1, the company currently has only some of the necessary infrastructure but has potential to grow. With only a little work, it can greatly optimize its current operations. Careful planning and some initiative will

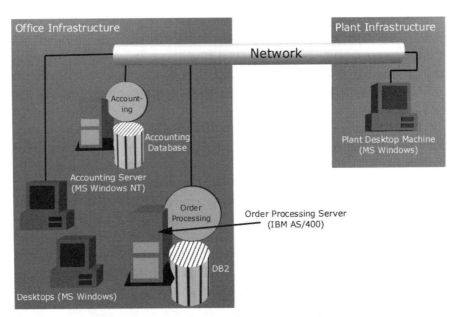

Figure 9.1   Smith Electrical Supply's initial computing environment.

permit the company to capitalize on the growing open source solution set and become an efficient e-business.

Phase 1: Building an Enterprise Application Infrastructure

The Smith company is already beyond the Tier 0 status. It uses computers to assist in its current operations assuring at least a Tier 1 classification. The office uses a computer program to handle the accounting, and the order processing system is definitely a step in the right direction. Even with these systems, however, problems are apparent.

To secure a Tier 1 status and to advance the business, Smith must continue to improve its computing environment. At this stage, enhancements to the infrastructure are needed. To capitalize on the available manpower, it must create a more efficient system. It must use technology to create an e-business infrastructure that can help the company grow.

The current Smith computing system is lacking some basic requirements to compete in the current market. The company has a basic network in the office with an access terminal in the assembly plant, but it has no Internet access or email system. Because no email system exists, nearly all processes require exchanging paper. Any paper process that can be made electronic is almost always a step toward efficiency.

The company should also have applications for each of its standard operational departments. Even though it is still a relatively small operation, things are being overlooked. Exact inventory tracking is difficult given the current manual system. This process can be enhanced with the use of an inventory application.

There is one problem that may be standing in the way of these enhancements. Perhaps the Smith management has already noticed the need for enhanced computer systems but lacks the knowledge to implement the necessary solutions. This can be a serious problem for smaller companies creating electronic systems within their enterprise. At this stage, the company has two choices. It may either use outside assistance in the form of consultants or it may directly hire a skilled IT employee. Either selection is suitable, but it would be wise to find an IT person to at least work on a part-time basis if the company plans to use technology for its benefit.

Business Case

Most of the business cases at this level are easy to analyze. The resolution of each problem will help to make the company more efficient. The extent to which this efficiency will actually help the bottom line is important to understand. Rational justifications of the costs of each enhancement must be found before any project is undertaken.

The implementation of an email system will help the operations of the company in many areas. The current ordering process requires that each customer account be verified before an order can be entered into the system. This means that a paper order must be given to accounting and then again transferred to order entry personnel. Employees will no longer be required to transfer a paper order manually between personnel. The order can be taken and simply emailed to accounting. Once verified, it can be forwarded to the appropriate party for processing. Used properly, an electronic trail of the order will exist. No longer will the paper order be lost in a stack on a desk.

The addition of an Internet connection enables the email system to become even more beneficial. Customers are given an additional option for placing orders. These orders can easily be checked and processed. Electronic orders can usually be processed more quickly than handwritten or paper orders. The increased efficiency will reduce the average order time and help to reduce mistakes made during the order entry process. These reductions in mistakes will help to decrease the number of orders that are delayed.

The Internet will not only help Smith to handle customer orders better, it will also provide a valuable tool commonplace in today's business setting. The Internet can be used to research competitors and may give the company insight into how better to serve their customers. Given the current e-marketplace, Smith can also expect to place orders from various vendors online and track those orders electronically.

An inventory system is an obvious step for Smith management. The implementation of an inventory system will reduce the mistakes made by plant managers using the manual process. The current inventory of parts and assembled components at any time can be easily determined. Knowing how much of a particular component is available will make ordering additional components more precise. The managers can analyze the inventory data along with the customer order data to determine when to increase or decrease stock before it becomes a problem. The likelihood of running out of an item unexpectedly will be reduced.

The current staff at Smith does not have the necessary computer skills to easily implement all of the required solutions. Since selecting the wrong technology or possibly destroying the current system will potentially cost the company a great deal of money, some outside help is required. The company has two choices, either of which is appropriate for its situation. It can either find a competent consulting company that it can establish a relationship with or it can attempt to hire a capable IT employee. Regardless of which is chosen, expertise is a necessity.

REQUIREMENTS SUMMARY

A secure network capable of accessing the Internet. The connection will be separated from other systems so it can easily be changed as the company grows.

The company must find either a consulting firm or an individual that is capable of installing and setting up the required solutions. The company or individual must be available after the installation, in case of problems or for further assistance.

A company-wide email system that is both internal and capable of sending and receiving email across the Internet. The system must be able to grow with the company.

The company's inventory system must be able to handle all the current needs of the company including tracking and reporting on all the components and assembled products sold and used by the company. This system must provide some means of external access, whether this access is through an API or directly through a database. The system must either be capable of expansion as the business grows or replacement (for example, by transferring the data to a new system).

Open Source Formula

Smith Electrical Supply is still relatively small and enjoys the luxury of selecting the products it wants to use. All of the listed requirements can be solved using open source software products. The right consultants or IT employees will result in an effective solution. The quality advancement of the open source products will enable a strong solution for the given scenario.

Given the list of tasks to complete, the company first looks into obtaining Internet connectivity. The actual type of connection selected is beyond the scope of this book, but typical connection types include DSL, ISDN, or a T1. Regardless of the type of connection, the business will typically be left with a router or modem that can be used to provide the local connection to the ISP.

Depending on the type of hardware provided to the company by the ISP, a firewall may be required to deliver a secure connection. If the device is a router, occasionally it will also provide firewall features. For Smith Electrical, the device is a router and does not provide firewall features. It is provided with certain IP addresses and other gateway and DNS information for configuration purposes.

Since the router does not provide such services, a firewall is required. A basic firewall design will be used, but the same hardware and software components can be used to create complicated and robust standard firewall and Demilitarized Zone (DMZ) network configurations. In reality, a company should research the different network designs and select one that works for its enterprise. The best open source configuration for a company this size uses a single machine with either Linux or OpenBSD installed. OpenBSD is the more secure OS, but Linux has more support and has a wider consultant knowledge base. Smith Electrical chooses Linux because its recently hired employee is more familiar with it.

The decision of how to handle email is also relatively complicated. Depending on the ISP being used, it may provide some email services. Most ISP services will typically limit the number of accounts allowed, the size of mail, and various other features of the service. Depending on company needs, this service may be usable. Smith has decided to handle its own email server. It has decided to purchase a domain name and has worked with the ISP to set up the necessary name server information to make this possible. Sendmail will be used as the email server or mail transport agent (MTA) on a Linux installation. Other mail servers could be used, but sendmail is feature rich and has become a standard.

The company can utilize the open source Zelerate AllCommerce Inventory Manager to maintain detailed inventory information. The Inventory Manager permits Smith's electrical components to be tracked through information like brand name, item description, shipping weight, and availability status. The system also provides the products to be searched by product ID and keywords. The Inventory Manager enables access by human operators through a Web-based interface that can also be displayed on wireless Web devices. Mobile access is highly useful for those pulling and stocking items. The application also stores its information in ODBC databases, such as MySQL, and can be integrated with external systems.

REQUIRED MATERIALS

- (1) ISP-supplied router.

- (3) Intel-based servers: (high-end) one of the systems with dual processors minimum PIII 500mhz CPU and 256 MB RAM; (mid-grade) one of the systems with a single processor minimum PIII 500mhz CPU and 128 MB RAM; and (low-end) one of the systems with a single processor minimum Pentium 100mhz CPU and 16 MB RAM.

- (3) Linux installations on each of the machines.

- (1) Open source firewall installation on the low-end machine (using ipchains, ipfwadm, or some other Linux firewall software).

- (1) Sendmail installation on the mid-grade machine.

- (1) Zelerate AllCommerce installation on the high-end machine.

- (1) MySQL installation on the high-end machine.

System Setup and Installation

Using the prescribed open source formula the installation is relatively simple for an employee or consultant with the proper skill set. The current company environment will likely pose no problems during the installation and setup phase. Most of the given requirements also do not require high performance hardware components, therefore reducing the overall cost and increasing the potential return on investment.

At this stage in the company's growth, no real test or production environments exist to contend with. Only two systems are in the current scheme that should not suffer a great amount of downtime: the order processing system and the accounting system. These systems will not pose a problem since most of the changes will occur on new hardware and will create functionality that previously did not exist. These factors eliminate the need for a test and production environment at this stage. The systems can be installed and configured separate from the current operations. Once everything has been tested, the existing Smith computer systems can be tied into the new network.

Once the Internet connectivity is established, the firewall and email server should take one skilled person less than a week to set up and install. The inventory management system is simple to set up, however the time-consuming task is populating the system with item and stock information. Since the requirements call for expandability, it is best to use separate machines for each of the systems. This allows for changes to any of the systems to be made with a lower risk factor for corrupting the other applications. The price of hardware components is low compared to the benefits of having each system separated. The firewall can use relatively low-end equipment, possibly hardware that already exists in the office. The send-mail server can use a mid-grade hardware setup since it does not have a high user load at this time. The inventory system should use a slightly higher class of equipment, since the system must be able to handle current needs with the expectation of some growth. The system can be configured as shown in Figure 9.2.

The last step for this project involves project completion or finalization. The employees must be trained to use the new systems. Training material may be required for reference until the employees are familiar with the proper usage of the software. Beyond the basic usage training, it is a good idea to document the entire installation. This information can be used in

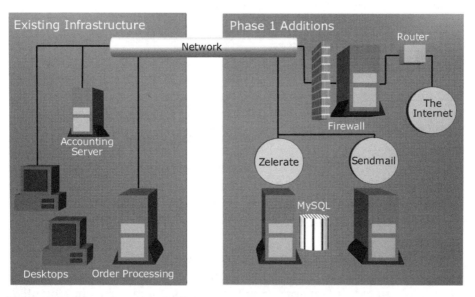

Figure 9.2 Phase 1 system architecture.

the future if any problems arise or if similar systems need to be built. Maintenance procedures must also be created. For this phase, the procedures consist of standard system backups for the inventory, order processing, and accounting systems. The email system should also be backed up periodically if the employees use email clients that maintain the user mailboxes within the server. One part-time individual can handle all the system maintenance tasks. Beyond these backups and basic system tuning, the programs should operate without intervention.

Results

The Smith Electrical Supply solution set provides all the necessary components to create the infrastructure for a basic e-business. Technology has been applied to all of the obvious business components within their enterprise. The operations and maintenance of the applications are trivial at this stage and require only periodic backups.

Upon completion of this phase, the business has a cluster of machines that provides the core functionality of the business along with a functional network. The network provides an email system and an Internet connection to all networked machines. Each of the installed applications will help the organization run in a more efficient manner. Less paper shuffling will help Smith process orders more quickly with fewer mistakes. This will provide the e-business strategy with the technology infrastructure to increase customer satisfaction and generate additional sales.

Phase 2: An Open Source EAI Solution

Maintaining a Tier 1 status may have been fine in the past, but it will take more before Smith can dominate the market. The steps implemented in Phase 1 created several stand-alone applications that work well but do not work together. To maximize the benefits of the technology, these processes must be integrated. Any manual task for which there is a business case to be automated must be automated. Automation permits the employees to focus on more important tasks within the business like generating revenues and delighting customers.

Integrating the current systems will move the company into either a Tier 2 or Tier 3 classification. The exact classification will depend on how the systems are integrated. If "one-off" point-to-point solutions are implemented, then Smith will be at the Tier 2 level. Point-to-point is not an optimal solution and does not provide a solid basis for technology growth. The company will likely need to re-integrate or integrate the point-to-point solutions at some point in the future. With careful planning, however, Smith can bypass Tier 2 and move directly into Tier 3. This tier is reachable if the integration solution that is utilized provides the features necessary to expand and change as the company grows. Absence of a flexible architecture will require significant time and effort in expanding the existing systems to meet the needs of the marketplace.

The current Smith computing environment requires further optimization. Employees must still transfer information between personnel. Some of these processes, shown in Figure 9.3, must be automated. In the current system, a single order must be received and checked by at least three people before it can be entered into the order system. Once it is entered, the plant must bundle the materials and the inventory must be updated to reflect the items that have been sold. After the plant is finished with the package, shipping information must be obtained from the accounting system. This system is will create the shipping labels and packing slips that are sent with the package. Even with the enhancements done for phase one, several manual steps remain where mistakes could be made.

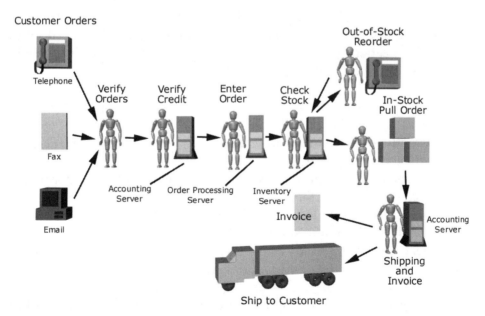

Figure 9.3 Smith Electrical Supply's ordering process.

This step from Tier 1 to Tier 3 is an ordeal. Often the current systems are uprooted and possibly replaced. Enhancements to various applications may also be done. Outside help may be required depending on the skills and qualifications of the IT staff that works for Smith. These tasks can be costly, but it is important to plan carefully and solve the problem correctly the first time. Trial and error on systems that the business relies upon for day-to-day operations is dangerous.

Business Case

Developing the business case for tasks at this level is important. Integration projects of any kind can be costly and potentially have an impact on all systems within the enterprise environment. The phase one enhancements showed clearly that the changes made would beneficially have an impact on the operations of the business. As the company grows, however, the cost to implement changes also grows. To prevent costly mistakes, estimates must be made for the business enhancements that will be achieved by any integration effort. These estimates can be used to determine which project should be done and to judge the successfulness of individual tasks.

The main justification for any of the Smith enhancements involves improved efficiency. This greater efficiency will reduce the order processing time from the current average of four days to potentially one day. Smith has done research and found that it could possibly persuade certain competitors' customers to purchase from Smith if it can handle two-day order deliveries. Neither Smith nor its competitors can currently do this. Minor optimizations within the company can help some, but a leap in efficiency is required to process orders quickly and consistently.

To reduce the order processing timeframe, the processes must be optimized. This will require integration and interaction between all of the systems currently involved in the order process chain. For optimum efficiency, orders must be entered into the computer system as soon as they are received. The new system must be able to verify the account information automatically and check the order for errors. Once verified, the new system should also be able to update the order processing system instantly. Orders can be noticed almost immediately as they are received. The plant personnel can enter into the system each order as it is filled, allowing for the automatic generation of the shipping material.

This approach allows for human interaction where it is required but removes this interaction when unnecessary. The new system will make the activities of taking an order, filling it, and shipping it a near real-time process. Only the problem orders will take longer than one day to process. Also, the possibility of these problems has been greatly reduced. The employees can focus on other tasks, rather than shuffling paper and checking orders. The Smith management determines that the cost of implementing these integration projects is less than the increase in income that can be achieved through new customers.

REQUIREMENTS SUMMARY

Integration platform that is highly expandable and maintainable. This platform must allow for the encapsulation of various business logic and data transformation rules. The platform must also offer tools and adapters that will decrease the installation and potential development effort that may be required.

As orders are received, they must be immediately entered into the computer system. The system must handle the processing of standard orders and deliver problematic orders to the appropriate personnel for special processing.

The account information for each order must be validated to ensure that the account is not extremely past due. Credit limits will be established and may be changed in the future. These limits may also vary between customers. The system must notify the appropriate personnel when problematic accounts are found.

The order must be inserted into the order entry system only after the customer account has been checked. Only those customers with adequate credit will have their orders placed into the system.

The new system must verify the necessary inventory and notify plant personnel if inventory of a particular item is low. The inventory limits and the inventory items may change in the future.

Plant personnel must be able to notify the system that an order has been filled. This notification will automatically update the customer's account, update the inventory, print shipping information, and print any packing slips that are required.

Open Source Formula

This phase of computer enhancements deals with integration. A single product used to create the necessary framework can handle all of the integration tasks. Several open source products exist that could be used for this purpose, and it depends on the enterprise environment as to which one should be selected. Each of these products creates the necessary architecture to integrate the existing applications easily and allow for future enhancements as the company grows.

Smith Electrical is not a software development company and does not have a large IT staff capable of implementing large integration solutions. Smith also has little interest in developing internal software solutions. For Smith, the best solution is one that is easily installable and has components to assist in the connection of applications with only minor development.

A message broker is the best possible tool set for this scenario. It easily provides the necessary adapters and server features to implement and maintain the required integration projects. Various application servers may be used, but most of the available open source and proprietary products are geared toward creating and maintaining Web sites. Smith currently sees no need for a complicated Web site and, therefore, does not need this functionality yet. EJB-style application servers could be used, but they often lack the integration tools available with message brokering products. The business environment and enterprise computing goals within Smith require the features of a messaging platform, preferably with message brokering capabilities, such as the Open3 E-Business Integration Server product.

REQUIRED MATERIALS

- (3) Intel-based servers: systems with dual processors minimum PIII 500mhz CPU and 256 MB RAM (integration test, integration production, and inventory test).

- (3) Linux installations on each of the machines.

- (2) Open3 E-Business Integration Server installation (one for test and one for production).

- (1) Zelerate AllCommerce installation (for the inventory test environment).

- (1) MySQL installation (for the inventory test environment).

System Setup and Installation

An integration task of this magnitude must be implemented carefully. The systems being integrated involve applications within the enterprise required by the company for day-to-day business. Interruptions in service for any of these systems will prove costly. For this reason, the most important step in the integration phase is the planning step.

The staff must determine early in the integration process how it will proceed with the actual integration effort. Often, it is wise to outsource most of the integration tasks. Enterprise-class integration architecture and setup is a complex task that requires expertise in many disciplines. Outsourcing the integration work permits Smith Electrical to maintain staff capable of making minor changes and maintaining the integrated systems. A full development effort or installation effort of this magnitude is required occasionally, and thus it is not cost-effective to hire full-time employees to handle all of the tasks. It is important, however, that the internal staff understands what the consultants are doing. Therefore, a consulting company must be chosen that employs a methodology to work closely with the employees. This ensures that the end solution is maintainable by the internal staff, requiring outside assistance only under extreme situations.

Smith Electrical currently has only one computing environment established, a production environment, which it uses to handle the day-to-day operations of the business. These systems must not be used to test against or to try new technology. The IT staff at Smith must establish an additional test environment. This secondary environment matches as closely as is practical the production environment. Usually, this involves the replication of the machines, databases, and software instances. The data within the test environment are sampled from the production data set. Occasionally, the entire production data set is copied to the test area.

Documentation must be ready for the consultants prior to arrival. All of the systems within the enterprise are documented. Because Smith extended the necessary effort during phase one, documentation of the existing applications is ready. Documentation must also be accumulated on the current data requirements and capabilities of each system within the problem domain. Items such as the current data formats and the expected data flows must be outlined. This information will be used to determine what systems can be integrated and how to proceed with that integration. These documents, along with the basic requirements, are best made available before consultants are brought in to assist.

Consultants are deployed once the environment and documentation is available to proceed with the actual implementation. Certain companies may want to bring in consultants to assist with the earlier steps, but the Smith Electrical Supply IT staff contains personnel capable of handling these preparatory tasks.

Each of the systems can be integrated one at a time in the test environment until the entire solution is available. The starting point is not extremely important, but often it is best to start with the most difficult items first, thereby decreasing the potential risk of pursuing a solution that is unable to be implemented. The Open3 server will be used as the integration server. It provides a multi-hub, multi-spoke architecture that permits highly flexible integration solutions. Adapters exist for the accounting and order processing systems through each of the applications' database. This provides a data-level solution, which will work for the applications being integrated. The DB2 system can be reached through several means including IBM's DB2 Connect or a third party DRDA gateway. The Open3/Zelerate AllCommerce adapter is used for the inventory system. The adapter enables the input and extraction of information between the inventory management system and other enterprise applications attached to the Open3 integration system.

Beyond the adapters, the integration project also has various rules and data transformation requirements. The data transformations are established by creating XSL stylesheets used to translate one data message into another. These stylesheets can also be used to call business logic elements embedded in the server architecture. These elements can handle the more complicated error checking and limit validations. If problems are found, the server can be set up to send email to various employees so the problem can be handled further.

After all of the components are integrated and everything is thoroughly tested, the solution is ready for the production environment. The new enterprise system architecture is shown in Figure 9.4. Again, the staff must be trained to use the new systems and reference documentation created for all facets of the project. Maintenance of this system should not require significant handholding. The IT personnel will continue to backup all the key components of the system. Minor changes to the server or other components can be tested in the test environment and then implemented in the production environment.

Results

The new integrated environment allows Smith employees to operate more efficiently. The sales staff is able to focus on sales rather than track orders and ensure an order is actually filled and delivered. The accounting personnel are no longer required to verify every order, and only problem accounts are brought to their attention. Problems are now found before

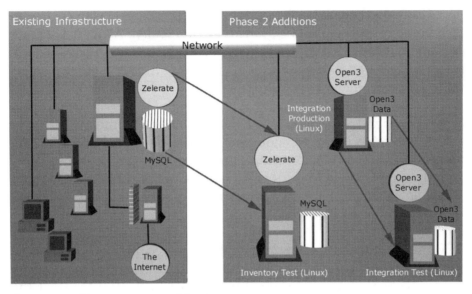

Figure 9.4 Phase 2 system architecture.

they become serious. The entire enterprise operates more smoothly, focusing on tasks that bring in new revenues and help the company grow.

The new environment also better enables Smith Electrical to analyze customer patterns and change to meet customer demands. Management can use the integrated system to create new applications or to generate various reports based on the newly available enterprise data. This allows them to discover potential patterns or problems within the company. Smith personnel can focus on improving the customer experience rather than spending their hours just to fill orders.

Phase 3: Connecting with Partners

The current computer system at Smith Electrical operates efficiently within the confines of the enterprise environment. This, however, does not mean that Smith should stop looking to improve its business operations. It is currently at a Tier 3 level of enterprise computing, but the changes made thus far have allowed Smith to increase in revenues and size. A Tier 3 status may be sufficient for its industry, but companies that do not wish to be overtaken by competitors should always look for ways to improve current operations.

The distinction between a Tier 3 and Tier 4 classification is the extent to which the company computing systems are integrated. A Tier 3 company has its internal systems completely integrated, which Smith currently does. To reach a Tier 4 status, companies begin to look outside of their own enterprise to further optimize business operations.

Smith Electrical has decided to examine its current operational environment to determine if any technological enhancements are suitable. Few optimizations are available within the enterprise, but enhancements within the supply chain or sales chain may be options. The current environment is shown in Figure 9.5. Both the suppliers and sales partners should be examined to see where integration options might exist.

Since the addition of the Internet in phase one, Smith has begun to see the power of placing orders electronically. Most of the orders to suppliers are now made through either email or Internet Web sites. Many of the orders that Smith receives from customers are also by way of email orders. A number of the suppliers offer automated ordering methods including EDI and Internet communication procedures. Inter-enterprise integration

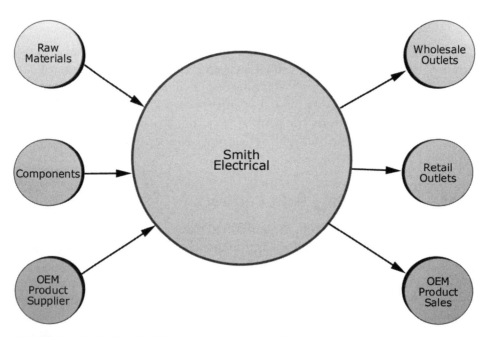

Figure 9.5 Smith Electrical Supply's sales and supply chain.

will help Smith Electrical further serve the needs of its customers and move the company into a Tier 4 status.

Business Case

What is gained by integrating with outside companies? For Smith, integration with suppliers allows them to react to customer needs more quickly. Integration with customers offers the customers another ordering option. This is an option that must be explored.

Although similar, integration with suppliers and integration with customers achieves two slightly different goals. Although both will benefit the customer, the primary goal of the supply chain integration is to simplify the ordering process. Orders can be automatically placed with suppliers as inventory runs low. Automated systems are also typically set up to invoice, handle payment notifications, and transmit shipment information automatically. All of this information can be automatically tied into the current Smith computer system. This greatly reduces the amount of data that has to be entered and tracked manually. Often the data would not even be available with the manual system.

The business case for supply chain optimization can be made by looking at the reduction in cost and increase in efficiency of the ordering process. Smith will be able to manage inventory more closely. Many of the accounts deliverable can also be handled automatically. The system will create fewer errors from suppliers. Employees can also be tasked with more important responsibilities. This reduction in overall operating cost will be passed on to the customer in the form of lower prices, beating any other supplier in the industry and potentially improving market share.

The customer integration offering is essentially a bonus for Smith Electrical. Because Smith is a wholesaler, it can offer integration scenarios to their customers. The software and process required to integrate the supply chain can be used to integrate the sales chain. Since the same technology is used, it does not cost that much more to offer the service to customers who are interested. This simply offers more options to customers and allows them to integrate their supply chain. Integration with a customer can also increase loyalty since the software creates a link that becomes essential for both businesses to operate efficiently.

The development of the supply-side and sales-side integration should only be pursued if Smith can find enough benefit to outweigh the cost of the project. The reduction in cost and the increase in customer loyalty can be factored into this equation. Smith can also count on increasing the number of customers it will be able to server, since it will be the only supplier that offers direct integration with its customers. The work required will likely be more than what was required for phase two, but the results will help Smith Electrical become the dominant player in its industry.

REQUIREMENTS SUMMARY

The B2B integration platform must be scalable and able to connect with the internal enterprise environment. The platform must support the ability for new businesses to connect to it. It is also essential that Smith can leverage the information from the B2B platform to its internal applications.

The platform must be able to integrate with suppliers already using EDI and XML transmission methods. Many companies have already invested heavily in technology for B2B and will be reluctant to spend more to connect to the system. Providing compatibility for these partners will be essential for the success of the site.

The platform must be able to communicate with clients using XML transmission methods. For the business partners that don't have a B2B infrastructure, Smith will standardize on XML messaging.

The platform should be relatively low cost to allow customers and other suppliers the ability to use similar technology to integrate directly with Smith. Selling the usage of the system to business partners is difficult enough without a huge investment requirement on the partner's end. A low cost system is better suited for appealing to the partners.

Open Source Formula

The primary component used for B2B-style integration is a common messaging method using agreed upon message formats. The standard in the past has been to use EDI messages typically transmitted through VAN services. A new standard is beginning to evolve which uses XML messages transmitted across the Internet using secure connections. The platform used for Smith must be able to handle both of these situations to connect with suppliers and customers.

Smith Electrical is already using most of technology required for this phase. It needs to only apply that technology in a slightly different manner.

The Open3 integration server product can be used to communicate using EDI and it natively communicates using XML. Because it is open source, those customers and suppliers that currently have no means to communicate electronically can use the same solution. Using technology that Smith is already familiar with will simplify the integration process.

Beyond the integration server, Smith will also set up a slightly more complicated but robust network design. Integrating with external entities in an extranet setting presents new security problems that must be considered before the project is even started. The current network environment uses one firewall to securely allow standard Internet traffic initiated from the office personnel. This network needs to be modified to allow external programs access to the integration platform safely. Several firewall and security configurations exist that should be examined. An in-depth discussion of the methods and procedures used to establish secure networks are beyond the scope of this book, so we will simply assume that more firewalls and DMZ will be required.

REQUIRED MATERIALS

- Some additional networking and firewall equipment.
- (3) Intel-based servers: systems with dual processors minimum PIII 500mhz CPU and 256 MB RAM (two for production and one for test).
- (3) Linux installations on each of the machines.
- (3) Open3 E-Business Integration Server installation on each of the machines.

System Setup and Installation

Integration with external organizations is usually more difficult than internal integration projects. Even when internal projects cut across departmental boundaries, at least the departments are within the same enterprise. When dealing with outside companies, the task of coordinating or persuading change can quickly become a daunting task. Some of this complication can be reduced by using outside consultants that have implemented similar projects.

Before beginning the project, the management at Smith must come to terms with the management of the outside companies and establish ground rules for conducting trade. The timeline for the project must be clearly outlined and agreed upon. Contact personnel from each company must be determined. All parties involved must understand any software installation or testing procedures that will be required. The trading partners must agree on a unified document exchange such as XML documents conforming to DTDs from XML.org. It may also be wise to establish a close relationship with one company to work with while creating the initial integration scenario. This will reduce the exposure and the amount of coordination that is required.

The next step in the installation of the software is to create the new network. Linux configured machines can be used that are similar to the firewall that was created during phase one. If this is not desired, then specialized firewall machines can be purchased to ease the installation. Typically, the internal network will still use a single firewall for Internet access. The software that will be accessed by external companies will be installed on machines that are separate from the internal machines. These machines will usually exist in a DMZ that is separated via firewalls from both the external network (the Internet) and the internal network.

This project also requires a vast amount of changes in the internal integration configuration. New rules and data transformations will be required. Various business processes need to be established to handle the new data that will be available once the project is completed. Most of this work can be done in parallel with the network setup and connection testing. The integration team should obtain the data layouts from the outside companies. These will be in the form of EDI mappings or XML schemas and DTDs. These layouts create the document format for the B2B applications.

Once the network is established, the company can begin creating a communication channel with one of the external companies. The test environment is used for the testing and installation phase of this project. For EDI channels, typically the communication channel will be through a Value Added Network (VAN) or via a direct connection to the external company. A VAN is somewhat like an email system, in that it securely handles the transmission of messages between a sender and receiver. The consultants will need to work with both the company they are integrating with and the VAN service to establish the necessary connectivity. XML channels are significantly more cost effective since they use the Internet rather than an external service. Once the Internet connection is established, only security and communication procedures need to be worked out. This new enterprise network configuration is shown in Figure 9.6.

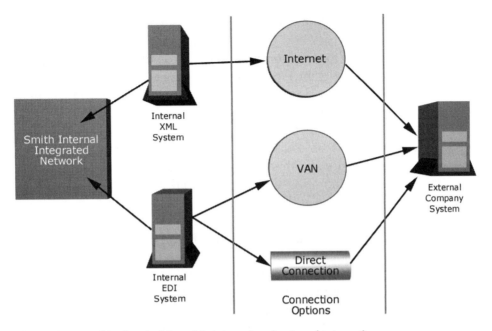

Figure 9.6 Smith Electrical Supply's internal and external Integration.

Establishing a connection and communication channel with one company will allow the rest of the solution to be tested. This must be done before proceeding with any other integration efforts. If the internal software is not set up correctly, it must be corrected as quickly as possible. Test orders and invoices are transmitted. The entire business process from start to finish is examined closely to ensure that everything is in proper working order. Once the tests are completed with the single company, the solution is moved to production. The new process is further tested to ensure that it is operating correctly. The first solution is always the hardest and the riskiest project to implement. Only after it has been thoroughly tested and used should further integration efforts be undertaken.

From this point, each company can be individually added first in the test environment and then moved into production. This process will be used throughout the lifetime of the implementation. New suppliers or customers that wish to be added into the network are first added to the test environment. They are then moved into production once the functionality has been tested and the connectivity is established.

This phase of advancement in the company's computing architecture will require the most work and the most documentation. Documentation will need to be created for the internal employees so they know how to use and maintain the new system. Once again they must be thoroughly trained to ensure that problems don't arise from misuse of the applications. Because external companies are now depending on its computing systems, just as it is depending on their systems, sophisticated testing and maintenance procedures must be established. Its trading partners must adopt these procedures. Failure at either end results in a failure to communicate. Developing and implementing these operational procedures will help to diagnose and fix problems quickly.

Beyond this internal documentation, information must also be compiled that can be given to suppliers and other partners that will hook into the new network. The information provides basic "getting started" information along with the mappings and schemas that Smith currently accepts. Certain IT personnel must be identified and tasked with assisting external companies with any problems they may have while using the new extranet environment.

Results

Inter-enterprise integration is arguably the most difficult phase in the creation of an e-business. This step turns the inward-facing e-business into one that crosses the boundaries of its enterprise. Nearly every facet of the Smith business is designed to use technology to help the company operate. This involves replacing and supplementing various manual processes with those that are automated.

Nearly the entire process from customer order through to order delivery has been automated. Partners can place orders through electronic channels. Smith can validate and process the order using entirely automated processes. If inventory is running low, the Smith computer system will automatically notify suppliers to send more materials. At this point, the order must still be assembled manually, but the customer can be invoiced electronically. Delivery notifications and payment information can also be transmitted electronically. Proper configuration of these systems enables many of the business processes to become entirely automatic and require very little human interaction. This enables the enterprise to respond at the speed of light and drastically improve the rate of business successfully accomplished.

Once the company is completed with phase three, the new system propels Smith Electrical as one of the e-business leaders in the industry. The company is chosen above other competitors because it offers services others in the industry cannot. Smith can operate significantly faster and seamlessly with other operations. Orders can be placed through phone, fax, postal mail, email, or electronically through the extranet. The employees of Smith are better able to serve the needs of customers and react faster to problems. Because everything is electronic, it can be tracked and found at any point in the process. The computer enhancements have helped Smith increase revenues and strengthen its position within the industry.

Phase 4: Building a B2B E-Commerce Solution

Smith Electrical's modifications and advancements have placed it in the upper echelon of competitors in its market. The current operations execute efficiently within the confines of the enterprise environment and through its partner connections. This, however, does not mean that Smith rests on its laurels. Competitors will work hard to match the work accomplished by the company. Therefore, Smith must continually improve its business operations. It is still a few steps away from the Tier 5 level of enterprise efficiency.

To reach the Tier 5 level is an admirable goal, but it is important that companies do not implement solutions just for the sake of implementing solutions. Companies nearing the Tier 5 category often make the mistake of implementing projects simply because they can or because the technology is interesting. Neither of these reasons are a justifiable factor. Although it is good to aim toward a more efficient operational environment, a valid business case must be made before making technological enhancements. Valid reasons may include ensuring the company's leadership in the market, increasing sales, and reducing costs. The potential outcome must justify the cost and risk of further enhancing the enterprise computing environment.

The sales process within Smith involves the creation of a 200-page catalog that customers use to purchase products. The company periodically updates this catalog to add new items and remove old ones. The computer system currently in place allows these updates to be done quarterly, but creating the catalogs and delivering them to all the business partners of Smith requires significant cost. The integrated trading partners from phase three are able to obtain an electronic version of the catalog, however most of the business' partners receive the printed copy. Smith realizes that an electronic version will not only save printing costs but also enable the business to update product listings continually for discontinued and new items.

Smith Electrical understands the importance of stronger relationships with its partners. As such, these partners are making recommendations about enhancements that Smith can implement to serve them better. One frequent recommendation missing in the Smith e-business architecture is a Web site for online orders. Currently electronic orders can only be made through email or via the extranet environment.

The management at Smith has decided to explore the possibility of creating a B2B portal for its industry. It has already implemented the extranet portion of the portal, so implementing the Web site portion of the system will be a straightforward task. This is another example of creating efficiency through a reduction in manual processes by creating an electronic option that is easier to use. The Web site also has the potential to broaden the customer base by tapping into a global marketplace.

Business Case

A B2B portal is a reasonable project to consider for Smith Electrical Supply. If completed correctly, the portal will allow Smith to reduce costs and potentially increase sales. The new portal will also increase customer satisfaction by allowing customers to have access to more information about their accounts. If the costs can be justified and the return on investment is significant, the portal will form an essential component to Smith's e-business strategy.

The obvious short-term benefit for the portal is the cost reduction to current business processes. Smith will be able to post the catalog of items it sells on the portal. At first, customers will be given the option of using either the paper version or the electronic version. A strategy is designed to wean customers away from the paper catalog to the electronic version. The electronic version will permit low-cost and more frequent updates than the quarterly changes that are made to the 200-page paper copy. Smith will reduce the costs in printing and be able to react faster to customer needs through an accurate and timely catalog.

The portal will also be beneficial to business customers, leading to an increase in satisfaction. Customers will be able to examine their accounts and current orders online. They will also be able place new orders and make payments. The integrated trading partners already do these activities electronically, but a B2B portal permits those that are not integrated directly with the extranet to have access to the same features. A B2B portal will also allow Smith to reallocate employees that were previously required to service these partners.

The Web site ordering method is also much more efficient than the traditional means of ordering by phone or fax. To Smith, an order made through the portal is essentially the same as an order made through the extranet. Very little manual interaction or processing is required. The main difference between the extranet and the B2B portal is that the trading partner's internal applications are not integrated with the portal. Therefore, business partners that place an order on the portal will also have to duplicate that order information into their own system. This isn't a large inefficiency, but one that can be eliminated through seamless integration in the B2B extranet.

REQUIREMENTS SUMMARY

Smith requires an online presence in the form of a B2B portal that can be used by all of the current partners. A B2B portal will permit those less technically savvy partners to engage in B2B transactions.

The portal must contain all the information that was previously listed in the catalog. The online catalog must be searchable by trading partners. The catalog must also be easily updated as the Smith product line evolves to meet the needs of its partners.

Existing customers must be able to manage their accounts through the portal. This includes the ability to place orders, view current orders including status information, view past orders, view payment history, and make electronic payments.

Open Source Formula

There are several open source software tools that may be used to build the B2B portal. Programming languages like Perl and Python may be used to build the system from the ground up. Application development environments like Enhydra, Zope, ArsDigita, and Apache Tomcat provide a higher level of functionality out of the box. E-commerce systems like Zelerate All-Commerce and Akopia Interchange provide the most rapid environment for setting up the portal.

Smith views the portal as an important project and speed of implementation is important. Smith is already using Zelerate AllCommerce to handle inventory management inside its enterprise and is having good success with the product. AllCommerce is also integrated into the Open3-based extranet, allowing the business logic from the extranet to be reused where it's necessary in the portal. Combined with their expertise, current implementation, and the ability to implement the project quickly, the AllCommerce product makes the most sense for Smith.

Since the portal is a Web application, Smith also requires supporting software systems for implementing an Internet site. It chooses Apache for the Web server, Linux for the OS, and MySQL for the database. Even though Smith is using the Zelerate product for its internal inventory management system, for security purposes and internal practices, it requires that the portal installation be separate from the current system. It is also wise for Smith to reuse functionality developed in the integrated extranet implementation. Therefore, the Open3 integration platform will be used to connect the portal to Smith's existing applications.

REQUIRED MATERIALS

- (8) Intel-based servers: four of the systems with dual processors (production and backup), four of the systems installed with RAID (production and backup), all with minimum PIII 500mhz CPUs and 256 MB RAM.

- (8) Linux installations, four for the web servers (production, backup, test, and development) and four for the database server (production, backup, test, and development).

- (4) Apache Web Server installations (one on each web server for production, backup, test, and development).

- (4) MySQL database installations (one on each database server for production, backup, test, and development).

- (4) Zelerate AllCommerce installations (one on each web server for production, backup, test, and development).

- (8) Open3 adapters for Zelerate AllCommerce installations (one on each web server and database server for production, backup, test, and development).

System Setup and Installation

The portal has a multi-tiered architecture (see Figure 9.7). Deploying a portal on the public Internet requires additional security considerations. The trading partners must be assigned secure login and passwords for access to the catalog and their individual accounts. Smith must ensure that there is no unauthorized access to ordering functionality or account information. Therefore, the Web server is set up to support SSL through an Apache module. A firewall is placed in front of the Web server that only allows requests through HTTP and HTTPS ports. Additionally, a firewall is set up between the Web server and the database server as a secondary measure of security.

The Web server is configured with the Zelerate AllCommerce application. AllCommerce is then configured to access the MySQL database on the database server. This permits the Web server to dedicate its resources to handling user requests and offload costly database processing to a separate system. The Open3 adapters are placed on both the Web server and database server. The Open3 adapter on the Web server permits the Zelerate-based portal to access functionality already present in the extranet system. The Open3 adapter on the database server handles data interchange between the portal and back-end systems like the inventory management and order processing system. The adapters provide seamless integration of the B2B portal with the technology infrastructure already in place at Smith. This enables an e-business design that is fully automated and information that can be accessed throughout the system.

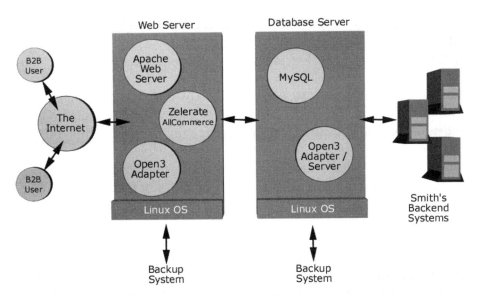

Figure 9.7   System architecture for the B2B portal.

Backup, test, and development systems are created with the same configuration as the production system. The development system permits the software engineers their own environment to build and update the software. Once a milestone of development is finished, it can then be moved to the test system where QA can verify its functionality and security. Once tested, the software is then moved to production. A B2B portal is a 24/7 business and must be available at all times. Therefore, backup systems are configured that can be quickly switched over to if any of the production systems fail. Additionally, the backup system provides duplication of the database to prevent data loss. The MySQL database permits replication, which makes system backups a simple process. To fulfill the first requirement, all of the trading partners have accounts created in the AllCommerce database. The Open3 integrated network enables the accounts to be created by pulling information from the legacy ordering system. End-to-end integration throughout the enterprise makes creating new systems like the B2B portal as painless of a process as possible. Once the necessary information has been added to the database, the trading partners are assigned login names and passwords.

The second requirement specifies all of the available products through the integrated extranet also be available through the portal. This is a simple process since the product information is already stored in the AllCommerce inventory manager. A data port is made between the AllCommerce databases. The requirement also specifies that updates can be made on a frequent basis to the catalog. AllCommerce provides an effective administration interface that permits existing products to be changed and deleted, and new products to be easily added. All of the changes are made to the back-end inventory management system and then transferred to the B2B portal.

The final requirement states that users must be able to manage their accounts and payments online. AllCommerce provides this functionality and can connect to several credit card processing systems to handle payments. For lines of credit, the legacy order processing system is accessed through the Open3 adapter and server to obtain account information. Custom logic is created in to allow trading partners to pay from credit cards or through their line of credit.

Once the system has been completed and tested by internal quality engineers, Smith implements a beta testing phase with three of its closest partners not currently integrated with the extranet. Beta testing permits actual users to find bugs and deficiencies in the system before it is available for wide release. These partners are friendly to the problems and glitches that may occur before the system is production ready. Smith's staff works closely with these beta users to finalize it for release to the other partners.

As with other phases of the project, Smith must incorporate changes in its business processes wrought from the creation of the B2B portal. Approximately 75 percent of the staff formerly responsible for handling production and creation of the printed catalog can be moved to other parts of the company. The remainder must be trained to support the electronic catalog. Also, business customer support must now be trained to handle issues with the portal, such as lost passwords or the users' inability to access account information. Finally, all trading partners must be provided with user guides and assistance in changing from the old way of placing orders through phone and fax to new and more efficient ordering system.

Results

The new portal allows Smith's partners that previously were not using the integrated extranet to place orders and manage their accounts. All trading partners are now able to benefit from the new electronic business initiatives enacted by Smith. The barrier to entry for new partners to use the portal is significantly reduced, requiring only an Internet connection.

Smith's trading partners are given a wide range of ordering methods far surpassing any other vendor in the industry. Those partners just being introduced to e-business or those that do not have the technological experience to use the extranet environment can still benefit from B2B portal. They can then eventually move to the completely automated system if desired, or continue to use the portal. Additionally, the portal provides a Web-based interface for the integrated extranet partners to login in and view orders and account information.

Smith is finally able to reduce the number of costly catalogs it produces. Sixty-five percent of the partners are now using the electronic systems to browse and purchase items. Smith expects that an additional 20 percent will be using the portal within the next six months. The printed catalog is changed from a quarterly to a bi-annual version, to support those partners that won't use the integrated extranet or B2B portal. Smith plans in two years to phase out the printed catalog. In preparation for this, it is developing an educational and training program to bring aboard those partners who are reluctant to use the new technology.

Smith has now reached the top level, Tier 5, of e-business efficiency. The reduction in cost and the increased customer satisfaction make the portal well worth the cost and effort required to create it. All facets of the business have been integrated internally and externally. All customers, even those starting their technological advancements, are able to benefit from the Smith enhancements. Smith has used technology to create an efficient and industry leading company. Through continued innovation and optimization, the company is positioning itself for strong growth and dominance in its market.

Phase 5: A Customer-Centric B2C Solution

Smith has achieved strong success with its e-business initiatives. Spurred by the results of previous phases, the corporate management is now ready to leverage its newfound position to mine untapped veins of opportunity. Smith has analyzed the business potential and realizes that the end-customer retail market is promising. The electrical component retail space is growing yearly by 28 percent. However, there is strong competition from traditional brick-and-mortar stores in its area of business. The company decides that traditional retail channels will be difficult to break into and that it does not have the experience or capital to succeed with this strategy. Smith realizes that there is opportunity to deliver value and service through a Web-based offering.

Of greatest concern to the management at Smith is the 25 percent of its business customer base that also sells to this retail market. By entering this space, Smith will become a competitor to its current customers. Smith is not willing to upset these partners and lose a large portion of its revenues. To avoid the loss, Smith decides to partner with these established retailers. The company's strategy is to gain retail experience through the partnerships and to broaden its offering by aggregating the products of its partners into a mega-B2C site for electrical components.

The management at Smith presents its ideas to the corporate board. Several of the board members are concerned that a B2C strategy will be difficult because of the recent shakeout of B2C companies in the broader market. They quote estimates of 95 percent of B2C companies to be out of business within three years. They plainly see that Smith is already moving strongly ahead in the supplier and wholesale markets. The board is concerned that forging into new territory may be costly to the core business. The management at Smith realizes that it will need to make a convincing case for the board and itself to go forward with the B2C catalog aggregation project.

Business Case

Smith talks with several of its partners that are retailers in the industry. Most agree that it is a worthwhile project and that it will be a revenue stream that will grow in the future. The partners like the fact that the online business strategy is rooted in brick-and-mortar companies that already have strong experience and brand awareness in the business. They also note that there are only fragmented competitors in the Internet space, and they carry limited product selection. Customers must shop at several online stores to purchase all of the items that they may need. Therefore, the competition is vulnerable to the conglomerate mega-site that Smith is proposing. Additionally, the customer base is technically savvy, the products are suited to online sales, and buying through a Web site can provide more choice and more value to the customer. The partners are excited about the opportunity to participate in the venture.

After more discussion and analysis, Smith and 14 of its partners decide to go forward with the site. All of these partners are already integrated through the extranet, so the additional communication required for catalog aggregation will be a simple process. Smith will pay for the costs to build, host, maintain, and market the site. The partners are required to submit their product information through the integrated extranet and be able to accept orders. The partners are required to provide fulfillment for their items. All of the items will be sold under a new company name that is owned and managed by Smith. Smith will receive a commission, between five to ten percent, for partner products that are sold through the site.

After meeting with its partners, Smith realizes that there will be approximately 12,000 products on the site. There will also be an estimated 50,000 customers that register in the first three months. There will be growth in the number of products and customers. The site must be able to maintain the initial demands for products and customers and also be scaleable for growth in the future. The site will contain the standard features inherent in consumer e-commerce sites, such as product search, shopping cart, and credit card payment. Smith also wants to do promotions through email, in a weekly newsletter sent out to those customers that opt-in to receive it. The email promotion will permit new products to be advertised and provide a regular reminder for customers to shop at the site.

REQUIREMENTS SUMMARY

The entire system must support an initial load of 12,000 products and 50,000 customers. The system must be scaleable and grow as the product and customer base grows. It must be also be maintainable, reliable, and secure.

Develop a set of partner documents that specify the communication format for product and order information. This is a B2B requirement, but it is essential for accomplishing B2C. Much of the failure in the first generation of the B2C space was a result of inattention to critical B2B and integration problems, such as supply-chain integration.

Aggregate the information from Smith's and its 14 partners' line of products into a Web-based B2C e-commerce system. The site must have standard functionality such as product search, manufacturer categories, detailed product information and graphics, secure checkout, and real-time credit card processing. The system must also be able to handle shipping charges for product orders that contain items from more than one partner.

Since Smith and its 14 partners will each handle their own fulfillment of products, functionality is necessary to manage and route fulfillment to multiple warehouses. The partners will be required to send two messages for each order through the integrated extranet. The first message will provide an estimate of the time to fill the order. The second message notifies that the order has been shipped.

It is Smith's job to take the communication from the partners and deliver email messages that notify the customer of when and what portion of their orders will ship. Smith must also implement an email campaign system that will deliver marketing-oriented email newsletters to those customers that wish to receive it.

Open Source Formula

Once again, Smith turns to open source software for its B2C solution. Applications that have been used in previous implementations will also be utilized for this project: Linux, Apache Web Server, MySQL database, Open3, and Zelerate AllCommerce. The B2C solution also requires customer relationship management functionality which will be provided by the Relata open source package.

REQUIRED MATERIALS

- (10) Intel-based servers: six of the systems with dual processors (production and backup), three of the systems installed with RAID (production and backup), all with minimum PIII 500mhz CPUs and 256 MB RAM.

- (1) Load Balancing hardware system such as products by Cisco or F5.

- (10) Linux installations, five for the Web servers (three for production, one for test, and one for development) and five for the database servers (three for production, one for test, and one for development).

- (5) Apache Web Server installations on the Web servers (three for production, one for test, and one for development).

- (5) MySQL database installations on the database servers (three for production, one for test, and one for development).

- (5) Zelerate AllCommerce installations on the Web servers (three for production, one for test, and one for development).

- (5) RelataMail installations on the Web servers (three for production, one for test, and one for development).

- (5) Open3/AllCommerce adapters on the database servers (three for production, one for test, and one for development).

System Setup and Operation

For the first requirement, the B2C site must support the data and user load. Smith provides the performance and scalability through a load-balancing architecture (see Figure 9.8). Smith decides to go with off-the-shelf server systems to save cost but maintain good performance. The production architecture will be composed of three Apache Web servers and three MySQL database servers. The Web servers will have load distributed through a hardware-based load balancing system. The database servers will be mirrors of each other and data will be replicated for consistency on a periodic basis.

To satisfy the second requirement, Smith and its partners agree to use XML document definitions specified by RosettaNet. RosettaNet provides a B2B framework targeted to the IT industry and Smith can utilize these specifications without need for modification. Smith will leverage the existing Open3-based extranet to support the exchange of messages between

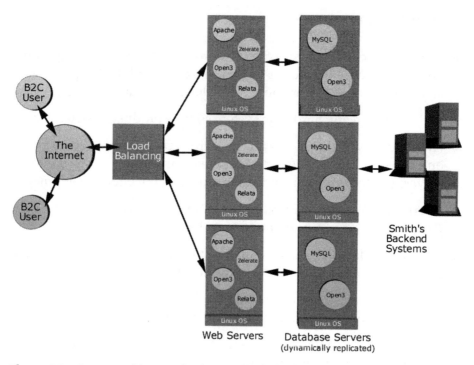

Figure 9.8 System architecture for the B2C implementation.

itself and its 14 trading partners. The additional messages sent from Smith to the trading partners are customer purchase orders. The trading partners will deliver to Smith product and inventory information for the Web-based catalog, a fulfillment time estimate for orders, and a notification when an order has been shipped.

To fulfill the third requirement, Smith will utilize the Zelerate AllCommerce package to build the Web site. The company has had good success with the package and is developing expertise with it. AllCommerce supports most of the functionality that Smith requires. Smith decides to write some custom code to handle multiple shipping charges. Customer orders may have items to be fulfilled from several different companies, these orders will require an individual shipment of products from each company. Therefore, the Web application must contain business logic that can determine how many vendors are involved in an order. Based upon this and the types of items that are ordered, the system can accurately tally shipping charges for the customer.

Providing the additional communication infrastructure between partners in the second requirement and the business logic to handle fulfillment in the third requirement completes a majority of requirement four. Complex orders can now be divided accurately amongst different vendors, encoded in B2B messages, and delivered to the appropriate recipient. The partner then returns a document estimating the fulfillment date, usually within 24 hours. At some future time, the partner sends another document with information that the order has been shipped. Smith is required to utilize this information to fulfill part of requirement five.

The fifth requirement provides customer attention through emails. Smith determines that its sendmail server configuration from phase one will be able to handle the load of sending order status emails to customers. The company creates custom code that generates an email to the customer when they place an order and when Smith receives the order information documents from its partners. Therefore, when customers place an order, they can expect to receive at least three emails. They will get one email immediately after they have placed their order. A second email, and potentially others if the order is through multiple partners, will be sent with an estimated shipping date. The third email, and again others if it is a multi-partner order, will be sent when the order (or partial order) has shipped. This email system provides a constant stream of communication to the customer, ensuring them that their order has been received and is being filled.

Requirement five also specifies that Smith creates an email campaign system for marketing to the customer base. The customers must have the ability to subscribe and unsubscribe from the list. The company builds a simple checkbox on the customer information page that allows the person to be added or removed from the subscription list. Smith then chooses the open source RelataMail package to handle their email campaigns. Subscribers are easily transferred to the RelataMail system through its import functionality. Smith assigns a person to create the emails on a weekly basis and utilize RelataMail for their processing. The email system provides management and reporting functions that allow Smith to track the success rate of the campaigns. Customers can be targeted based on specific preferences, delivering the personalization that the new era in B2C demands.

Results

Smith's previous phases and technical design enables the company to build the system rapidly. By working from the integrated partner architecture established in phase three, the often difficult problem of coordinating partner communication is significantly eliminated. The project undergoes significant testing to ensure that the workflow and partner interaction will work as expected. Two of the partners have required special assistance to get their systems integrated for the exchange. Since Smith already had the integrated extranet in place prior to starting phase five, the company is able to devote resources to assisting these two companies. Additional testing simulates user load and verifies that the system will be able to handle the expected number of users. Smith finds that the system is more than adequate and is satisfied with a site launch.

Smith and its partners announce the site to their customer base. When the site enters production, there is significant traffic of eager customers ready to browse and buy. The project's testing phase was able to eliminate all of the major bugs and most of the minor ones, so the customers are treated to a solid online shopping experience. The focus on delivering customer value, service, and an enjoyable shopping experience begins to pay off. Customers are returning and recommending the site to friends. The cost savings enabled by the security, reliability, and flexibility in the open source software leads Smith to estimate that it will recoup its initial investment quickly. Its partners are enjoying a new revenue source and are excited about the growth potential. The mega-site will be a difficult project for another company to replicate and Smith is eyeing dominance in the Web marketplace.

Summary

The examples and information provided in this chapter have shown the potential of growing a company by utilizing the power of open source technology. Smith was able to grow from a Tier 1 competitor to a Tier 5 industry leader. It became the measuring stick used by all other companies in their industry to determine success. When necessary or prudent proprietary solutions were used or integrated into the evolving open source infrastructure.

By utilizing the commercial resources and entities that are associated with the open source solutions, an enterprise can greatly ease the growth process. The commercial side of open source can also make the technical solutions feel more like standard commercial solutions by adding enhanced support and tools. The final chapter provides a reference to the commercial companies that champion open source software. Look to these companies to provide updates, support, and consulting services that your enterprise demands for its e-business solutions.

Open Source Companies

Individuals and companies create open source software. The early success of open source can be attributed to personalities like Richard Stallman and Linus Torvalds. They created software communities of individuals to pool their talents and develop great products. Developers, sequestered by geography but united by code, lent their time and talents to create software that rivaled their closed source counterparts. It is the effort of these individuals that have laid the foundation for open source to become mainstream.

In the past five years, open source companies have joined in the effort. Commercial companies have devoted resources toward the development and testing of software in many of the open source communities. Leaders of the early open source projects have started many of the commercial enterprises. The business side of open source is proving extremely beneficial to the movement and for the use of open source software in the enterprise.

There are two types of companies that create business around open source: Participant Companies and Parasitic Companies. *Participant Companies* are those that sponsor projects, lend developer support, and actively work to make better open source projects. *Parasitic Companies* commercialize open source products but do not contribute their resources to create better open source software. Often Parasitic Companies will merge proprietary products with open source products and fail to mention that some of their software came from the open source community. Participant Companies are the ones who are maintaining the spirit of the open source movement and are leading the software with great expertise to the enterprise. It is the Participant Companies that will provide the best service and support for creating e-business solutions based on open source software.

Open source software exists not because someone has marketed and hyped it, but because it can provide solid, reliable, and tested solutions. You'll find that working with open source companies is a different experience from proprietary vendors. Why? The reason is that open source companies don't make their money from selling expensive licenses. They drive their revenues by delivering solutions based on the software products. Anyone who has sat through endless marketing drivel to buy a license for a proprietary product will understand how refreshing it is to see companies who take a solution-oriented approach to their customers.

The following pages list Participant Companies who have made great strides to bring open source into the business world. These companies provide service and support demanded by mission-critical e-business projects.

NOTE   The information contained in this chapter is current as of February 2001. Check each vendor's Web site for up-to-date information.

ActiveState

580 Granville Street
Vancouver, BC
V6C 1W6 Canada
Phone: 604-484-6400
Fax: 604-484-6499
www.activestate.com

ActiveState was founded in 1997 by Dick Hardt. The company is private and headquartered in Vancouver, BC, Canada with offices in the United States and Australia. ActiveState develops popular tools to empower software engineers utilizing open source programming languages like Perl, Python, Tcl, and XSLT. Its Web site reaches over 1.5 million downloads each year. ActiveState serves small, medium, and large customers including HP, 3Com, Microsoft, and Disney.

Products

ActiveState provides quality free tools like ActivePerl and ActivePython that assist in the usage and development of the Perl and Python programming languages. ActiveState also provides the ActiveState Programmer Network, a portal ActiveState products. ActiveState also sells commercial products including ASPN Komodo, ASPN Perl, and PerlMX Enterprise.

Services

ActiveState provides commercial support services for its products. Support services include PerlDirect and The Perl Clinic, which provide Perl-based assistance, and also PythonDirect, which provides Python-based assistance.

Anteil

160 South Progress Avenue, #3D
Harrisburg, PA 17109
Phone: 877-675-4689
Fax: 717-657-6142
Email: info@anteil.com
www.anteil.com

Anteil provides customer relationship software based on the OpenSource-CRM.org community. Jim Capp founded Anteil in 1999, and the company is strategically partnered with VA Linux. Its CRM solutions deliver a low-cost alternative to proprietary CRM systems that are often a large expenditure for the enterprise.

Products

The OpenSourceCRM.org software forms a basis for Anteil's product line. The open source software contains features like campaign and event management and facilitation for corporate communications. The software can be leveraged not only to support basic customer service but enhance it through an Internet-based architecture.

Services

Anteil provides consulting and support services based on the OpenSource-CRM.org software. This includes project management, consultation, integration, custom development, and management services.

ArsDigita

80 Prospect Street
Cambridge, MA 02139
Phone: 617-386-4100
Fax: 617-354-8581
Email: info@arsdigita.com
www.arsdigita.com

ArsDigita was founded in 1997 and provides Web-based solutions based on the ArsDigita Community System. ArsDigita is headquartered in Boston with offices in England, Japan, Germany, and throughout the United States. ArsDigita enterprise solutions are deployed in companies like Siemens, America Online, and The World Bank.

Products

The ArsDigita Community System is an integrated suite of components for building Web-based applications. It includes components for e-commerce, user collaboration, personalization, content management, and marketing analysis. The platform has been created for the rapid development of B2B and B2C e-commerce applications.

Services

ArsDigita provides professional services for project management and implementation based on the ArsDigita platform and a wide variety of back-end database systems.

Caldera

240 West Center Street
Orem, UT 84057
Phone: 801-765-4999
Fax: 801-765-1313
www.caldera.com
info@calderasystems.com (product and sales inquiries)

Caldera, Inc. is a public company (Nasdaq: CALD) that provides software and service solutions for Linux. Ransom Love and Bryan Sparks founded the company in 1994. Caldera recently acquired portions of the Santa Cruz Operation, Inc., a historically significant participant in the Unix OS. Based on the acquisition, Caldera is now forging new territories in unifying Linux with Unix.

Products

Caldera's OpenLinux product is a Linux distribution engineered for business customers. The OpenLinux product line also includes OpenLinux eDesktop, a suite of desktop productivity solutions, and OpenLinux eServer, a suite of server offerings include web, file, network, and mail servers. The Caldera Volution is a Linux management product for remote management of Linux server networks. Caldera's open sourced products include LIZARD and the Caldera Open Administration System, both available at www.openlinux.org.

Services

Caldera's OpenLearning services provide education on Linux-based e-business solutions. Caldera also provides support services for its products including a support knowledgebase, installation, legacy software, and commercial enhanced services.

Digital Creations

607 William Street, Suite 201
Fredericksburg, VA 22401
Phone: 888-344-4332
Fax: 703-995-0412
Email: info@digicool.com
www.digicool.com

Digital Creations provides content management solutions based on the Zope platform. The first version of the Zope platform was created by Digital Creations in 1996 and, thereafter, released to the open source community. Zope has significant support in the development community and continues to grow in use.

Products

Beyond the open source Zope.org platform, Digital Creations also creates customized vertical software packages based on the Zope software.

Services

Digital Creations provides consulting services based on the Zope application server. They provide short-term consulting and long-term project implementation. Digital Creations have also developed courses for training on the Zope platform.

EverySoft

920 Scenic Drive
Midland, MI 48642
Email: sales@everysoft.com
www.everysoft.com

EverySoft was founded in 1997 and provides a popular open source auction engine known as EveryAuction.

Products

There are two primary products, EveryAuction and EveryChat. EveryAuction provides online auction capabilities. EveryChat is a popular lightweight chat script that is compatible on all major platforms. EveryAuction and EveryChat are licensed under the GNU GPL.

Evidian

300 Concord Road
Billerica, MA 01821
Phone: 877-5EVIDIAN
Email: info@evidian.com
www.evidian.com

Evidian is a subsidiary of Groupe Bull and is based in Massachusetts. The company provides proprietary application, security, and fault management solutions. Evidian has provided the open source JonAS EJB Implementation available on the ObjectWeb Web site (www.objectweb.org).

Intalio

2000 Alameda de las Pulgas, Suite 250
San Mateo, CA 94403
Phone: 650-345-2777
Fax: 650-345-8787
Email: info@intalio.com
www.intalio.com

Intalio, Inc. is a private company founded in 1999 that provides business process management software. The company is the major sponsor of Exolab.org, a group of software projects dedicated to building open source components of the J2EE platform. Intalio also sponsors the Business Process Management Initiative (www.bpmi.org), an organization of companies dedicated to developing standardization for business process management internal and external to the enterprise.

Products

Intalio's flagship product is the n3 Business Process Management System, a platform that is partially powered by the Exolab.org open source software. The cutting-edge n3 system enables companies to develop and operate business processes throughout the enterprise.

Services

Intalio provides business process management services throughout the lifecycle of business process development.

International Business Machines

1133 Westchester Avenue
White Plains, NY 10604
Phone: 914-499-1900
Fax: 404-238-6628
Email: info@ibm.com
www.ibm.com

IBM is the giant of computing. The company has recently devoted one billion U.S. dollars to the Linux OS. IBM has provided a significant amount of resources to the open source community, contributing to projects like Apache Xalan and Apache Xerces. IBM's alphaWorks site also provides open source software, mainly tools for Java and XML (alphaworks.ibm.com).

Jabber.com

1899 Wynkoop Street
Denver, CO 80202
Phone: 303-308-3231
Fax: 303-308-3215
Email: services@jabber.com
www.jabber.com

Jabber.com provides enterprise-class products and services based upon the jabber.org platform for instant messaging. Jabber.org provides a client/server platform that allows clients to communicate with zero latency. Instant messaging has become a standard part of major portals like Yahoo, MSN, and AOL. Jabber provides the best open source solution for instant messaging and can connect with the major IM systems. Jabber.com began in March 2000 as a subsidiary of the public company Webb Interactive Services, Inc (Nasdaq: WEBB). Jabber.com employs several of the Jabber.org developers, ensuring that their contributions are returned to the open source community.

Products

Jabber.com extends the Jabber.org instant messaging software with commercial products aimed at small businesses, enterprise customers, and service providers.

Services

Jabber.com provides professional services for enterprise customers and service providers. The services include installation, custom configuration, management, and training of Jabber software.

JBoss Group

Email: support@jbossgroup.com
www.jbossgroup.com

The JBoss Group is an organized group of the top jboss.org developers that sell products and services around the JBoss open source platform. The company is in its infancy of corporate development, however the JBoss open source software is quite mature. Look to the JBoss Group in 2001 to grow and service the commercial sector.

Kaivo

600 17th Street Suite 2125-South
Denver, CO 80202-5421
Phone: 303-539-0200
Fax: 303-539-0201
Email: info@kaivo.com
www.kaivo.com

Kaivo was established in 1984 and is based in Denver. The company provides training, consulting, and development services based on open source products including Jabber instant message software and the Zope application development platform.

Services

Kaivo provides consulting and development services for prototyping, application development, and integration. They also offer educational courses for open source software including Jabber and Zope.

Lutris Technologies

1200 Pacific Avenue, #300
Santa Cruz, CA 95060
Phone: 877-688-3724
Fax: 831-471-9754
Email: info@lutris.com
www.lutris.com

Lutris Technologies was founded in 1995 to develop the Enhydra platform as a cutting-edge application server. In January 1999, Enhydra.org was created to which Lutris released the Enhydra system to the open source community. Lutris is establishing itself as one of the major players in Java and XML software through an open source strategy. Enhydra is moving toward a full J2EE platform, a significant market where 90 percent of the application servers in the enterprise are powered on Java technology.

Products

Lutris Enhydra 3.5 is a Java/XML application server for Internet and wireless Web applications. The architecture permits rapid application development and a tiered design that separates data, business logic, and presentation.

Services

Lutris provides several enterprise support programs and incident level support. Installation support is provided with the purchase of the Lutris Enhydra product. The company also provides consulting services for application architecture, systems development, e-business strategy, creative and design, system deployment, and maintenance.

Open3 Technologies

777 South Wadsworth Boulevard, 2-204
Lakewood, CO 80226
Phone: 303-298-8552
Fax: 801-697-4779
Email: info@open3.com
www.open3.com

Open3 Technologies provides e-business integration software and services based on the Open3.org platform. Open3.org is an open source software system based on Java Enterprise and XML to enable EAI and B2B integration. Open3 Technologies is a sponsor of Open3.org and launched the community in 1999. The company promotes the platform to businesses around the world to enable quality low-cost integration solutions.

Many of the open source applications for e-business have adapters to the Open3.org platform. The adapters permit these applications to connect and share data with other systems, greatly enhancing their adoption into the enterprise. Open3.org, through open source, is enabling the broadest adapter set possible in an integration platform.

Products

Open3 Technologies provides commercial products based on the Open3.org platform. These products include message brokering, B2B software, and tools to deploy rapid and effective integration solutions.

Services

Open3 Technologies provides commercial support, e-business consulting, and technical implementation services for EAI and B2Bi projects. The company employs an acclaimed methodology to leverage integration between existing software infrastructure and new technology.

Red Hat

2600 Meridian Parkway
Durham, NC 27713
Phone: 888-733-4281
Fax: 919-547-0024
Email: orders@redhat.com (product orders)
www.redhat.com

Red Hat was started in 1994 and is headquartered in the United States in Durham, North Carolina. It also has worldwide offices in the United States, Asia, Europe, and Australia. Red Hat has made significant contributions to open source, especially for the Linux platform. Red Hat Linux is a strong leader in many Linux markets.

Products

Red Hat provides several Linux-based and Linux-related products.

Red Hat Linux. The widely used distribution for installing a Linux-based workstation or server.

Red Hat Professional Server. A massive package with ten CDs (version 7.0) for setting up a mission-critical Linux server.

Red Hat Alpha Deluxe. A Red Hat Linux version for the Compaq Alpha platform with Alpha tools.

Red Hat Enterprise for Oracle 8i. Red Hat Linux optimized for Oracle 8i to be used as a database server.

Red Hat High Availability Server. Clustering solution for Red Hat Linux for scalability through load balancing and reliability through fault tolerance.

Services

General support. All distributions include installation support with many of the packages including additional support.

Corporate support solutions. Various support solutions such as Web server, e-commerce, and onsite consulting.

Engineering. Services for GNU-based development, optimization, and hardware and software certification.

Sendmail

6425 Christie Avenue, 4th Floor
Emeryville, CA 94608
Phone: 888-594-3150
Email: info@sendmail.com
www.sendmail.com

Sendmail, Inc., is the primary commercial software developer based on the open source sendmail application. The open source sendmail application was originally developed in 1979. Sendmail, Inc., is headquartered in California with offices in England, France, Germany, and Hong Kong. Sendmail, Inc., provides development expertise on email standards for their adoption into the open source software package. Sendmail, Inc., leverages the open source application to deliver commercial products, value-added bundling, and services.

Products

Sendmail has several products to facilitate email messaging in the enterprise.

> **Sendmail Advanced Message Server.** Provides an enterprise and service provider solution for reliable and robust Internet messaging solution.
>
> **Secure Switch.** Provides an additional layer of security to prevent unwanted intrusion to the corporate mail servers.
>
> **Multi Switch.** A management solution to configure, monitor, and update multiple sendmail servers from a single interface.

Sendmail, Inc., also bundles its products into value-added platforms, such as a Red Hat Linux Dell server for Internet messaging.

Services

Sendmail provides incident support and several program support solutions which provide a variety of services from setup and installation to expert consulting for custom mail systems.

Stratabase

34314 Marshall Road
Abbotsford, BC
V2S.1L2 Canada
Phone: 800-475-3349
Email: info@stratabase.com
www.stratabase.com

Stratabase was founded in 1998 by Trevor Newton and provides CRM solutions based on the open source Relata software. Stratabase is headquartered in British Columbia, Canada, and is a publicly traded company (US OTCBB: SBSF). The mission of the company is to provide a cost-effective open source CRM system that is competitive with enterprise-class proprietary offerings.

Products

Relata is a suite of CRM tools. Relatamail is the first component of the system and handles email communications. Additional components are being developed, the second component is to be released in the early part of 2001 which provides sales force automation functionality.

Services

Stratabase provides professional services and technical support for the installation, customization, and deployment of its product line.

Sun Microsystems

901 San Antonio Road
Palo Alto, CA 94303
Phone: 650-960-1300
Fax: 650-336-0646
Email: info@sun.com
www.sun.com

Sun Microsystems is a giant public company (Nasdaq: SUNW) that provides hardware and software solutions. Its Java programming platform has become the dominant system utilized for enterprise software. Sun's major contribution to open source is openoffice.org, a suite of desktop office productivity tools competing strongly against Microsoft's Office platform.

SuSE

580 Second Street, Suite 210
Oakland, CA 94607
Phone: 888-875-4689
Fax: 510-628-3381
Email: info@suse.com
www.suse.com

Roland Dyroff, Thomas Fehr, Hubert Mantel, and Burchard Steinbild started SuSE in 1992, based in Germany. SuSE is one of the earliest Linux vendors, selling software on floppies in 1993. SuSE is a popular Linux distribution and contains the YaST installation tool and over 1,500 supporting applications. SuSE has offices in Europe (Germany, France, Italy, U.K.), South America (Venezuela), and the United States.

Products

SuSE provides products based on Linux-based software bundles.

SuSE Linux 7.1 Personal (available 2/2001). Product includes 60 days of free installation support.

SuSE Linux 7.1 Professional (available 2/2001). Product includes 90 days of free installation support.

Services

SusE provides consulting and support services for Linux and several open source products.

Professional services. Includes consulting and project implementation to provide integrated solutions for Linux and other open source software. Their specialties are in network services, Internet and email infrastructure, and high availability and performance of Linux-based servers.

Business and advanced support services. Provides full-service technical support for Linux, Apache Web Server, Sendmail, Samba, and other major open source applications.

Turbolinux

8000 Marina Boulevard, Suite 300
Brisbane, CA 94005
Phone: 650-228-5000
Fax: 650-228-5001
www.turbolinux.com

Turbolinux, founded in 1992, is a well-funded private company that provides Linux-based software solutions. IDC listed Turbolinux as the fastest growing Linux company in market share from 1998 to 1999. Turbolinux is headquartered in the United States and has offices around the world including Japan, China, Korea, Taiwan, Australia, Germany, England, and Central and South America.

Products

TurboLinux provides Linux distributions and enterprise clustering solutions for Linux.

Turbolinux Workstation. Linux distribution aimed at software developers.

Turbolinux Server. Linux distribution for high performance and e-commerce, available for Intel, Compaq Alpha, IBM S/390, and IBM zSeries platforms.

Turbolinux Cluster. Clustering technology for Linux.

Turbolinux EnFuzion. Clustering solution that utilizes parametric execution on a computer network for calculation-intensive applications.

Turbolinux DataServer. Optimized Linux for databases such as Oracle 8i and IBM DB2.

Services

TurboLinux provides support, consulting, and educational services for Linux.

Support services program. This is a customizable offering of various support packages for Turbolinux' products.

Professional services program. Through professional services, Turbolinux provides clustering and high performance solutions for Linux, application development, and system integration.

Education services program. Educational curriculum for Linux-related studies.

VA Linux Systems

47071 Bayside Parkway
Fremont, CA 94538
Phone: 877-VA-LINUX
Fax: 510-226-8833
Email: info@valinux.com
www.valinux.com

VA Linux was founded in 1993 and is publicly traded (Nasdaq: LNUX). VA Linux specializes in Linux servers and other Linux-based hardware. Its contribution to the open source community is primarily through the Open Source Development Network (OSDN). The OSDN is the largest community of open source projects and provides a free infrastructure for project management and code distribution.

Products

VA Linux sells a variety of custom configurable hardware systems based on the Linux operating system. VA Linux provides enterprise enhancements to the Linux operating system to ensure interoperability with other major applications. The VA Cluster Management software provides a central management console for server clusters. The OSDN provides a Web-based infrastructure for remote collaborative development.

Services

VA Linux provides a variety of services including Linux, e-commerce, integration, and security consulting. The company's Initial Code Offering service facilitates proprietary software vendors to move their proprietary code to open source. VA Linux also provides extensive support services for hardware, Linux, and other open source software.

Zend Technologies

P.O. Box 3619
Ramat Gan 52136
Israel
Phone: 972-3-6139665
Fax: 972-3-6139671
Email: info@zend.com
www.zend.com

Zend Technologies is the major commercial company backing the PHP Web programming language. Zeev Suraski and Andi Gutmans, cofounders of Zend Technlogies with Doron Gerstel, rewrote the PHP 2.0 code to create PHP 3.0 and later the Zend Engine for PHP 4.0. PHP provides an open source solution for building dynamic Web applications.

Products

Zend Technologies provides commercial software that enhances and extends the open source Zend Engine. Zend products include:

Zend Cache. The Zend Cache increases the execution speed of a PHP application by storing a compiled version in the Web server's persistent cache registry.

Zend Encoder Unlimited. This product protects source code for distribution by encrypting it.

Zend IDE. This is an integrated development environment for Zend that provides tools like editing and debugging of Zend applications.

Zend LaunchPad. This product assists with configuring, monitoring, and managing the PHP development environment.

Services

Zend provides incident support for Zend products and PHP.

Summary

Open source software no longer resides solely within the domain of software developers. When your enterprise considers deploying solutions based on open source, consulting, support, and education services from one or more of these expert companies can save considerable time and money in your e-business solution. Choosing open source software and open source vendors over proprietary ones will ensure the growth and advancement of the open source movement.

E-business and open source will continue to evolve, and growing together each will benefit the other. The time is now to engage open source enterprise solutions.

Index